THE

EVERYTHING

BUILD YOUR OWN
HOME PAGE
BOOK

Create a site you'll be proud of,
without becoming a programmer

Mark Binder and Beth Helman

Adams Media Corporation
Holbrook, Massachusetts

Acknowledgments

Pam Liflander; Alicia Lehrer; Max and Harry;
Sharon McDonnell; David Adler and Equitable Travel;
Jeri Johnson; Adam G. Gertsacov, Boss Clown, Acme Clown Company;
the WELL, Brad Hyson, Executive Director, Apeiron Foundation;
DJ Delorie at delorie software for "Making it harder to hate computers";
Christina Murphy; the Kevins—Kevin Donlin, owner of Guaranteed Resumes, and Kevin McNeely.

An Everything Series Book. The Everything Series
is a trademark of Adams Media Corporation.

Published by Adams Media Corporation
260 Center Street, Holbrook, MA 02343
adamsmedia.com

ISBN: 1-58062-339-5

Printed in the United States of America.

J I H G F E D C B A

Library of Congress Cataloging-in-Publication Data available upon
request from the publisher.

This publication is designed to provide accurate and authoritative information
with regard to the subject matter covered. It is sold with the understanding that
the publisher is not engaged in rendering legal, accounting, or other professional
advice. If legal advice or other expert assistance is required, the services of a
competent professional person should be sought.
    — From a *Declaration of Principles* jointly adopted by a Committee of the
American Bar Association and a Committee of Publishers and Associations

Many of the designations used by manufacturers and sellers to distinguish their
products are claimed as trademarks. Where those designations appear in this
book and Adams Media was aware of a trademark claim, the designations have
been printed in initial capital letters.

Illustrations by Barry Littmann and Kathie Kelleher

This book is available at quantity discounts for bulk purchases.
For information, call 1-800-872-5627.

Contents

CHAPTER 4: BEFORE YOU START / 53

CHAPTER 5: MAKING COOL WEB PAGES 101 / 71

CHAPTER 6: MOVING FROM WEB PAGE TO WEB SITE / 85

CHAPTER 7: MAKING EVEN COOLER WEB PAGES / 91

CONTENTS

CHAPTER 12: DESIGNING AND MAINTAINING YOUR SITE / 197

CHAPTER 13: BUSINESS ON THE WEB / 227

CHAPTER 14: WEB PAGE AND WEB SITE CREATION TOOLS / 249

CONTENTS

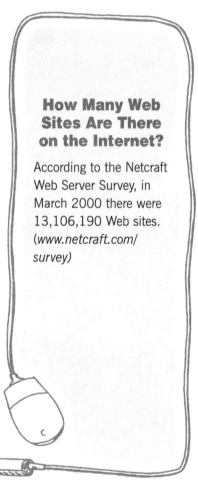

How Many Web Sites Are There on the Internet?

According to the Netcraft Web Server Survey, in March 2000 there were 13,106,190 Web sites. (*www.netcraft.com/survey*)

A few years ago, "Click me" didn't mean much to anybody. Multimedia meant a slide projector and atonal music at an avant-garde dance performance. A web was something that a spider made, and while it was pretty to look at, you'd probably sweep it out of your kitchen.

Today, the Internet is everywhere. The World Wide Web is pervasive. The browser wars between Netscape and Microsoft's Internet Explorer moved from rabid arguments between computer widget-heads into the headlines as the Justice Department brought an antitrust suit against Microsoft. You go to the mall and see a sign in the Gap for Gap.com. You hear radio ads for Yahoo! When you watch the TV news, the newscaster says that you can find out more at the station's Web site.

Today, anybody can have a Web site. Even you.

You might not have millions of dollars or thousands of personnel resource hours, but in less than an hour you can post something online. You can have your own beginning Web site. It might not be much, just a little tiny note posted on the gigantic electronic bulletin board that is the Internet. But that's your note. That's your spot.

You don't need to program. You don't even need to spend money. (Although learning something about how the Web works and spending a little money here and there wouldn't hurt.) All you need to do is take a little time to connect to the Internet and begin.

We have a question for you: What do you want to say?

You've got 2 megabytes, or 10 megabytes, or 25 megabytes, or 100 megabytes of space on the World Wide Web. You've got a computer that's faster and better than the best computers that existed 10 years ago. You've got digital pictures, digital sound, multimedia capabilities, and, of course, words.

What do you want to do on the World Wide Web today? It doesn't have to be big. You could post a list of your favorite movies. Or pictures of your 10 cats. You might want to create an online advertisement for your business or offer for auction your Great Aunt Edna's rocking chair that's been sitting in the garage for the past decade gathering dust. Maybe you'll get lucky and create the latest dot-com corporation that will sell for a billion dollars!

It sometimes seems as if every corporation is getting online these days, that the Web is nothing but commerce or a gigantic advertisement. But it's more than that, it's communication.

Imagine taking a digital photo of your baby and uploading that. Your father-in-law could see the pictures of the baby whenever he wanted. Your yoga class could be flooded by people looking for enlightenment. You might hit on a site name that a start-up company wants and is willing to pay $50,000 for the rights to.

So, what's stopping you? Maybe it seems too hard. That's where this book comes in. Yes, there are things you can do on the Internet that are incredibly tricky and take expert programming and months of debugging. We'll tell you about some of those options, but you're probably not going to go down that tunnel. It would take too long.

You can have a basic Web site in an hour. Working only a few hours a day, you can have an pretty cool Web site in a week. Imagine what your site will be like a year from now. Or better yet, don't imagine it. Start it.

You can put yourself on the Web today. The next question is, "What's it going to cost me?"

Well, aside from this book, which we hope you've already bought, it could cost you as little as an hour and no money.

Free? And an hour? No way.

Yes, way!

Of course, this is a fat book. If you read the whole thing, it'll take longer than an hour. And we're also going to tell you many ways that you can spend money to improve or augment your Web site. There are software tools that make building an entire Web site a snap. There are services that will help you put your business online professionally. But you don't have to start there.

In a few minutes, we're going to show you how to put up a Web page for free in an hour. So, what are you going to post?

Our Web Site Philosophy

1. Start it today. Don't wait until you get it perfect. Get something up online right away.
2. Continuous improvement works. If you catch a typo on your home page, fix it. If you think of something better to put on, change it. Unlike books or magazines, you don't have to run to the printers every time you want to make a change.
3. Add but don't subtract. Leave old materials online. One of the most valuable uses of the Internet is as an archive. Take advantage of it. Too often businesses and people choose to erase their past and start over. A wealth of knowledge is lost every time someone erases a Web page.

The word "post" is used on the Web in exactly the sense of a Post-it note or posting something on a bulletin board. You're sticking something into your Web space.

I Want a Web Site!

If you have a computer and an Internet service provider (ISP), this book will help you get a simple Web page up in one hour. Or you can have an entire Web site up within 24 hours! If you don't have a computer or an ISP, we can do it, but it will take a little longer.

How is that possible?

The World Wide Web isn't as difficult as it seems. All the tools for you to build a Web site are within your reach. You probably have many of them already built into your computer.

You're kidding, right?

Nope. Getting a basic Web page up online is about as easy as typing up your resume. Maybe easier, because you won't need to make up any impressive-sounding job titles or remember exactly when you worked flipping burgers.

How do I start?

Trying out the exercises in this book would be the next step. As you begin to develop your Web site, you'll make mistakes. Don't worry. You should be making plenty of mistakes. That's good, because that means you're learning. If you don't make any mistakes, chances are you haven't begun trying.

Our philosophy about Web site development: DON'T WORRY ABOUT GETTING IT PERFECT THE FIRST TIME!

That's right. Our experience shows that for individuals and small businesses (the ones who don't have a few hundred grand to throw at the Web) the best way of developing a Web site is slowly and incrementally over time. When you first develop your online presence, you won't be supremely fabulous. You'll just be visible. After a while, though, you'll begin to shape your Web site.

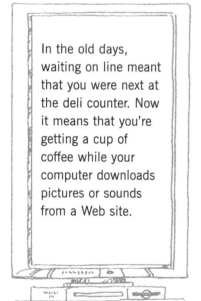

In the old days, waiting on line meant that you were next at the deli counter. Now it means that you're getting a cup of coffee while your computer downloads pictures or sounds from a Web site.

You'll make changes. You'll discard what doesn't work and find new ways of communicating. In short, you'll be creating yourself anew online.

"Creating yourself anew online." That sounds pretty significant.

Yes, it does. But it doesn't have to be burdensome.

If you're planning a Web site for your business, it's a bit like giving your office or store a makeover. You're going to be presenting yourself publicly. You want to look good—professional. You want to make sure you don't have any mistakes, right?

If you're setting up a Web site for your family, you don't want to forget about Uncle Harvey. You don't want to get Cousin Jane's birthday wrong.

If you're setting up a Web site as a hobby, you don't want to be criticized by everyone else in your field, right?

Perhaps more than anywhere else in today's world, the Internet is a place that thrives on controversy. If you're getting e-mails from your customers, competitors, or colleagues, that means that they've seen your site. That means it's working.

Hold on, I'm getting lost here... What do you mean by "it's working"?

The World Wide Web is about communication. One of our favorite metaphors is that it's a big bulletin board. You can put anything that you want up on the bulletin board, but will anyone see it? Or more to the point, will the right people see it?

After you've created your Web site, we'll give you detailed information about how to get more people to see your Web site, and how to get the right people to see your Web site.

How Big is a Megabyte?

A megabyte is 1,000,000 bytes. Just to give you a sense of how much that is, the last time we saved this book to disk, it took up 968,192 bytes—just a few bytes short of a meg.

Privacy Online

There is no privacy online. You can assume that the weirdest (and nicest) people in the world have access to your Web page. Don't post anything that you wouldn't want your mother to know about.

Quick, Let's Make a Home Page

Before we go any further, let's just get a quick home page online. It's not going to be elegant. You might want to delete it as soon as you're done, but it'll be a start.

1. Turn on your computer.
2. Log on to your Internet service provider.
3. Open your browser and type in: http://edit.yahoo.com/
4. Sign up for My Yahoo! They'll ask for all kinds of personal information. Feel free to make stuff up if you don't plan on using this home page again. We entered "Everythingbook" as our user name.
5. Go to http://geocities.yahoo.com/home/
6. Click on "Start Building Now"
   Note: Our Web address will be: www.geocities.com/ everythingbook
7. Fill out more forms and then accept the Terms of Agreement.
8. Click on "Yahoo Page Wizards."
9. Click on "Personal Page."
10. Follow the steps:
    a) Pick a color.
    b) Enter your name.
    c) Pick an image from your computer or use their picture.
    d) Enter your e-mail address.
    e) Enter a description of the page, and then describe your interests.
    f) Enter three favorite links.
    g) Describe your family and enter any family links.
    h) Describe your friends and enter any links to friends' pages.
11. Decide if this is going to be your home page or just an auxiliary page. If it is your home page, it will be named "index."
12. Have a look at the page!

Terms of Agreement

Nearly everybody has terms of agreement, but does anybody read them? If you're planning on using a service, read these terms carefully. Yes, it's boring legalese, but you might find that you're giving away your content or leaving yourself open to scads of unsolicited e-mail. If you don't like the terms of agreement, don't sign up.

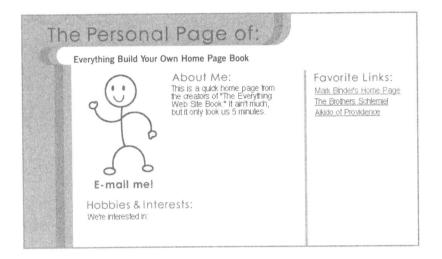

It isn't pretty, it's not even that informative, but it's online at: http://www.geocities.com/everythingbook/index.html.

What Is the World Wide Web?

Often confused with the Internet, the World Wide Web is only the visual part of the Internet: a collection of linked pages of information filled with colorful graphics, text, sound, animation, and advertisements from all over the world. These pages, which offer links to other pages with related information and allow a lot of jumping around, can belong to companies, organizations, government agencies, or individuals.

Each page consists of computer files, which may include text files, graphics files, sound files, and so on. Each group of pages belonging to a specific company, individual, or entity is called a Web site. Traveling between these oceans of information is often called "surfing the Web."

Those funny-looking addresses beginning with www that you see on television commercials, print ads, buses, and billboards are addresses for Web sites, so you can look them up easily on the Web. The Internet was started in 1969 as a project of the United States Department of Defense's Advanced

The entity that set technical standards for the Web is the World Wide Web Consortium, or W3C for short. Its members include all the big software companies involved with the Internet and the Internet Society. The W3C's Web site (www.w3.org) contains a wealth of information about the Web and coding HTML, as well as many useful tutorial pages.

Women are almost one-third of the current Internet users—9.9 million—more than three times as many as in late 1996. Men and women browsed the Internet for different reasons, with men outnumbering women in sports and product information—the biggest gap—as well as news, hobbies, entertainment, and games. Women outnumbered men in health/medicine and travel content.

Research Projects Agency. Called the ARPANET, the idea was to have a decentralized computer network that linked the agency with military contractors and universities doing related research. Conceived as a computer network that could withstand nuclear attack—it had no main central computer—the ARPANET strayed away from its military research origins as more American universities joined the network to share resources. Eventually it split into two networks: one for general research, one for military purposes.

The National Science Foundation also got into the act, setting up five supercomputer centers for research and connecting them with the ARPANET. The foundation later designed its own faster computer network in 1986, the NSFNET, with smaller regional networks to connect researchers. The mid-1980s was a time of tremendous growth for what began to be known as the Internet, fueled by the trend toward smaller computers for individual users instead of giant computers. Many different countries joined.

In 1990, the ARPANET closed as the Cold War began thawing rapidly and its original purpose was lost. The National Science Foundation began to manage the Internet and removed prohibitions against using the network for profit the following year, which changed the face of the Internet forever. Meanwhile, the handful of big commercial networks operated by private companies that had sprung up inside the Internet evolved into Internet service providers to serve the general public as the idea dawned that this could be really big business.

In 1991, the World Wide Web was born. Its father was a British researcher, Tim Berners-Lee, who was working at CERN, the European particle physics laboratory in Geneva, Switzerland. His idea was to let scientists share and locate information easily using one standard program, despite different computer platforms, across a worldwide network of connected computers. He created HTML (Hypertext Markup Language), the code Web pages are written in, and HTTP (Hypertext Transfer Protocol), which allows Web pages to be transmitted to users over the network.

When the software program Mosaic was invented in 1993 at the National Center for Supercomputing Applications at the University of Illinois at Champaign-Urbana, an easy-to-use way to find things on the World Wide Web suddenly appeared. Mosaic let users point a computer mouse at something interesting, click, and then find that information immediately. The first graphical browser, which let users find information through a simple point-and-click interface—without typing text commands—Mosaic forever changed the look of the Internet, which before this consisted of not-very-exciting-looking reams of text. (They were probably exciting to the scientists who needed them, but left something to be desired for the average person.)

The invention of Mosaic was crucial in bringing the Internet to the masses. The two big browsers we have today, Netscape Navigator from Netscape Communications—most of whose designers worked on Mosaic—and Internet Explorer from Microsoft Corporation, are its descendants. They added to many of Mosaic's original features and are much faster.

Thanks to the Web and Mosaic, which made it much easier to find and view information, two more pieces were in place for the Internet's shift from its origins as a research and military tool to a new medium for the general public. Millions of pages are now on the Web—the number is multiplying at an astonishing rate—as companies, nonprofit organizations, countries, cities, and everyone imaginable grasped the enormous potential of the Internet and raced to create their own Web sites.

Who's on the Internet?

Anywhere from 30 to 50 million Americans were regularly using the Internet in 1997, depending on what study you read. In a study by FIND/SVP, a New York market research firm, half of this group used the Internet daily, while two out of five used it weekly. In addition, over nine million Americans have tried the Internet but are not current users. According to *The Industry Standard* (citing *The Computer Industry Almanac*), there were 147,800,000 Internet users worldwide at the end of 1998, with 52 percent (nearly 77 million) living in the United States.

Many Internet users noted they were watching less television, reading fewer magazines and newspapers, and watching fewer

Uses of the Web

To better understand what you want to do, consider how other people use the Web.

- **Research.** The *Encyclopedia Britannica* is online, and so is your local newspaper. But a lot of information comes from individuals like you who are putting their own experiences online.
- **Shopping/Selling Products or Services.** Think about how you look for items online. Are you looking for the best quality or just the best price?
- **Entertainment and Game Playing.** You can watch movies online or play chess with somebody in Norway. Tease yourself or your children with puzzles, riddles, quizzes, or multiplayer games from action adventure scenarios to golf, poker, and backgammon.

videos in 1997. The biggest proportion of current Internet users (35 percent) said their television watching had dwindled. Sixteen percent said their magazine/newspaper reading had fallen off, while 19 percent said their video watching had slackened. Only 10 percent were listening to the radio less, perhaps because it's easy to have a radio in the background while Web surfing.

Some Frequently Asked Questions about the Web

There are some basic terms you need to grasp that will explain a bit more how things work on the World Wide Web. Without understanding these terms, you will truly be lost. Understanding them, you will learn how to add to and improve your overall experience.

What is a Web page?

When you're browsing the Web, a Web page is what pops up when you type in a URL (Uniform Resource Locator—a Web address). In the background, a Web page is a text file written in HTML (Hypertext Markup Language) that tells a Web browser how to form the page on the viewer's computer. It can contain text, links, pointers to graphics files, and scripts that do cool tricks.

What is a Web browser?

A Web browser is the software that you use to look at Web pages and sites. Most people use Netscape Navigator or Microsoft's Explorer. There are also other graphical browsers, like Opera and CyberDog, and text-only browsers like Lynx.

Who is a Webmaster?

You are! Anybody who builds and maintains a Web site can call himself or herself a Webmaster (or Webmistress, if you prefer). It's the catch-all term for the person who is in charge of a Web site. They're the ones who are responsible for everything that is posted online. In a small operation, they do all the work. They write the HTML pages, they handle the graphics, they do all the uploading, and they answer the e-mail. In a big operation, they're probably just the site's manager, overseeing employees.

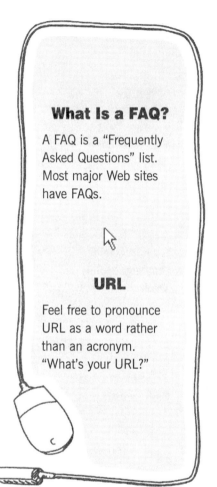

What Is a FAQ?

A FAQ is a "Frequently Asked Questions" list. Most major Web sites have FAQs.

URL

Feel free to pronounce URL as a word rather than an acronym. "What's your URL?"

Sound like you? Well, maybe not yet. Maybe you're just a WiT (Webmaster in Training). Don't worry. Even the greatest Webmasters had to begin somewhere. That's what this book's for, to train you to go out and do it for yourself.

What is the difference between a Web site and a Web page?

A Web site is a collection of one or more Web pages. A Web site can be a single Web page or thousands of them. Most Web sites have a home page and a variety of other pages linked to them. They may also have image and multimedia subdirectories. Some Web sites, like search engines, may actually generate their own Web pages on the fly. That means that on those sites, the pages you see aren't stored in HTML but are generated from data stored on the site.

There are two ways to design a Web site. You can either start on a page-by-page basis and link pages together, or you can envision the entire Web site and then plan and design what you need.

We recommend a combination of both methods. Beginners will tend to work on a page-by-page basis until they learn what works and doesn't work for site design. Advanced Web designers will look at an entire site, determine what it needs, and go from there.

What is a home page?

A home page is the front page of a Web site that appears when you type its Internet address. People often use the term home page to refer to the entire Web site. Sometimes it looks like a table of contents, with links to different areas of the site. Many Web sites have dozens, even hundreds or thousands of pages. You can reach an interior page without accessing the home page first if you know the URL for that page, or you can follow the directions on the home page to jump around.

In Internet Explorer, click on Preferences and choose Web Browser/Browser Display. In the Home Page box, type a new Address.

In Netscape, click on Preferences, choose Navigator and type the address into the Home page location box.

Web Browsers

Your Web browser has a default home page that opens whenever you open a new window. This is typically set to that browser manufacturer's Web site. You can change the default page to any home page you'd like.

It's a simple matter to set your browser to open a Web page on your computer. Instead of typing in a URL, use the pathname. Open the file from your browser, click in the Netsite/Address window and copy the pathname. Then paste that into the home page box. Every time you open a new window in your browser, the page on your computer will be displayed. If you have a dial-up connection, this is a good way of managing your links before your computer automatically logs you in.

What is hypertext?

Hypertext is the name for the system of linked pages that make up the Web. Web pages are written in HTML (Hypertext Markup Language), a programming language your browser reads, and uses links to easily connect to related information either on the same Web site or on a different site. These links to other Web pages or to sound, image, or video files—also called hot links or hyperlinks—can be either words or phrases, pictures, or icons on a Web page.

Links are generally underlined and blue in color (although this can be changed). In fact, your cursor turns into a pointing hand when it is on a link, while the Internet address of that new page appears in the lower left corner of the page. Links you've already seen will change color afterward, a handy reminder that you've been there, done that.

When you reach a Web page, your browser translates the information and commands in the HTML file it receives—plus files for pictures, sound, or video that may be on the page—into readable words and viewable graphics.

What is an Internet address?
What is a URL?

The long addresses for Web sites follow a format, starting with "http://" and followed by "www" (without the quotes). For example, "http://www.xyz.com" is the Internet address, or URL (uniform resource locator, pronounced you-are-el) for the fictional XYZ Company. Let's break it down. Think of the prefix "http," which stands for Hypertext Transfer Protocol, as a command to your browser to connect with the Web and find the site whose name follows.

URLs are often lengthy because they can specify the name of a directory and the name of a file or document in the directory. These appear separated by front slashes in the URL. For example, typing the URL "http://www.xyz.com/products/widget" will show the page for the document named "widget" in the directory called "products" on the Web site of the XYZ Company. Because every page within a site has its own URL, you can type the URL for a specific page, if you know it, to find that page without going to the

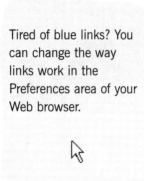

Tired of blue links? You can change the way links work in the Preferences area of your Web browser.

Fortunately, most domain name servers are not case sensitive. You can type in *www.adamsmedia.com/* or *WWW.AdamsMedia.com/* and get the same Web page.

site's home page first. This saves a lot of time because you don't have to explore the whole Web site to reach that page.

You must type a URL EXACTLY the way it appears in the Location, Address, or Netfinder box—no matter how weird it looks—including every bit of punctuation, the whole string of letters, or sometimes numbers and capital letters in the middle. Otherwise, you won't find that site. This is probably the single main reason for not finding a Web site and the major cause of people throwing up their hands in despair and complaining they can't find anything on the Internet.

Remember, if you bookmark a Web site, you never need to type its long, complex address again! You can find it in one click. By the way, most URLs are entirely lowercase. But if one includes some capital letters, which means the host computer is case-sensitive, use them.

While "http" is how an address signals to your browser that the location is part of the Web, other prefixes signify other parts of the Internet. For example, an address that starts with "news:" means it is a newsgroup. For example, "news:rec.arts.movies.current-film" tells your browser to find the discussion group on current films called "rec.arts.movies.current-film." File Transfer Protocol (files to be downloaded) can also be accessed by URLs that begin with "ftp://"

What is a domain name?

The domain name is the registered name for an Internet address. The very end of an Internet address, or top-level domain name, shows the domain, or type of organization supporting it. The top-level domain names are: com, which means it is a business; gov for government; edu for an educational institution; net for a computer network; mil for military; and org for a nonprofit organization.

The first part of the domain name is called the second-level domain name, which precedes the top-level domain and shows the specific organization or person to whom the site belongs. For example, in "nytimes.com," the domain name for the *New York Times*, "nytimes" is the second-level domain. In "census.gov," the domain name for the U.S. Census Bureau, "census" is the second-level domain.

Top-Level Domain Names

Currently, the only available top-level domains are:

.com
.org
.net

The existence of other domains has been under discussion for some time. At present, the community that decides these things seems deadlocked and unable or unwilling to move forward and authorize new domains.

13

Your Resources

You have a lot of resources at your disposal. It's a good idea to know what you've got before you start. Don't worry if you don't know all the answers. Don't worry if you don't have any of these items. The idea is to know what you have—and what you don't have.

1. What kind of computer do you have? (If you don't have a computer, where can you use one and what kind is it?)

2. How fast is your modem?

3. Who is your Internet service provider (ISP)?

4. Do you have a Web space included with your ISP account?

5. Do you have a scanner? A digital camera? A video camera?

6. Does your computer have video or audio input?

7. Do you like to draw?

8. Do you like to write?

9. Who do you know who can help you with your Web site?

10. Are there computer or Internet classes you'd like to take at a local community college or library?

The most important resource you need to create your home page is this book. Next, you need to access the free Web site that we've provided. It will link you to all the software you need to create your site. The Web address is: *www.adamsmedia.com/everything/homepage.asp*.

Each domain name is unique in the world. Each is coupled with an Internet Protocol (IP) address, a series of numbers that refers to a specific host computer in the routing system of the Internet. Typing in these numbers will bring up the same Web site as typing its Internet address, but generally only a computer, not the average person, knows the numbered IP address.

Different countries have country codes, two-letter endings to their domain names, such as "fr" for France, "uk" for United Kingdom, and "it" for Italy. When there is no country code, a location in the United States is implied. Some American domain names do have "us" as an ending, preceded generally by a state and city or county.

Domain names are like online gold. If you have a memorable online name you're in business. Amazon.com, for instance, is named after the largest river in the world. After building its brand as a research resource, The Mining Company (www.miningcompany.com) changed its name to About.com. When it's time to register a domain name, take your time and pick the best one.

Some Enchanted Domain Names

The South Pacific islands of Tonga, Nieu, and Norfolk Island are among the nations who register their two-letter country domain names to noncitizens who pay a fee: $25 per year for ".nu" from Nieu (pronounced new-way), $1,000 per year for ".ni" from Norfolk Island. The majority of country names limit domain names to citizens. As a result, some Americans have domain names like "go.to" and "internet.nu."

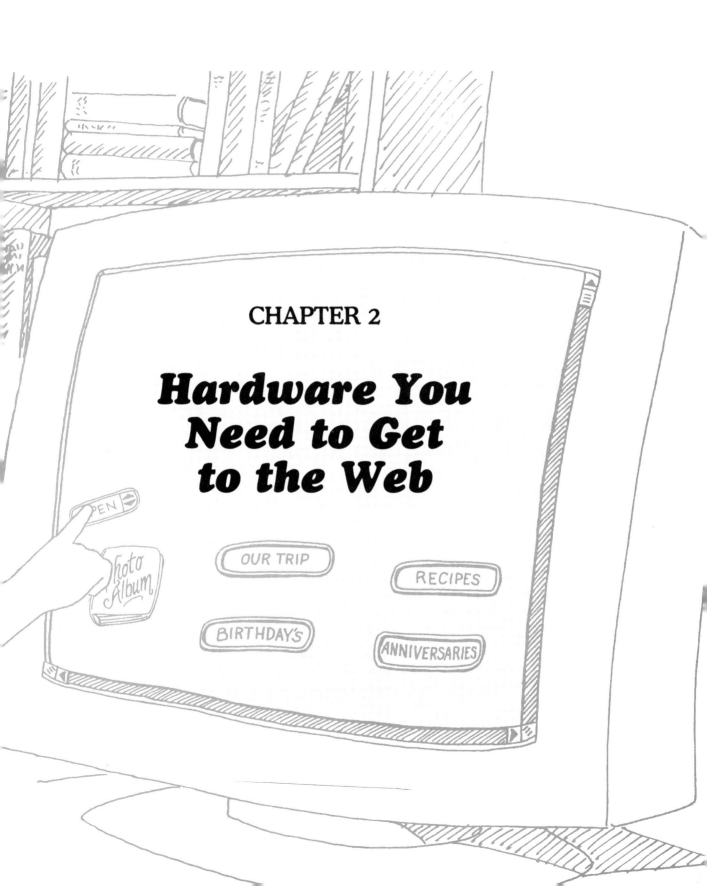

CHAPTER 2

Hardware You Need to Get to the Web

If you're going to build a Web site, you're going to need to cruise the Web. Here's the hardware and software you need to find an Internet service provider (ISP) and connect to the Internet. If you already have a computer and an Internet service provider, you can skim or even skip this chapter.

In each of these options, there is no hardware to buy and no software to maintain. Unfortunately, you're limited by the hours of the library, school building, or cafe.

If you're serious about building Web sites and staying up to date, here's what you'll need.

1. A computer or television set. A computer that can run Windows 95, Windows 3.1, or a Macintosh will work. Because the Web is so rich in images, which take longer to download than text, you'll need more memory and probably more hard disk space than what usually comes with an older computer.

   A growing number of people are using their television for Internet access. If you subscribe to WebTV or similar services that use a set-top box atop your television, you get the added thrill of reading a Web page or your e-mail lying on a couch from across the room.

2. A modem. This is an electronic device that lets your computer talk to other computers and obtain information over telephone lines. Most new computers now come with pre-installed modems. If you belong to a company, university, or school network, however, Internet access may be delivered through a network card inside your computer, which then talks to the company's or school's own network that communicates with the Internet. If you connect via cable modem, you'll also need an ethernet card.

3. A connection to the Net. In the old days, everyone used a telephone line. Any analog line, which tends to be used in homes, is generally needed. With cable modems and other connection methods (like satellite Internet connections) you may not need to use your phone.

4. Software. You need telephone dialer software to dial the Internet, communications software called TCP/IP (Transmission Control Protocol/Internet Protocol) so your computer can communicate with the Internet, and a browser that finds Web pages to display on your screen. The software will generally be supplied by your Internet service provider when you sign up, except perhaps for the browser. If you choose Windows 98 or an online service, a browser will be included.

5. An account with an Internet service provider. This can be a national, regional, or local provider that offers full Internet access, or one of the commercial online services, such as America Online, CompuServe, Prodigy, or Microsoft Network, that offers original content to members plus a gateway to the Internet. If you use a cable modem, your cable company will be your ISP.

What Kind of Computer Do You Need?

The World Wide Web was initially designed to serve the needs of the lowest common denominator. Until a few years ago, anybody with an old computer and a slow connection to the Internet could use it effectively.

Now, however, with more and more focus on graphics and multimedia, you'll probably want to use the latest browser, plug-ins, and nifty design software.

Absolute minimum hardware

Yes, you could use an old 486 PC or a pre–Power PC Macintosh. They'll work fine for Web design and content creation—especially if you decide to write your own HTML. Using these old machines with a slow modem would be a humbling experience. Your Web site won't be filled with intense graphics because you won't be able to stand the long wait.

Free, Inexpensive, and Inconvenient Access

Anyone can get access to the Web without spending a penny. Almost every library has a bank of computers with a fast connection to the Internet. If you're in school, chances are your university has a computing room. You can also go to an upscale copy shop or an Internet cafe and pay an hourly fee. (Check the Yellow Pages or do an online search.)

1. You'll need a bare minimum of a 486 PC (which is no longer sold new today but available secondhand) with at least 8–12 MB (megabytes) of RAM (random access memory, or memory for short) but preferably anywhere from 16–32 MB of RAM. The preferred Pentium processor commonly sold today is a 586, which has more power and so is even better but not necessary. A 386 with a handful of MB and Windows 3.1 is possible, but you'll miss a lot and won't be able to use the latest browsers. For a Macintosh, you'll need at least a System 7 with at least 8–12 MB of RAM but ideally 16–32 MB.

2. A hard disk with at least 400–500 MB. The size of your hard disk determines the amount of permanent space on your computer for storing files and programs, and this should do. But if you plan to download a huge number of files or play lots of games (with or without your kids), you'll want more room, say 1–2 gigabytes.

3. A video card that supports 256 colors and a high-resolution VGA graphics display for clarity. You can still see the Web if your video card supports only sixteen colors, but your browser may not show pictures. To see pictures the way their designers intended, you'll need a 256-color card.

4. A 16-bit (or 32-bit) sound card (SoundBlaster or compatible) and speakers (or a headset). There is lots of sound on the Web—music, radio, and interview clips—but if you can live without this, you can skip the sound card. If you plan on listening in privacy without blaring sound in front of your family or others, get a headset.

5. A color monitor (15" is standard, but 17" is sharper and no longer so expensive), keyboard, and mouse. These generally come with your computer.

6. A printer. An inkjet, which produces good quality, or a laser printer, which produces excellent quality but is much more expensive, is preferable. Don't get a dot matrix printer, which produces poor quality, is slow, and needs paper fed one sheet at a time. If you don't need

to print out Web pages in color, buy a black-and-white printer, which is cheaper.

7. A CD-ROM drive (16X or higher; X refers to the speed). It's not necessary to reach the Web, but a great deal of software, including Internet connection software and children's educational and game programs, are available on CD-ROMs.

Excellent and inexpensive machines

Any computer you buy today will blow away last year's model. Because of this, used editions of last year's models will be incredibly inexpensive. We don't really recommend buying top of the line machines for premium prices (unless you're a professional graphics or multimedia designer and the speed of rendering and processing makes a huge difference in your workload).

Today, all computers come with CD-ROM drives, sound cards, and more memory and hard drive space than was possible five years ago. So buy whatever machine you like.

Repeat after us: "The more memory, the faster and more efficiently your computer will run." Get at least 64 megabytes of RAM.

1. For less than $1,000 you can get a Windows 98 machine with a 500+ MHz processor that will rock every single Web creation application. It will have gigabytes of memory, a built-in sound card, a built-in video card.

2. For under $1,000 you can also buy a Macintosh iMac, which is a superb all-in-one solution and has the added benefit of including an excellent bundle of software.

3. Buy a 17" monitor. If your eyesight is poor, you'll be able to blow up the images. If your eyesight is good, you can have more screen real estate.

4. Consider buying a CD-ROM burner (or a DVD burner when they become inexpensive). You don't need this for the Web, but it's a great way of creating permanent backups. These CD-ROMS will be especially useful if you use a large number of images and need to archive them.

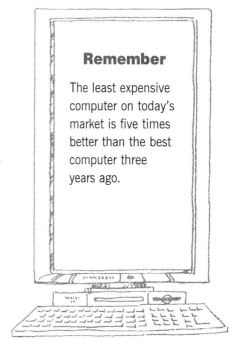

Remember

The least expensive computer on today's market is five times better than the best computer three years ago.

Choosing a Computer

When you buy a computer, comparison shop. Read articles in magazine and newspaper technology sections on computers and computer magazines, which always run articles on "Best PCs," "PCs Under $1,000," and "Best New Product," etc., and review different brands. Talk to computer salespeople at several stores, ask questions about how the products differ, and what they recommend for your needs and price range. If you want to buy by mail order, obtain several catalogs, not just one.

Don't be swayed by the latest, most expensive models that come on the market. You can always upgrade your computer with fancy new software and other accessories such as a faster modem, bigger monitor, and better sound card. You can also buy a more advanced model later when you can afford it or want loads of extra features. Don't think you have to buy a new machine every year or so; many computers are still thriving several years after they were bought.

Leasing a computer is an option. Paying a small monthly amount over the term of a 24-month or 36-month lease may be more affordable in the short run. When the lease ends, you can either buy the computer at a specific percentage of the sales price or lease a newer, more sophisticated model. But read the fine print carefully in the leasing agreement, which is subject to credit approval because it is in effect a loan, to see exactly how much more the computer will cost in the long run. Leases vary widely from different computer makers, so be sure to comparison shop here, too.

When you're ready, buy—or lease—the model with the best mix of features that suits your needs and fits within your budget.

The iMac vs. a cheap PC

Beth and Mark have been having the Macintosh vs. PC war for years. Before he wrote this book, Mark was a dedicated Macintosh user. In the interest of research, he bought an inexpensive Windows machine. Here's his analysis of the advantages and disadvantages of each machine.

The Bad News

Buying a computer from a chop shop that puts it together for you has its downside. The low-budget machine Mark bought didn't work very well, and Mark learned that unless the hardware malfunctioned, basic repairs would cost $50 an hour. After much complaining, the store agreed to take the computer back—for a 15 percent restocking fee.

iMac—$999

The iMac is the Volkswagen Beetle of computers. It looks cool but doesn't really fit into every lifestyle. Somehow it seems too cute to be a serious machine, but with a 350 MHz processor, it rocks. (*Note:* According to Apple, a 350 MHz iMac would actually be faster than a 350 MHz Pentium machine.)

The iMac keyboard is a little too dainty, and its round mouse is even less ergonomic than your basic repetitive motion syndrome mouse. It also comes with 64 MB of RAM, but there are frequently automatic upgrade programs available.

That said, the iMac is truly easy to connect to the Internet. It comes with a built-in 56K modem and a 10/100 Base-T Ethernet card, which means that you can either hook up a cable modem or cruise through the phone lines at top speed.

For Web designers, the iMac has a slew of preinstalled software.

- AppleWorks 6 is one of the simplest and most useful single-product suites. It includes word processing, drawing/painting, spreadsheet, and database functions. Its "Save As HTML" feature is usable, but not the best.
- MetaCreation's Kai's Photo Soap is just plain cool. This is a graphics image processing program. Think of it as PhotoShop but with a California-style user interface. It's the easiest way to get the red eye out of any of your photos before uploading them
- Adobe PageMill 3.0. This is a basic WYSIWYG (what you see is what you get) HTML page generator. For laying out simple pages, adjusting images, and creating links, PageMill is superb.

Finally, built into the Macintosh operating system is an easy-to-use Web server with a (supposedly) unbreakable firewall. In other words, if you follow the simple steps, you can use the Mac OS Personal Web Sharing system to serve Web pages on the Internet without any uploading. Of course this requires a constant connection with the Net and may slow down your computer.

iMac DV

If you're buying an iMac, consider spending another $400 for the iMac DV. It comes with a 400 MHz processor, 128 meg of RAM, a 13 gigabyte hard drive, and DVD. Best of all, it includes iMovie, one of the easiest ways to edit movies digitally. Then, you can upload the movie to the Web.

Local computer store's PC special—$801

Mark didn't go to a major chain store. He found this machine assembled by a small company in Rhode Island. For just over $800 (including tax) he got an AMD K6-2 450 MHz machine with 64 MB of RAM. It too had a 56K modem and an Ethernet card (though he had to make a special request).

The LCS machine came with a 10 gigabyte hard drive and a 44X CD-ROM drive, which were nearly twice as big and twice as fast as the iMac's 6 gig hard drive and 24X CD-ROM. It also has a floppy disk drive, which the iMac spurned.

For software, the LCS machine came with the Corel WordPerfect Suite, which included Corel's excellent word processor WordPerfect 8, as well as spreadsheet, presentation, and database programs. Not the best HTML export features, but serviceable.

CHAPTER 3

Connecting to the Internet

There are a number of ways to connect to the Internet. As a rule, you can't connect to the Internet without a modem. At first glance, the exception seems to be WebTV, which allows you to access the Web through your television, but the WebTV box is nothing more than a computer and modem. So whether it's a traditional telephone modem or a cable modem, you'll need to pick from one of these options.

Telephone Modems

Telephone connections are still the most popular and least expensive method to connect to the Internet. In all probability, your new computer comes with a built-in modem.

If you're buying a modem, keep in mind that modems come in different speeds, can be external or internal, and are made by many different manufacturers for desktop computers or laptops at varying costs. Some have additional features and can act as fax, voice mail, and speakerphone systems.

You'll want at least a 56 Kbps modem (kilobits per second, or a theoretical speed of 56,000 data bits per second). The Web is filled with images, sound, and video clips, which take a lot of time to download. Don't settle for a slow 28.8 or 14.4 Kbps modem unless you have the patience of Job and the tolerance of the late Mother Teresa.

When you buy a modem, make sure it is Hayes compatible, which means it is standard and should work with your computer. If you have an older 386 computer, most modems made today will not be compatible; a 486 or Pentium, however, will be able to use the fastest modems around. Also, make sure your Internet service provider will support your modem's speed. If you have a high-speed 56 Kbps modem but your ISP is at the 33.6 Kbps speed, you'll be cruising at the slower 33.6.

Telephone modem tips and tricks

- If you want your telephone and your modem to share the same line, consider using the phone company's voice mail service. Instead of getting a busy signal when you're using your modem, callers will be able to leave a message.

Note: One of the selling points for cable modems is that they eliminate the need for a second phone line, hence justifying their higher cost. However, you can't send or receive faxes from a cable modem. You may still need a second line if you plan on sending and receiving a lot of faxes.

- If you have only one telephone line, make sure your modem is connected to the telephone jack in your wall from its line in or line jack for a clearer connection. Your telephone and answering machine should be connected to the modem's line out or phone jack.

- If you have call waiting, dismantle it while using your modem. Otherwise, an incoming call is likely to break your online connection; worse, you may end up with no call and no online connection. Dismantle it by adding *70 (or *71) before your telephone number in your dial-up connection (in Windows 95 go to "Dial-Up Networking," then "Dial Properties.") If you have pulse, not tone dialing, use 1170 or 1171. Call waiting will resume when you finish Internet usage.

- Internal modems are a little cheaper than external modems. They also save precious desk space. However, they are harder to install; you have to open your computer. It's best to have a computer expert do this instead of trying it alone.

- If you have a laptop computer, you may want an internal modem or a credit card-sized PC card modem, which fits into the card slot. This makes it easier for travel than lugging around an external modem.

If you have a fax modem, your top fax speed will be 14.4 Kbps, despite the higher speed for your modem.

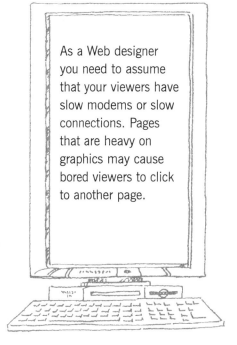

As a Web designer you need to assume that your viewers have slow modems or slow connections. Pages that are heavy on graphics may cause bored viewers to click to another page.

- Ask if your ISP can support a faster modem connection, such as 56K or ISDN.

- If you have trouble connecting with your modem, or keep getting disconnected, check all the modem settings with your ISP to make sure all information has been entered properly. If this doesn't work, call your telephone company to see if you have noise on your line. If you do, perhaps they can fix your line. Sometimes, switching your modem to a slower

Internet Service Providers

National

AIS Network
www.solutionprovider.net
847-882-0493

AT&T WorldNet
www.att.com/worldnet
800-967-5363

Blue Sky Internet
www.blueskyweb.com
503-669-1497

Brigadoon.com
www.brigadoon.com
425-586-2497

Concentric Network
Corporation
www.concentric.net
800-745-2747

EarthLink Network
www.earthlink.net
800-395-8425

FlashNet
www.flash.net
800-352-7420

Global Net
www.globally.net
703-715-1829

GTE
Internetworking
www.gte.net
888-GTE-SURF

HoloNet
www.holonet.net
510-704-0160

IBM Internet Connection
www.ibm.net
800-888-4103

InterNET Resource
NETworks
www.inr.net
603-880-8120

Kampus Networks
www.kampus.net
888-826-1985

MCI Internet
www.internetmci2000.com
800-550-0927

MindSpring Enterprises
www.mindspring.com
800-719-4332

Netcom On-Line
Communication Services
www.netcom.com
800-638-2661

Nova Internet Services
www.novaone.net
214-904-9600

PSINet
www.psi.net
800-827-7482

Sprint Internet Passport
www.sprint.com/sip
800-747-9428

TOAST.net
www.toast.net
888-TOAST-ME

UniDial Communications
www.unidial.com
502-244-6666

Voyager Online
www.vol.com
800-864-0442

WebTV Networks
www.webtv.net
800-GO-WEBTV

ZipLink
www.ziplink.net
947-888-5465

The Internet Access
Company (TIAC)
www.tiac.net
617-276-7200

Regional Internet Service Providers Serving Major U.S. Cities

Boston
Cyber Access
Communications
www.cybercom.net
617-876-5660

Galaxy Internet Services
www.gis.net
888-334-2529

The Internet Access
Company (TIAC)
www.tiac.net
617-276-7200

Chicago
I Connect
www.iconnect.net
847-662-0877

InterAccess
www.interaccess.com
312-496-4400

The Ads
www.the-ads.com
815-741-1645

Urbancom.net
www.urbancom.net
708-687-2090

Denver
Denver.net
www.denver.net
303-573-5020

Rocky Mountain Internet
www.rmi.net
307-332-3755

Houston
Compass Net
www.compassnet.com/index.html
713-776-0022

Netropolis Communications
www.netropolis.net
713-977-9779

Regional Internet Service Providers Serving Major U.S. Cities (continued)

Southwestern Bell Internet
Services
www.swbell.net
972-238-3600

Los Angeles
aNet Communications
www.anet.net
800-395-0692

BNS Internet
www.bassett.net
714-227-7503

BeachNet Internet Access
www.beachnet.com
310-823-3308

Brand X Internet
www.brandx.net
310-395-5500

Direct Net
www.directnet.com
213-640-6246

InterWorld
Communications
www.interworld.net/
default.htm
310-726-0500

Pacific Bell
www.pacbell.net
800-708-4638

Miami
CyberGate
www.gate.net
800-NET-GATE

Internet Providers of
Florida
www.fla.net
305-273-7978

Netpoint Communications
www.netpoint.net
305-891-1955

New York
ASANet Internet Service
www.asan.com
718-539-2362

BrainLINK International
www.brainlink.com
718-805-6559

bway.net
www.bway.net
212-982-9800

Erol's Internet
www.erols.net
888-GO-EROLS

GAIN-NY
www.gainny.com
212-779-8715

Interport Communications
www.interport.net
212-989-7448

i-2000, Inc.
www.i-2000.com
800-464-3820

Internet Quick Link
www.quicklink.com
212-307-1669

Link America
Communications
www.link-net.com
212-334-0331

Panix
www.panix.com
212-741-4400

Spacelab Net
www.mxol.com
212-966-8844

San Francisco
BAIS (Bay Area Infoserve)
www.bais.com
408-447-8690

Pacific Bell Internet
www.pacbell.net
800-708-4638

Sirius Connections
www.sirius.com
415-865-5000

Verlo Northern California
www.wco.com
800-226-3848

Seattle
Emerald Net
www.emeraldnet.net
206-363-1818

Seanet
www.seanet.com
206-343-7828

Washington D.C.
Cornerstone Network
www.cstone.net
800-325-9848

Erol's Internet
www.erols.net
888-GO-EROLS

The Hub Internet Services
www.knight-hub.com
703-553-6790

Verio Washington D.C.
www.veriodc.net
888-VERIO-DC

speed will ease things. Other times, removing another appliance, such as a fax machine, from the same telephone line will help reduce interference.

- A modem works by switching digital data from a computer into analog data for transmission over telephone lines, then to digital data for the other computer and back again to analog data. A 56 Kbps modem runs so fast because the data sent over telephone lines in the first place from the ISP remains digital. Even with a 56 Kbps modem, uploading data—transferring files from your computer to another computer—remains at the 33.6 Kbps speed.

Cable Modems

Hundreds of times faster than a traditional modem, cable can far surpass the super speedy T1 lines businesses often use, which run at 1.5 Mbps (one-and-a-half megabytes). Because a cable connection means you are permanently connected to the Internet over the coaxial cable used for your television, you don't need to dial up your ISP every time you want your computer to go online.

If you have a cable modem, you may also be able to use your computer as a Web server. Since your connection to the Net is always open, you could access a portion of your computer directly from the Net—no more uploading. Naturally, some cable companies prohibit this sort of usage. You'll need to check your cable modem contract to find out the specifics. Also, cable modem upload speeds are slower than download speeds.

The bad news about cable modems is that they're more expensive—about $40–50 a month—which is at least two to three times the cost of a traditional Internet service provider.

Also, you may not live in a part of the United States that has cable Internet access at this time. Check with your local cable company for more information.

ISDN (Integrated Services Digital Network)

Much faster than a traditional modem—four to nine times as fast as many home users' modems—ISDN runs at up to 128 Kbps, more

Don't buy a cable modem. The cable modem itself typically costs $300 or more, and different cable companies use different modems. Some cable companies include modems in their connection costs, while others will rent them to you for about $10 a month. Chances are that within the three years it would take to pay off a cable modem, the technology will change. Maybe a new form of fiber optic connection will be available in your area.

than twice the speed of a 56 Kbps, because it uses a special, completely digital telephone line. It's also more expensive, both in terms of installation and monthly charges, although this varies widely depending on where you live. Buying a special ISDN terminal adapter is also required.

Ask your telephone company if it supplies ISDN, which is now available in most urban and suburban areas. One advantage, besides the speed, is that you can use your regular telephone line while using ISDN at the same time.

Until recently, most ISDN was priced out of the reach of ordinary consumers. Now, firms like Pacific Bell (www.pacbell.com) on the West Coast are offering ISDN for as little as $26 a month.

Satellite Dishes

A satellite dish can also offer very high speed, about 200–400 Kbps for downloads, but you'll still need a standard dial-up connection to upload. The dish itself costs several hundred dollars.

T1 Connection

You might want a T1 line, with an always-open up and downstream connection of 1.5 Mbps speed for a dedicated line. But you probably won't want to pay the piper. T1 comes with a hefty price tag—at least $1,000 per month. The advantage of T1 is that it makes Web hosting a breeze. While cable modems offer a fast downstream connection (from the Internet to your computer), the upstream is considerably slower. T1 is used to post information from your computer upstream to the Internet. Many corporations, as well as some Internet cafes and even apartment buildings, sport T1 lines.

ADSL Connection

Asymmetric Digital Subscriber Line (ADSL), also called DSL or XDSL, is a new technology that uses ordinary telephone lines but can achieve tremendous speeds of up to 6 or 7 Mbps. Found only in a few trial areas of the United States, DSL uses the non-voice

Cable Rates

Check your cable rates. We found that it was less expensive to order a cable modem plus basic cable than it was to order a cable modem by itself.

ISDN

ISDN uses existing telephone lines and divides them into multiple digital channels. This allows you to make phone calls, send faxes, and surf the Internet simultaneously.

part of the telephone line, which means you can talk on the telephone while Web surfing.

One company ramping up a nationwide DSL campaign is Telocity (www.telocity.com/).

Prime-Time Internet: Working the Web on Your TV

As of this writing, users of WebTV don't have their own Web space included in the cost of their service. That said, there are plenty of free Web hosting sites available online that WebTV users can access.

WebTV can be cheap, fast, much easier than a computer, and even lets you print pages in color. At only $99 for WebTV Classic, the original version (plus a wireless keyboard for about $50–$80), and $250 for WebTV Plus, the advanced version and its keyboard, it's a bargain whose quality has won many rave reviews in computer publications. Since six e-mail accounts come with each unit, it's easy for a family to share. Of course, the Web pages, e-mail, and newsgroups displayed are the size of your television screen— pretty impressive if you own a 31" screen.

Sold in electronics stores, WebTV looks like a black cable box, which you plug into your telephone line and the back of your television. Turn it on and off with its lightweight wireless keyboard or its remote control if you prefer. There's no mouse, so you zip around with up, down, and side arrow keys, which automatically jump to links if you're on a Web page, and with scroll up and down keys. To find a Web page, press a "go to" key and a window pops on the screen so you can type its address.

WebTV Plus comes with a 56K modem, a 167 MHz 1.1 GB hard disk, and 8 MB of RAM. All of this means it both connects to the Internet fast and sends pages rapidly, and its picture and word quality is superior to WebTV Classic, which has no hard disk and the speed of a 28.8 modem. The versions sold by Sony, Philips Magnavox, and Mitsubishi look slightly different but operate the same way. These companies licensed the revolutionary technology invented by WebTV Networks, a Palo Alto, California, start-up formed by three Apple Computer veterans. The first WebTVs were introduced in late 1996 and sold for about $250 plus the keyboard.

Faster is better. If you're going to spend a lot of time working on the Web, bump up your connection speed. If you've got a slow modem, spend the money and buy a faster one. Keep an eye out for cable and DSL options. The faster your connection to the Web, the less time you'll spend waiting for pictures to download and the less time you'll spend waiting for your computer to upload your files.

The monthly rate for unlimited Internet access is $19.95 for WebTV Classic, which is more or less the going rate for all-you-can-eat plans from many Internet service providers and commercial online services such as America Online and CompuServe. (It drops to $9.95 monthly if you use your own ISP.) It's $24.95 for unlimited monthly access for WebTV Plus, or $19.95 if you use your own ISP. Certain color printers from Hewlett-Packard and Canon can be plugged into the back of the WebTV box.

Heads or Tails: Commercial Online Service or Internet Service Provider?

As a Webmaster-in-Training, the amount of free Web space provided with your Internet account is only one small reason to sign up with a provider. If you choose to serve your Web site on a commercial host, the few megabytes that your ISP gives you is simply extra unused space. Choose your commercial online service or Internet service provider based on your computer-savvy, comfort level, and what you enjoy.

Differences are blurring between commercial online services and Internet service providers, as some content that began on commercial online services has expanded to the Web to draw a bigger audience. For example, The Motley Fool, a personal finance site, started on America Online but now is on the Web. Also, some Internet service providers offer a limited amount of content and recommended links, particularly local or regional providers.

Commercial online services

Many people like the fact that each commercial online service is its own self-contained small world. You'll only meet fellow subscribers in discussion forums and chat areas, which fosters a reassuring feeling of safety and belonging to a community. Some subscribers, in fact, venture only rarely, or perhaps never, past its cozy confines to the Internet.

Of course, this is somewhat misleading, since at 10 million subscribers, America Online, the biggest online service, can hardly be considered a small town where everybody knows each other's

DSL

Although DSL offers high-speed continuous Internet connection, the actual DSL connection speed depends on the distance of your home from the phone company's central office. The closer you are, the faster the connection speed. You may also need to rewire your home for optimal DSL speed. While DSL is very much in the news, since it uses existing copper wires, it will ultimately become obsolete as users demand faster and bigger pipelines.

Users of cable, DSL, ISDN, or satellite modems will typically have a limited number of choices for Internet service providers.

name. But many subscribers to online services enjoy certain discussion forums centered around common interests—plus friendships and contacts formed with fellow members—that they are unwilling to give up for an Internet-only account.

All commercial online services offer parents ways to protect their children from sexually explicit and other objectionable material.

Many people prefer to get their feet wet through an online service, then later move to an Internet service provider when they feel more independent and adventurous. While you can access the Internet if you subscribe to an online service, it doesn't work the other way around. An Internet user can't reach the content and services of an online service unless he or she subscribes to the service. That is, the Internet user can send mail to people if he or she already knows their e-mail addresses or reach the online service's home page on the Web, but not its members-only content.

Internet service providers

Internet service providers often offer faster access and fewer service shutdowns because none has anywhere near the number of subscribers as America Online's millions. In contrast to a privately owned commercial online service, no one owns the Internet, it has no members, and anyone can get to it with the proper software, which is offered by countless different providers. Many Internet users assert that they have found a strong sense of community on various Web sites and in newsgroups without subscribing to a commercial online service.

Set up your own domain name with e-mail forwarding, or use a free e-mail service like Hotmail (www.hotmail.com).

America Online (www.aol.com)
Web Space Available: 2 megabytes per screen name for a total of 10 megabytes over five accounts.
Cost: $4.95, $9.95, $19.95 (yearly discounts available)
The biggest online service, America Online (AOL) is easy to use and install, its content is well-organized and appeals to many

Shop for Service and Price

Don't get attached to your ISP or commercial online service. If you sign a long-term contract, pay attention to when the contract expires and shop for service and price. The easiest way to avoid getting stuck with one ISP or online service is to use e-mail addresses that are independent of the ISP.

different age groups and interests, and there are lots of colorful graphics. Its content is divided into different topics, called channels; each can be found quickly on the main channel menu or by typing in the proper keyword.

For example, the Entertainment channel contains sections on movies, television, music, comedy, fiction, and the arts. You can read movie reviews from the *New York Times* and Joel Siegel, celebrity gossip at the Daily Fix, David Letterman's Top Ten Lists, and hear interviews with movie stars and directors and attend premieres at Entertainment Asylum. Fans can discuss genres, such as action or science fiction, and stars at many forums. Career help can be found at the WorkPlace channel, which offers resume tips, regular discussions with small business owners and professionals in various industries, and job postings.

Investment advice, financial news, and analysis are offered by the Finance channel's The Motley Fool, whose experts have written several books on investing. Tax help and forms, mutual fund ratings and reports, and insurance advice are also available at the channel. In the Families channel, parents can obtain advice from experts and each other on many child-rearing topics. Its timesavers section enables busy parents to pay bills, plan vacations, and handle other tasks in one place, while a genealogy forum teaches how to research your family tree. Hobbyists meet and exchange tips in the Interests channel, which also offers a food area with recipes, a pet care forum, and an auto center with expert advice and price deals.

At the Travel channel, you can book airfares, hotel rooms, and car rentals from Preview Travel, explore travel bargains, and share prize finds with others in various forums. Arts and leisure, including book and movie reviews and gossip, can be found in the Influence channel, while AOL Today offers the top news headlines and top AOL features of the day. Meanwhile, the Lifestyle channel offers a women's network, communities where you can find others with similar interests, plus a Love@AOL section featuring personal ads.

Breaking news, the *New York Times* newspaper, and ABC News are located at the News channel. Reference help, such as

Although long scorned by Internet pros, AOL is still the largest and most powerful force in the Internet. Its recent merger with Time-Warner makes it even more powerful.

encyclopedias like Grolier's, Compton, and Columbia, homework help on different topics, and for-credit college courses from the University of California can be found at the Research & Learn channel. For the more playful minded, the Games channel lets users play action games with others across the world, exchange tips, read reviews, and buy games.

Starbucks, Eddie Bauer, and 1-800-FLOWERS are some of the name-brand merchants at the Shopping Channel, but there are many more selling computers, clothing, books, sports equipment, and gifts.

A special Kids Only channel offers homework help from online teachers, chat rooms, and a variety of puzzles, trivia, and word games. Besides these channels, which come with the 4.0 version of AOL—if you have an earlier version, you may not have all of them—the Internet button is the jumping off point to the Internet, including the World Wide Web, newsgroups, and Personal Publisher, which gives you free tools to design and publish your own Web site. The People channel lets you meet people in real-time chats, which can be general or organized by topic.

America Online's Web site (www.aol.com) offers a detailed index for help on all features of AOL, whose software can be downloaded from the site.

Its membership is considered more diverse in age and more middle-of-the-road than CompuServe, which it bought in 1997. A huge surge in membership followed its decision to offer unlimited monthly access and resulted in constant busy telephone signals that prevented many members from using it for hours at a time and delayed e-mail service. Since then, however, AOL has focused more on improving its network and keeping current members than attracting new ones.

AOL also has its own integrated Web browser, which is a version of Internet Explorer. Unfortunately, that means that Web pages look slightly different on AOL than they will in Netscape or even the latest version of Internet Explorer.

If you are serious about running a Web site, it's a good idea to sign onto AOL from time to time just to check how your home page looks. Fortunately, if your friends or relatives have AOL, they may let you borrow a screen name. You don't even have to live in the same state to use this feature. Be aware that only one screen name can be logged onto any AOL account.

CompuServe 2000 (www.compuserve.com)
Cost: $9.95–$19.95 (yearly discounts available)

The recent "deals" offered by computer stores nationwide have put CompuServe into more homes than ever before. In exchange for signing with CompuServe for three years, computer buyers have received rebates of $400 off the purchase of a new computer. This savings has made the immediate cost of getting online considerably lower. Users are still required to pay a monthly fee to CompuServe. (Typically, CompuServe pricing ranges from $9.95 per month to $19.95 a month, with a discount if you sign up for a year. Rebate users are required to sign up at a fixed rate. If they cancel before the end of 36 months, they will be required to repay a portion of their rebate.)

The oldest online service, which started to serve the public in 1979, CompuServe has a reputation for an older, more serious, more business- and professional-oriented, and more international audience than AOL. Since its purchase of CompuServe, AOL has pledged to let the older service keep its distinct identity. It's known for over 1,000 highly specialized discussion forums devoted to over 60 categories, including work at home, journalism, music/arts, family services, travel, and many computer and Internet issues. Databases offering business information and thousands of magazines, newspapers, and trade journals at per-article or per-hour rates are a real boon to researchers.

Business and legal experts, as well as authors, show up for conferences—real-time chats—whose subject matter is far removed from what often passes for chat online. *Time*, *Money*, and *Fortune* magazines and newspapers such as *USA Today* are also found on CompuServe.

Available in 185 countries, CompuServe has no separate children's section, but there are educational forums.

MSN—Microsoft Network (www.msn.com)
Web Space Available: 12 MB
Cost: $21.95/month unlimited access

If you own a PC with Windows installed, chances are you've bumped into MSN. In fact, it's nearly impossible to log onto the Internet from an alternative provider without a lot of trouble.

If you own a Macintosh, you can't access MSN.

Formed in 1995 by the Microsoft Corporation, who belatedly realized the importance of the Internet, much of the content on MSN is available free at its Web site (www.msn.com). This includes MSNBC, a news outlet and joint venture with NBC, which has a cable channel as well; Sidewalk, a guide to local events and restaurants in certain cities; and Cinemania, movie reviews and interviews.

MSN also offers Expedia, an extensive travel resource for making reservations and a guide for researching destinations, and the Internet Gaming Zone, which offers many games, from classic board and card games to action and combat simulation (some games charge fees). MSN also includes the Encarta encyclopedia, Microsoft Investor (which helps users track their stock investments), a shopping area, chats, and new programming that has changed often since MSN's launch.

Prodigy Internet (www.prodigy.com)
Web Space Available: 6 MB
Cost: $9.95–$21.95
(Discounts available for one-year commitment)

One of the earliest online services, Prodigy underwent an overhaul to become more Internet-oriented. Prodigy Internet is an Internet service provider that divides popular Web sites into channels—each topic also features links to related newsgroups and chat rooms—to make Web surfing organized and easy.

Prodigy Internet has incorporated the old Prodigy Classic's content such as Business & Finance, Education, Entertainment, Computing, Games, Home & Family, Music, News, Reference Center, Travel, and Sports. There is also a special Kids Zone, while a Shopping section includes merchants like J.C. Penney and Amazon.com. The Communications section offers message boards, e-mail, and chat.

Prodigy has recently begun offering its members a number of premium features, including:

- 5¢ Anytime Long Distance
- Internet Call Manager (ICM)—lets you know who is trying to call when you're online so you can either take the call or let the caller know you'll call back ($4.95/mo.).
- Prodigy Unified Messaging—receive all your e-mail, voice mail, and fax messages in your Prodigy Internet mailbox ($12.50/mo.).
- Prodigy Learning Center—offering interactive, online courses on the latest applications from Microsoft, Lotus, Adobe, and more (from $9.95 per class).
- Prodigy MailLink—a free service that lets you easily check your e-mail from anywhere without dialing into Prodigy's network (free to members).

EarthLink (www.earthlink.com)
Web Space Available: 6 MB
Cost: $19.95/month unlimited access.

EarthLink is one of the largest non-content–oriented ISPs. In other words, they'll give you the connection to the Web, help you get started, and leave it at that.

EarthLink does offer an "Integrated Environment" that combines e-mail, Web browser, chat and messaging software, and a file upload tool in one easy-to-use, easy-to-customize package. It also offers easily customizable individual user profiles for multiple accounts, nationwide dial-up numbers, and location profiles for laptop users. EarthLink is known to be reliable and user-friendly.

A straight Internet service provider is more like an unguided tour of the Internet. Many users start with an online service, then jump to an ISP when they feel ready. Many, in fact, keep both so they can still take part in favorite forums or avoid changing their e-mail address.

What kind of account do I get with a national or local Internet service provider?

Web Space Available: Varies with ISP; typically between 5 to 10 megabytes.

Cost: $5 to $50, depending on the service.

When you sign up with an Internet service provider, you should ask for a PPP (Point-to-Point Protocol) or SLIP (Serial Line

Internet Protocol) account. This means your computer is really part of the Internet network and lets you use the most popular browsers, Netscape Navigator and Internet Explorer, which do all kinds of fantastic things.

UNIX shell accounts, which let you access the Web as text-only, used to be the only way to connect to the Internet before PPP and SLIP. Most Internet service providers will still give you a UNIX account for an older computer, which needs no special software since it runs all programs you need on the provider's computer, not yours.

How to select an Internet service provider or commercial online service

1. Decide if you want a commercial online service (such as America Online, CompuServe, Microsoft Network, or Prodigy) or a straight Internet service provider (ISP). Because online services have their own private content and serve as guides to the online world in general, they can be a good choice for newbies, or people new to cyberspace.

2. Ask if it is a local call to reach the ISP. It is important for an ISP to have a POP (Point of Presence) connection in your local calling area. You can expect a much higher telephone bill if there isn't. If you have a regional, not national, ISP, make sure there is a local number that you won't be charged extra for using.

    Sometimes an ISP's local access numbers might be changed to 800-numbers. Users assume these are free or local calls, then are surprised to receive $90–$100 monthly telephone bills for usage instead of $10–$20. When they check, the 800-numbers turn out to cost $6 per hour. Check with your telephone company to make sure the telephone number your modem is dialing is in fact a local call.

3. Ask the basic rate. Find out how many hours per month this rate includes and the per-hour rate for extra hours. Ask the monthly rate for unlimited access.

Determine which is the best deal for you based on whether you will be a heavy or occasional user. A good idea is to start with the basic rate, then see what your bill is. Those hours always pile up faster than you think. Most ISPs now charge about $20 for unlimited access but will charge half that for only a couple of hours per month.

4. Decide if you want a national or local/regional ISP. They vary wildly. If you live in a city, you probably can choose between national and local providers. If you live in a rural area, you may only have a local ISP. National ISPs, because they are offered by very large companies such as AT&T, MCI, IBM, and Sprint, are stable. Local ISPs go out of business much more often. National ISPs have bigger technical support staffs, but local ISPs may give more attentive service and be more willing to go out of their way for you. Local ISPs often host community chats and offer resources involving their regions.

   If you travel a lot and want Internet access on the road, a national ISP is your best bet. They most likely have a POP in big cities, plus 800-numbers for smaller towns that lack access through a local telephone call.

5. Make sure all the software you need to connect your computer to the Internet is supplied by the ISP. This should include a Web browser, connection software, an e-mail program, a newsreader to read newsgroups, and an FTP (File Transfer Protocol) program to move files between computers connected to the Internet.

6. Talk to sales and support departments at the ISP before signing on with them. Find out if there is 24-hour technical support. You don't want to be stuck with an Internet glitch at 2 A.M. or on Sunday with no support available. Ask the staff a list of questions to see if they are knowledgeable and polite. If you prefer to e-mail technical support queries, ask how long a response takes.

How Do I Find a Local Internet Service Provider?

A directory of over 3,000 providers, divided into categories by area code, state, and country, with links to profiles and costs, can be found at The List *thelist.internet.com*. It is published by Mecklermedia, a publisher of Internet trade magazines. Remember to check how many dial-up numbers the provider has within your local calling area.

Internet Service Provider Checklist

1. How much Web space do you really need?
2. Do they help you set up your Web site?
3. Do you want something simple to use?
4. Do you want the cheapest possible rates?
5. Do you need multiple e-mail accounts or Internet filters to edit out content for younger audiences?
6. How fast is your modem?
7. How reliable are their connections? Do you connect at top speed?
8. Are the ISP's phone lines always busy?
9. Does the service log you off if you're inactive for a period of time?
10. Do you want to support local businesses?

7. Look for an easy, automated process to install and configure your software and instructions written in plain English. A simple online registration, where you fill in various numbers and other information your ISP gives you, is what you want.

8. Talk to other people about their ISP. Do they often have trouble connecting? Do they get frequent busy signals? Do they get disconnected often? Do they think technical support is helpful? Ask friends, colleagues, or family, or ask the ISP to supply customer references.

9. Find out the fastest modem speed the ISP can accommodate. If you have a 33.6/56 Kbps modem or an ISDN line, make sure your ISP can support these higher speeds.

10. Do your research. Consult the ISP's own promotional materials; read their ads in the Yellow Pages (under Internet Services) and in business and technology sections of newspapers and magazines; check out their Web sites; read articles comparing ISPs. See what computer trade magazines and business and technology sections of newspapers and magazines have to say about their differences. Some offer blow-by-blow comparison charts. The television network, CNET, has an excellent comparison list on the Web (www.cnet.com).

11. Ask if there is a setup charge. So many ISPs have no setup charge that it seems unfair to pay one.

12. Find out what percentage of newsgroups your ISP includes. Some include only a fraction. If you planned on discussing your favorite hobby and its newsgroups are omitted, you won't be a happy camper. Ask if any particular categories are left out.

13. Ask about the peak hours for usage. Try an ISP at those times to see if you get through or if you get constant busy signals or frequent disconnections.

Finding the Internet in Public Places

The Internet can be found in some surprising places nowadays. Besides many of the almost 10,000 public libraries in the United States that offer free access if they have Internet-connected computers, you can surf the Web and send e-mail for a fee at airports, cyber cafes, copy shops, auto dealerships, even the mall.

Public libraries with Internet access, including many in small towns and rural areas, vary greatly in their policies. While many allow anyone to come in and use their computers, others require a library card, which can cost a fee. The time limit is usually a half-hour, although you can continue if no one else is on the waiting list in some libraries. In New York City, the New York and Brooklyn Public Library systems—which cover 100 libraries—you don't need a library card and can print out ten pages free. (They even supply the paper.) Free classes on how to use the Internet are offered at public libraries. Many organizations such as Webgrrls, a networking group for women interested in Internet issues with chapters in many cities in the United States have continuing education programs, and community centers offer very cheap classes.

At airports serving New York (Kennedy, LaGuardia, and Newark), Chicago, Houston, Orlando, Baltimore-Washington, D.C., Oakland, and Minneapolis, among other cities, passengers and visitors can Web surf or send e-mail at almost 200 ATM-style kiosks. The rate for the machines, located in main terminals or in TWA Ambassador's Clubs and Continental President's Clubs, is $.35 a minute plus a $1.95 access fee, payable by swiping a credit card. The company that installed the kiosks, TouchNet Information Systems in Kansas City, upgraded them from offering fax and copying services only.

In Los Angeles, San Francisco, and Newark, there are large stand-alone Internet stations from QuickATM, a Berkeley, California, company, which cost $2.50 for 10 minutes. The terminals are also

Be sure to take advantage of the trial offers of free service for a limited time. Try more than one to see if you like it, can get around well, and find its support staff helpful. If you're really sneaky, you can get away for a year or so just by trying out new Internet services with different credit cards.

convenient for travelers with laptop computers who normally have to hunt for data hookups to check e-mail or snatch a quick Internet break before a flight. You can also sip and surf at many cafes nationwide that offer Internet access as well as coffee, pastries, and often sandwiches as well—making the word "wired" doubly meaningful. In New York these include Cyber Cafe in SoHo, a loft-like space, alt.coffee in the East Village, a Beat-type coffeehouse with comfortable couches, chairs, and eccentric fixtures, and Internet Cafe in the East Village, a funky space with loads of Internet reference books and a large dog. Directories of Internet cafes, with addresses, phone numbers, and links to their home pages, are on the Web at Cyber Cafes of Europe (www.xs4all.nl~bertb/index.html) and Cyber Cafe Guide (www.easynet.co.uk/pages/cafe/ccafe.htm), an international guide.

Early in 1998, a major mall developer began installing Internet kiosks and giving free CD-ROMs to its shoppers to alert them of merchant discounts at its malls and permit online buying, Web surfing, and e-mail. The Simon DeBartolo Group, which owns or manages over 200 regional and local shopping centers nationwide—including the nation's biggest, the Mall of America, plus The Forum Shops at Caesar's Palace in Las Vegas, and Newport, in the New York area—is also rolling out cyber cafes in its malls. These 3,500 square-foot cafes have an average of 40 computers and kiosks. The cyber cafes will be run by Cybersmith, a New York chain of technology stores.

How Else Can I Get the Internet for Free?

Besides public libraries, colleges and universities give their faculty members and students free Internet access, as do many companies with their employees. More and more high schools and grade schools are getting wired as well. An increasing number of community organizations also let local residents use their Internet-connected computers for free, or cheaply.

CONNECTING TO THE INTERNET

Some cities have "freenets," where people register for free and get limited Internet access with lots of local content. Then there are companies that offer free unlimited Internet access. In the San Francisco area, @Bigger.net has offered access to area residents, in exchange for a setup fee of about $60–$70, for the past few years. Tritium Network, based in Ohio, offers access in certain cities in exchange for viewing ads running along the bottom of the screen like a news ticker and monthly surveys on users' buying preferences.

But a number of firms that promised free Internet access folded after a couple of months, some, sadly enough, with users' setup fees. So be suspicious toward any firm touting free access and look up their track record. As is so often the case, what seems too good to be true often is.

NetZero (www.netzero.net)
888-279-8132

NetZero may just blow away pay-for connection providers. It's free. That's right FREE. NetZero offers free local-access dialup Internet connections throughout the United States.

How can it be free? Along with NetZero's Internet access, you have to run an application called the ZeroPort, which is something akin to AOL's welcome screen. It takes you to your e-mail and works as a search engine, stock ticker, and shopping pointer. In other words, they're hoping to seduce you into buying things through the ZeroPointer.

NetZero's a new service and worth looking into. The bad news for Macintosh users is that as of press time, NetZero works only on PCs.

Bluelight.Com (www.bluelight.com)

Bluelight is one of the latest ISPs to offer free service. It is advertising supported, so you will see a small banner on your screen showing advertisements when you are online. You don't have to click on or otherwise interact with the advertisements for the service to remain free.

Free Web space is offered through geocities.yahoo.com// and briefcase.yahoo.com//.

Questions to Ask Before Picking a Provider

1. Do you prefer to surf the Web and write your e-mail on your television because you've never really warmed up to computers?

2. Will you be on the road a lot, Web surfing as you go?

3. Can you access your e-mail remotely with this service?

4. How available is tech support? Does it cost extra?

Making the Connection

Connecting to your Internet service provider or online service

Follow all the printed instructions from your ISP or online service on how to install its software and configure it properly. Pay particular attention to the information you are supposed to enter to log on for the first time.

Some, particularly the commercial online services, offer highly automated software that is simple to install and basically runs itself, asking you to choose a local access number and password and little else. Others require more work. Call the technical support line of your provider if you have any problems connecting.

Of course, if your modem and your telephone share the same line, you will not be able to execute their instructions during the phone call and will have to hang up. Two telephone lines make this much easier.

Connecting with Windows 98

Windows 98 offers a fast, easy way to connect to the Internet and sign up for an ISP (or use the ISP you already have) due to its Internet Connection Wizard.

1. Click "start," then "programs," "online services," and follow the instructions of the ISP you pick. The Connection Wizard will automatically configure your computer and install any special software your ISP requires.
2. If you already have an ISP that is unlisted but no sign-up software, click "start," "programs," browser icon, then Connection Wizard. Follow its instructions, and it will automatically set up your account.
3. Either way, to connect to the Internet from now on, click "start," "programs," "Dialup Networking," and your ISP icon. Type your user name and password (unless saved on your computer), then click "connect."

Connecting to an ISP with Windows 95

The good news is your system already has everything it needs to connect to the Internet. If you have the Internet Setup Wizard software, the connection process is a lot easier. The Internet Setup Wizard may be in your computer or part of a product that enhances Windows 95 called Microsoft Plus!.

If you don't know if your computer has Microsoft Plus!, do this:

1. Click "start" on the vertical row of icons on the left side of your screen. Click the "programs" menu, then "Windows Explorer." If you find a "Plus!" folder on your C:\ drive, make sure the "Microsoft Internet" folder includes "Internet Tools."
2. Click "start," then "programs," then "accessories." Click "Internet Tools." You should see Internet Setup Wizard (Hooray!). If you didn't find that "Plus!" folder on your C:\ drive—or other drives if you have them—you don't have Microsoft Plus!. You should buy and install it in the correct drive. (By the way, you can also use the Internet Jumpstart Kit, available from your ISP or your retailer, to connect to the Internet.) Then, follow these tips.

If you have Microsoft Plus!, do this to configure your system:

1. Click "start, then "programs," "accessories," "Internet Tools," and "Internet Setup Wizard." Then, click "next." (Unless your modem is not set up yet—in that case, set it up ASAP.)
2. Choose the option that states you have an account with a different service provider, then "next."
3. Type the name of your ISP, then click "next."
4. Type the local access telephone number of your ISP, including area code. Choose "bring up terminal window after dialing," then click "next."

Where Do I Get Software to Connect to the Internet?

In all probability, it's already on your computer.

1. Click the Windows Start button on the bottom left of your screen, then highlight "Find" and "Files and Folders." Type "Internet" and see if anything comes up.
2. Ask your Internet provider for a floppy disk or CD-ROM. (Of course, if it comes on a CD-ROM, you'll need a CD-ROM drive to run it.) Sometimes you'll find a free sample in your mailbox, in a magazine, or given out at events on the street because some providers find this a good way to win more customers.
3. Use an America Online CD-ROM. You've got dozens of them, right? Just be sure to cancel later if you don't want to use AOL.

5. Type your user name (login name), which is the first part of your e-mail address—for example, "jdoe," leaving out the "@mindspring.com" part—and password. Then, click "next."

6. Choose the way you obtain your Internet Protocol (IP) address. (Your ISP will tell you either it is a fixed address or that they automatically assign it each time you log on to the Internet.) Click "next."

7. Type the Internet Protocol address of your Domain Name Service (DNS) server. (This is a series of 12 numbers, which your ISP will give you.) Also, type the address of an alternate DNS server, if your ISP gave this to you. Click "next."

8. Choose "Use Internet Mail," then type your full e-mail address and name of your mail server. (Your ISP will give you this.) Click "next."

9. Type "Internet Mail Settings" in the box in the big Exchange Profile box. Click "next." Click "finish." You're done. Congratulations!

Now, to connect to the Internet for the first time, do this:

1. Double-click the "Internet" icon on your screen.

2. Click "connect" in the big Connect To box.

3. After it says "status: dialing" and then connects, type your user name, password, and other information given to you by your ISP in the big Post-Dial Terminal Screen box. Click "continue."

4. It will say "connected" at a certain modem speed if you're lucky and all the required information was typed properly. You can now minimize, but don't close, the Connect To box—closing it means your connection is lost and you will have to start from 1.

If you don't have Microsoft Plus! (or the Internet Jumpstart Kit), you may have to do more work to configure your system. OK, a lot more work, as the following shows:

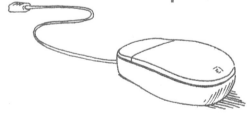

1. Insert the software from your ISP into the appropriate drive of your computer.
2. Establish Dial-Up Networking. Click "start" button, then choose "settings," and then the control panel. Click on the "add/remove programs" icon. Choose the Windows setup tab, then click on "communications." Click the "dial-up networking" box, which allows you to connect to other computers over telephone lines, then click "OK."
3. Install TCP/IP. This sets up the proper language (or proto-cols) to allow communication among computers on the Internet. Click "start," then "settings," then "control"—just like you did in step 2. Click on "network" to see a box that lists network components. Click "add" for a list of network component types, then click "protocol," then "add." Select "Microsoft," then TCP/IP, and finally click "OK." To make sure you have done this correctly, at the control panel—click "start," then "settings" to reach it—click "network" to see TCP/IP listed under "configuration."
4. Configure your connection to your ISP. At the control panel, double-click on "network." Click "TCP/IP" and then select "properties" to see a box with six different cate-gories. On the "IP address" option, click on "obtain an IP address automatically" if your ISP has told you to do so. (If not, type in the address, a series of numbers.) On the "DNS configuration" option, disable DNS if your ISP has told you so. (If it hasn't, type your ISP's name in "domain," your user name in "host" box, and the IP address of your ISP name server in "DNS server search order." You can usually ignore the rest of the options, which are at a default setting.
5. Establish your dial-up connection to your ISP. Click "my computer," click "dial-up networking" and also the "make new connection" icon. Fill in the boxes, typing in a name for your ISP (its real name or a nickname will do), seeing if your modem type appears, then click "next."

This is the information you'll need to log on!

:-) IP address
:-) domain name
:-) mail server
:-) news server
:-) type of IP address (static or dynamic)
:-) dial-up telephone number
:-) e-mail address
:-) host name

Type the access telephone number of your ISP; no area code is needed if it is a local call. When you see a message stating you have made a new dial-up connection; click "finish."

6. You're almost done (whew!). Click "my computer," click "dial-up networking," and choose the new connection icon you just created. Make sure all the information you typed earlier is there, then click "properties." Click "general" to verify your ISP's local access number and your modem type. Click your new connection icon, and type in your user name and password (plus your ISP's local access number, in case it's missing).

7. Click "connect"—you'll hear your modem dialing, which will be music to your ears at this point—and stare exultantly as "connected" at a certain modem speed comes up.

Congratulations! You've connected successfully to the Internet. Reward yourself somehow, you deserve it. Don't worry, you don't have to do this again—unless you get a new ISP.

Again, because there is so much variation, pay attention to how your specific ISP tells you to connect.

Connecting with a Macintosh

Apple takes pride in being "Internet ready." Users report that they are able to get online within minutes of turning on their iMac. Apple's Internet Assistant will walk you through all the steps you need to connect to the Internet. It's incredibly easy to use.

Connecting to America Online

America Online offers a highly automated connection software. Do this to install:

1. Insert your diskette or CD-ROM into the appropriate drive of your computer.
2. Go to the Start menu, then choose "run."
3. Type d:\ setup" to start the installation.

Users of Mac OS 9 and above have access to iTools, which includes:

- a free e-mail address (yourname@mac.com) that can be accessed online or forwarded to another e-mail address
- KidSafe, a Web site blocking tool
- iDisk—20 megabytes of storage on Apple's Internet server. This can be used to store home pages, images, or even as a private disk backup system. It is a bit slow, however.
  - Home Page, a three-step home page creation tool.

4. Click "install." After this concludes, click "OK." Then, double click the AOL triangle icon. Reboot your computer if this icon doesn't come up.
5. If all the information on the next screen is accurate, click "yes." If not, click "no."
6. Click "OK." Your modem will now dial into AOL's toll-free number so you can select a local access number.
7. Carry out the online instructions. Type your area code and choose a local access number from those which appear. AOL will disconnect at this point.
8. Dial in with your new local access number. Type your registration number and password (see the diskette's packaging) and the remainder of the online registration form. Congratulations! You're an America Online member now. Sign on with your password whenever you return.

Connecting with WebTV

The easiest of all is saved for last (and just goes to show you how the lack of a computer simplifies everything). Connect your set-top box, which looks like a black cable box, to your telephone line and television with the cords that come with it. Then fill out the online registration form and you're ready to Web surf. No software, no installation, no configuration. Congratulations!

A wireless keyboard, which uses arrow and scrolling commands to navigate instead of a mouse, is a good bet to buy instead of using the online pop-up keyboard. If you have an older television, you'll have to buy an accessory called an RFU adapter.

Pick Passwords Wisely

You will need a handful of passwords in your journeys around the Internet. If you use a cable modem, you won't need a password to log on because your connection is hard-wired. You will, however, need e-mail and FTP passwords.

For traditional ISP users, the most important password is the one you pick when you connect to your ISP for the first time. It can be saved on your computer if you don't want to type it every time you go on the Internet or get your e-mail.

Old Mac Users

If you have System 8.x or earlier, the special software you need to connect to the Internet is:

1. MacTCP or TCP/IP control panel. System 7.5 and higher comes with MacTCP. But if you have an older version, it's best to upgrade to 7.5. If you have system 7.5.3, TCP/IP is pre-installed.

2. MacPPP or FreePPP (system 7.5.3 needs FreePPP instead).

Many Web sites will ask you to pick passwords as well so you can use their bulletin boards and read their special content, and they can track your visits to their sites. To prevent you from forgetting your password, some sites will ask you to think of a question and its correct answer to verify that it is really you.

The best type of password is one you can easily remember but hard for others to guess, over five letters and/or numbers long. Computer security experts recommend these tips in choosing passwords so other people will not be able to access your account and read your e-mail:

:-) Don't use your full name, first or last name, initials, or any combination of these in any order
:-) Don't use your user name
:-) Don't use your telephone number, birthdate, address, or social security number
:-) Don't use the name of your child, spouse, girlfriend or boyfriend, pet, favorite sports team, or any other obvious personal information someone who knows you may guess
:-) Don't use a word in the English dictionary
:-) Don't use the same password for every system; if you don't want a different password for every system, at least use several
:-) Don't tell anyone your password; if you do, change it immediately
:-) Don't carelessly display your password (for example, taped to your computer monitor or atop or under your desk)
:-) Use a combination of letters and numbers
:-) Use a word that has deep personal meaning for you but which almost no one knows (for example, a word your child has invented; a name from your distant past, such as your first pet, the street you lived on as a child, a character in a favorite book)
:-) Write it down and keep it in a safe place (for example, your wallet, unless you tend to misplace it often, or under lock and key)

Password

Be sure to pick a different password to access online sites than your e-mail and ISP password. In other words, when you log into your travel agent software site, use a different password than when you check your e-mail.

CHAPTER 4

Before You Start

E ven if you already know what you want your Web site to look like, we recommend that you take some time to plan and browse. Start off by surfing the Web, seeing what's out there, and then think carefully about what you want in a Web site. Once you know what you have in mind, see what else is out there in that category. You can set goals, timelines, and even budgets. Or you can just skip all that and start designing your pages.

Surfing the Web

The best thing you can do before you start designing your Web site is to do something you've probably already done before—surf the Web. Yep, get online and start clicking.

Wait! Before you get lost in cyberspace, you're clicking for a different reason. This time you're looking at Web sites from a design standpoint. Instead of just trying to find out more about your favorite breed of dogs, we want you to look at the dog's Web site *critically*.

Your goal: To steal good ideas and concepts and avoid bad mistakes. Isn't theft bad? We'll get to the bad kind of theft later on. Nobody can own a good idea. And many other people have made the same mistakes you're likely to. So why not profit from other people's experience? After all, that's why you bought this book in the first place. We're simply recommending that you do a fair amount of research online, keeping in mind the fact that you're about to build or improve your own Web site.

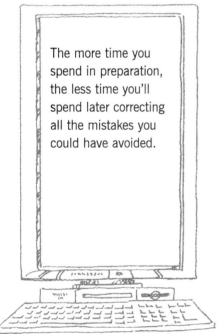

The more time you spend in preparation, the less time you'll spend later correcting all the mistakes you could have avoided.

Take a note pad (or use your word processing program) and jot down some ideas. Make sure you keep track of the URLs for sites you'd like to copy. One of the nice things about the Web is that although content is copyrighted, the code that produces the content—the HTML programs underneath—really can't be copyrighted. There just isn't that much variation. So down the road you might just borrow their code rather than write your own.

Browser Wars

Web Browsers are software programs that scan the Internet to locate Web pages and show them on your screen. They also

Questions to Ask as You Surf

1. Does this Web page look good?

2. Is the text clearly presented? In other words, do the words make sense? Why does the site even exist?

3. Am I bored?

4. How long does it take to download? (Am I bored waiting?)

5. Are the graphics appropriate? Are they just throwing in pictures because you're supposed to have them?

6. Is it easy to find what I'm looking for?

7. Is it easy to get back to the home page?

8. Can I contact somebody if I want to?

9. How difficult was it to find this page in the first place? Was it one click from your search engine, or did you have to spend a lot of time looking for it?

10. Is the information in the site current? Are you looking at calendar dates from last year?

11. Is the information in the site relevant to the site? This is different from the question, "Is the information in the site relevant to me?" If the site is about dogs, then why is there something about horses?

12. What do you wish they did differently?

13. What do you really like about the site?

respond to commands to perform many other tasks. There are two kinds of Web browsers: text-based and graphical. Most people use graphical browsers (the kind that display pictures), but text browsers are not uncommon and have the advantage of increased download speeds.

The most popular browsers, Netscape Navigator and Internet Explorer, are locked in a dog-eat-dog battle to outdo. Not only that, everything keeps changing. America Online bought Netscape but still uses a version of Internet Explorer as its default browser. Each browser keeps offering more and easier features to win the hearts of users everywhere. As a result, the most recent versions are workaholics: they handle e-mail, read newsgroups, create Web pages, find people and businesses, connect you to search engines, send customized news and information, and let users work together easily by sharing documents.

The higher the number of the version, the more recent a browser is and the more features it has. For example, 3.0 is more advanced than 2.0. The 5.0 version of Explorer and 4.7 version of Netscape Communicator were the latest and greatest when this book went to press. You don't have to have the absolute latest version of a browser, but you will be able to do more with it. Many Web pages note they can be seen best with a certain browser or version: "Netscape and Internet Explorer 3.0 or better."

Some sites note, thoughtfully, that users of other browsers, such as AOL, which (for now anyway) has its own version of the Internet Explorer browser, or text-only browsers, can click to view their pages properly. Web sites look different depending on the browser you use, which creates a challenge for Web designers and adds to the infinite variety of the Web. Both Netscape Navigator and Internet Explorer work on many operating systems, such as Windows 95, Windows 3.1, Macintosh, and UNIX. Specific system requirements, including the amount of memory and disk space your computer needs to use the browsers, plus detailed descriptions and technical support to answer likely questions, are located on the Web sites for Netscape (www.netscape.com) and Internet Explorer (www.microsoft.com/ie).

Cool Web Sites

Coca Cola:
www.cocacola.com
Yahoo! Search Engine:
www.yahoo.com
Netscape:
www.netscape.com
(notice how much the Netscape site looks like the Yahoo! site)
Microsoft:
www.microsoft.com
Apple Computers:
www.apple.com
The New York Times on the Web:
www.nytimes.com/

Browser versions

Because browsers come in many different versions, it is sometimes hard to keep track of which version offers what features in addition to browsing the Web. Netscape Navigator comes either as a stand-alone product or as part of a package called Netscape Communicator, which lets you create Web pages, share documents to work with others, even make telephone calls without paying long-distance charges in addition to e-mail and newsgroups. Microsoft Explorer is (as Microsoft maintains) part of the operating system and is included free with Windows. It is also available for the Macintosh.

Here is a short list of some of the major features in recent browsers:

Netscape Communicator

E-mail and newsreader programs, Web page design, customized channels for news and information, instant messaging, sharing documents to work together and synchronizing with devices like the Palm. Standard Edition is free; Professional Edition for companies is not after a 90-day free period.

Netscape Navigator 4.0 Stand-Alone Edition

Customized channels for news and information.

Netscape Navigator 3.0 Gold

E-mail and newsreader programs, Web page design.

Netscape Navigator 3.0

E-mail and newsreader programs.

Netscape Navigator 2.0

E-mail and newsreader programs.

Internet Explorer 5.0

E-mail and newsreader programs, customized channels for news and information, instant messaging, sharing documents to work

Questions to Ask about Commercial Web Sites

1. Which are the most interesting?
2. Why do they exist?
3. What are they selling?
4. Is it easy to find what they're selling?
5. If they are providing a service on the Web, does it work?
6. Is the site fun? Does it have to be fun?
7. How long did it take to download?
8. What annoys you about the site?
9. What do you like best?
10. Would you return to this site? Why?
11. Would you bookmark this site?
12. Would you pay $10 million for the Web site?

together. New features include search assistant, customization of site-visit History, offline browsing, simplified use of multiple connections.

Internet Explorer 4.0
E-mail and newsreader programs, Web page design, customized channels for news and information, instant messaging, sharing documents to work together.

Internet Explorer 3.0
E-mail and newsreader programs.

Internet Explorer 2.0
E-mail and newsreader programs.

How do I get a browser?
Browsers are either free or fairly cheap. As a result of the antitrust lawsuit against Microsoft, both Netscape and Internet Explorer are probably already installed in your operating system. If you have Windows 95 or 98, both Microsoft products, you definitely have Microsoft's Internet Explorer browser. As Microsoft likes to point out, you do not have to use the browser that comes with your computer, however, and may choose another you like better, as many do.

A browser is probably also included in the connection software from your Internet service provider when you sign up for an account. The ISP will give you Netscape or Internet Explorer, or its own more limited version of one of these very common browsers, as America Online does. If you have WebTV, its own browser is built in.

You can also download some browsers for free from its maker's Web site. Set aside some free time: the download takes a couple of hours on a slow modem (six hours estimated for Explorer, two hours estimated for Netscape) and may be a pain in the neck if installing software is not one of your natural gifts.

You can also buy a browser. Stores and mail order retailers sell CD-ROM versions. Netscape's and Explorer's Web sites can also ship a CD-ROM for just a few dollars in shipping charges.

Why would I want an old version of a browser?

If you were just an ordinary Web surfer, you wouldn't want an old version of a browser. If you're interested in becoming a savvy Webmaster, you may want to download old versions to see how your Web site looks in those versions. New versions incorporate more and different interpretations of HTML (for instance, cascading style sheets are visible in Netscape version 4.0 but not in 3.0).

Why doesn't everybody just upgrade to the latest and greatest browser? A bunch of reasons. Downloading and installing Web browsers can be confusing and time-consuming. The browser makers come out with new ones every 6 to 12 months. How much time does the ordinary person want to spend keeping up with the browsers?

Also remember that there are millions of old computers out there that don't have the 30 or more megabytes of disk space to download and install a bloated gee-whiz new browser.

Other browsers besides Netscape and Explorer

Yes, there are other browsers, but you would almost never know it from all the press the big two get. Some work just fine for older computers because they require a lot less memory (RAM) and speed. Some show graphics; others, however, only show text—meaning you miss all the color, images, sounds, and excitement of the full Web experience. (Since you also miss all the delays when these images and sounds load, you can hop around pretty fast with a text-only browser.)

A list of a few of the lesser-known browsers, which have their loyal fans, follows.

Opera (www.operasoftware.com)

Opera continues to improve. Version 3.6 only needs 6 MB of RAM and runs fine on an older 486 PC with Windows 3.1. It works on a 386 and even a 286, and takes up a little more than one tenth the disk space of Netscape and Explorer. (No Macintosh version yet.) Plus, Opera is designed to help disabled people by allowing them to customize the windows, making type large enough for anyone to read.

Maintain Browser Neutrality

We highly recommend that you try and stick to browser-neutral Web programming. Stick to straight HTML, because if you choose one browser over another, you'll lose a sizable chunk of your Web audience. That means avoiding some really nifty features like Microsoft's ActiveX and Front Page extensions.

No e-mail program is included, however, so you'll need to get one. Opera also won't show sites with heavy animation and interactive elements the way Netscape or Explorer do.

Lynx (www.fdisk.com/doslynx/lynxport.htm)

Lynx rocks. It is the fastest browser on the market. It also shows NO graphics. (That's why it's so fast.)

Lynx is text-only browser that requires no mouse, just arrow keys to jump to links and view a link plus other single-key commands. Lynx dates back to the good old days before the Web was born, when people used the UNIX operating system on the Internet. It can be used on Windows 95 if your standard browser is not working well. It cruises around much faster than the latest browsers because of its lack of graphics, only needing a 386 PC with a slow (under 14 Kbps) modem, which is truly impressive.

It requires so little power because the program runs not on your computer but on a UNIX server. Your computer merely shows the results. If you are using Lynx on a UNIX operating system, you will need telnet software.

In place of a picture, the word "image" or brackets will appear, letting you imagine what might have been. If you have a UNIX shell account from your Internet service provider, Lynx and its e-mail program, Pine, will come free.

Palm browsers

People are just beginning to browse the Web on personal data assistants (PDAs) like the Palm VII and other palm computers running Windows CE. How do you handle problems like tiny screen size?

Our recommendation: Don't worry about it. People are only just getting used to the idea of going online. The AOL/CompuServe computer discount is going to put PCs in everybody's home a lot quicker than spending several hundred dollars for something that can be dropped or easily stolen. When your Aunt and Uncle start thinking about buying a Web client, that's when you should begin designing parts of your Web site for them. By then, hopefully, there will be some standards.

For the Webmaster

Opera prides itself in sticking strictly to the HTML standard, so it's a good test case for any odd Web page designs. If a Web page doesn't work in Opera, then it's probably not "good" HTML.

Test your site in Lynx. It's good discipline to find out whether the thing works without any pictures, Java, or multimedia.

How do I get it to browse?

After you have installed the browser—by downloading it or following instructions on the installation package that comes with the CD-ROM—and connected to your Internet service provider or commercial online service, just double-click the browser icon on your screen to launch it. Look for a capital "N" for Netscape, or a small "e" for Explorer.

Try a command, which can be found in the toolbars—the horizontal rows of icons and verbal commands—at the top of your screen. Many commands are duplicated in both icons and verbal menus, which may either delight or confuse you. Your browser shows it's busy working for you when you see an hourglass or a clock replace the cursor on your screen. You will also see changes in the browser icon at the top right corner of your screen, called a status indicator. For example, on Netscape, you can admire a status indicator that looks like a comet cruising through the sky.

The following commands refer to the 4.0 versions of both Netscape Communicator and Internet Explorer, unless just one is specified. Older versions or different browsers will have similar functions and more-or-less similar commands, except for a text-only browser like Lynx, where you will use single-key commands because there are no icons.

Icons Toolbar

This is the row of icons (pictures) near the top of your computer screen, below the Menu toolbar. Each is a command you can click on.

Back

This returns you to the Web pages you've seen before the current page. Click "back" once to reach the immediately previous Web page, keep clicking for the page visited five pages ago, ten pages ago, etc. Copies of pages you've viewed are stored in order in your hard drive's cache, which is why clicking on "back" is much faster than reaching a Web site in the first place.

Learn More about Browsers

Two excellent Web sites with news and product information on browsers are CNET's Browser.com (www.browser.com) and Mecklermedia's BrowserWatch (www. browserwatch.com).

Forward

This takes you to the next Web page you have already seen, once you have started viewing past pages stored on your cache. It is not used to view a new page you have not yet seen.

Stop

This immediately stops browser action so a new page won't continue to download or an image or sound clip on a page will be prevented from downloading. Use this when you've made a mistake or are just plain tired of waiting for those pages or sound clips to kick in.

Reload (or Refresh)

This gives you the most current version of a page, handy if the site's content changes often. It's also handy if you are viewing an older version stored in your cache.

Home

This returns you to the Web page at the very start of your journey. It's generally either the home page of the Netscape or Explorer browser or a page you have selected as your home page.

Search

This will bring up several search engines at once, such as Yahoo! and Lycos. This way you don't have to type in their Internet addresses or bookmark them.

Print

This will print the current Web page, e-mail message, or news-group posting you are seeing. (But only if you have a printer hooked up!)

History (in Explorer only)

This shows a batch of recent Web pages you have visited with links to those pages. Just click on the name of the desired page. (In Netscape, you reach your history by clicking on

"Communicator" in the Menu toolbar, then clicking on "history." Or, click "Go" in the Menu toolbar, and see a shorter list of recent Web sites visited since you launched your browser. Either way, click on the page you want.)

Channels (in Explorer; Netcaster in Netscape Communicator)

This offers a batch of Web sites—news, business, and entertainment—whose current content can be sent to you on a regular basis so you don't have to search for it. This is the Microsoft and Netscape version of push technology and lets you decide how you want to receive the content. For example, you may want it full screen, as a screen saver while your computer is idle, or in a small window. You can also decide how often you prefer updates.

Mail (in Explorer; Mailbox for Netscape Communicator)

This is for sending and receiving e-mail, reading newsgroups, and composing Web pages. In Explorer, these features are bundled into a package called Outlook Express. (In Netscape Communicator, "discussions" is the newsgroup icon, "composer" is the Web page composer icon.)

Fullscreen (in Explorer only)

This means the Web page you are viewing will now be much larger than just the size of the window. It also means a few more icons will appear on your toolbar, such as "print" and "edit." Since all icons will now have no text commands attached, rest your mouse on one for its description to appear.

Guide (in Netscape only)

This brings up five easy ways to find information on the Web, including categories from the search engine Yahoo!; a people finder to look up telephone numbers, street addresses or e-mail addresses; a business finder to look up telephone numbers and addresses; "What's New" and "What's Cool," new sites that just came on the Web and

interesting sites such as Cool Site of the Day, Category of the Day, cool sites grouped by category, even This Day in History. It's an easy way to keep track of new or noteworthy sites on the Web (or just amuse yourself).

Security (in Netscape only)

This indicates by showing a closed lock whether the Web page you are viewing is secure, meaning you can safely purchase on it. An open lock means the site is not secure.

Component Toolbar

This is the row of icons at the bottom of your screen. If you have Netscape Communicator, each icon will refer to a different part. The ship steering wheel icon is for the Navigator browser. The mailbox icon is for sending and receiving e-mail. The balloons with messages inside are for reading newsgroups. The paper and pen icon is for composing Web pages. Rest your mouse over each icon to see the description.

In Explorer, "Mail" is for sending and receiving e-mail and reading newsgroups; "Channels" is push technology. Rest your mouse on each icon and its description will appear.

Menu Toolbar

This row of commands at the top of your screen lets you move around the Web and your files and perform many tasks. Each has a pull-down menu with a variety of choices. You'll notice some do the same thing as the row of icons (pictures) below. It's a matter of choice which to use. For example, in Netscape Communicator here are commands you can click on:

- *File.* The "open page" command lets you type an Internet address and takes you to that Web site. "Send" means you can e-mail the Web page you are viewing to a friend or colleague. "Print" lets you print the Web page. "Edit" means you can edit—change or move around words or sections—in the page you are viewing. "Quit" allows you to end your browsing.

- *Edit*. The "search Internet" command lets you find a topic or keyword on the Web, if you don't know the Internet address, by giving you a variety of search engines to choose from. "Search directory" lets you locate people's telephone numbers or e-mail addresses in a variety of directories. "Find in page" means you can zero in on a specific word in a Web page you are viewing. Commands such as "copy," "cut," and "paste" let you duplicate or move around words or sections after you highlight them.

"Preferences" allows you to change the first page you see when you start Web surfing. So if you've tired of admiring the beauty of your browser's home page, you can type the Internet address of the Web page you'd prefer to start with—or start automatically with the last page you visited earlier—by clicking your browser icon and following the instructions.

You can also change the number of days your browser will track the Web sites you have visited. It will even conveniently finish an Internet address you have begun typing, like a friendly elf, by typing the preferred number or by clicking your browser icon in the "preferences" menu. The look of Web pages, such as colors, font size, and the toolbars themselves, can be altered by clicking on the "appearance" option.

- *View*. This lets you change the look of Web pages, including "reloading" with the most current version of a page, stopping the display of images, enlarging or reducing font size, and displaying only the toolbars of your choice.
- *Go*. This will take you to the last Web pages you have viewed (click "back"), the next already viewed Web page (click "forward"), or your home page ("home"). By the way, "back" even numbers your recently viewed sites in order.
- *Communicator*. This reaches the various components—the Navigator browser, Messenger for e-mail, Collabra for newsgroups, Netcaster for push technology, Conference for sharing documents for working cooperatively—and enables you to make telephone calls over the Internet. (The caller and

Four Kinds of People Who Should Never Be Allowed to Build Web Sites

1. People who never finished building the back yard bird feeder.

2. People who are incredibly frustrated when computers do stupid things.

3. People who don't like to stare at computer screens for hours on end.

4. People who regularly subject their guests to four-hour slide presentations about their vacation to Timbuktu. (Actually, maybe they should, as long as we don't have to visit their site!)

recipient will need sound cards and microphones for Internet telephony.)

- *Help.* This offers a variety of assistance including how to get technical support for problems, information on updates, and increased computer security.
- *Location (or Address or Netsite) Box.* This long white box under the Icons toolbar is where you type in the Internet address of a page you want to see. Start with "www" because the "http://" that begins a Web site address is implied. In Explorer, you can also type a keyword or topic, preceded by "?," "go" or "find" (for example, "go Paris" or "?U2" for the rock band). First, click inside the box so that little up-and-down line appears on the side. Then type the address. Last, hit "enter" on your keyboard.

If you make a mistake typing the address, click at the start of the mistake, drag it across the screen, then hit your "delete" key, which will erase the mistake, now highlighted.

Bookmarking a site

If you're a Webmaster, you want people to bookmark your site. Why? Because that means that your site is important to them or that they want to find your site quickly. Your information is so special, so unique, that they're willing to return to it—or at least they think they will some day. If you haven't already used your bookmark feature, try it out.

In Netscape click "Add Bookmark" from the bookmark menu.

In Internet Explorer, click "Add Page To Favorites" from the Favorites menu.

File Edit View Go FaxMenu Help
Add Bookmark ⌘D
Guide ▶
Search ▶
Directories ▶
Banking and Finance ▶
Business Resources ▶
Computers and Technology ▶
Education ▶
Entertainment ▶
General News ▶
Hobbies and Lifestyles ▶
Local Information ▶
Shopping ▶
Sports ▶
Travel and Leisure ▶

Back Forward Reload
Location: http://markbinder.o

Over time, notice which of your favorite bookmarks you actually use and which you don't. Those are the sites you come back to for one reason or another.

Ask yourself the Webmaster questions, "Why do I come back to some sites and not to others? Why are some sites more useful than the ones you bookmarked that you never revisit?"

Thinking about What You Want

You know you want a Web site. Maybe your neighbor has one, or your granddaughter. Maybe your business competition has one. Maybe you like tinkering around with software. Maybe you're just curious. All of those are really superb reasons to develop a Web site. But the more specific you can be about your goals, the more likely you are to achieve them.

Perhaps you want to do a family photo album online. You might start with a simple desire to publish your poetry and end up with an elaborate Web site that brings you fame and fortune. Maybe you're looking for new business, and think that the Internet is the answer.

Finding Similar Sites

All right, you've got a fairly good idea. Time to surf again. Why? Before you waste all your time and energy producing a Web site, it might be a good idea to see if somebody else has already done exactly the same thing you planned. Right?

Of course, if you're going to put your grandchildren's pictures online, you can probably skip this part. Chances are slim that somebody's duplicating that. Still, you might want to see what's out there. How did other people show off their grandchildren?

Remember, your goal is to steal good ideas and concepts and avoid bad mistakes. Be sure to bookmark the sites that you like, and the ones that look good.

Browser User Tip: Organize Your Favorites/ Bookmarks into Categories

In Internet Explorer click on "Organize Favorites." In Netscape, click on "Bookmarks" in the Netscape menu. Create bookmarks for:

Excellent-looking Web sites to steal code from

Lousy looking Web sites

Transportation (trains, planes, busses, subways)

Computers and Software

Games

Relatives

Hobbies

Should I Hire Someone to Do My Web Site?

Maybe. For some people hiring a professional may be the best choice. For instance, if you've read this far and are really bored but you need a Web site for your business, the answer is probably yes. If you've read this far and are excited by the idea of building your Web site, or if you don't really need a Web site, then the answer is almost certainly no.

Even if you decide to hire someone to build a site for you, you haven't been wasting your time reading this book. You're developing the vocabulary and understanding that will help save time and money.

Seven reasons to build your site yourself

1. It's easy; really. That's what this book is all about.
2. It saves you money. No need to pay someone to do something you can do.
3. It's an online adventure.
4. You'll learn a lot.
5. You'll have the satisfaction of doing it your way.
6. It's an excuse to stay inside on a sunny day or something to do late at night when everyone else is asleep.
7. You'll know how to fix problems yourself.

Seven reasons to hire a professional to build your site

1. It saves your time. They'll be the ones doing all the work.
2. Nothing to learn. You don't need to learn anything else.
3. No need to buy software or hardware. You won't need to purchase a scanner, a graphics program, or a new computer.
4. You're likely to get a professional, quality Web site.
5. There is no learning curve. They've already done the learning.
6. It can be faster. Not only will they save you time, it's part of their job to do this work. So, if they do a good job, your Web site will be up and running sooner.
7. There's someone else to blame if anything goes wrong.

How to find someone to design a Web page

You can hire a Web design firm or even your ISP to design a site, but first ask their prices and see if you will be charged a project fee or hourly rate. Web designers want to design high-paying Web sites for corporate clients, not small $1,000 jobs. Many people recommend that the way to find a low-cost designer is to ask a local university or continuing education program that offers classes in multimedia design to suggest some quality, inexpensive Web site designers. These may be college students or recent graduates who are skilled and perhaps designing sites part-time or full-time. Grab them now before they are out in the real world and commanding market rates in this very popular field.

Sample Web Site Goals

The purpose of our Web site is:

1. To improve our business by generating new customers.
2. To show our grand-children off to the world.
3. To sell our house.
4. It's a fun way to invite friends to our wedding.
5. I'm an artist; I don't need a purpose.
6. To sell Nantucket Baskets and publish my articles on the technique of Nantucket Basket Weaving.
7. Because Coca Cola is supposed to have a Web site.
8. To teach people something they didn't know.
9. To start an Internet business, make a billion dollars in the initial public offering (IPO), and then retire to Bali.
10. Because it's there.

According to some professional Web designers, there are two ways to make Web pages: the easy way and the right way. The easy way is to buy an HTML coding program.

If you don't want to program, this is the way to go. Later in this book we give you a detailed list of some of the best, simplest, most expensive, and least expensive tools available. We go into a lot of detail about HTML generators later in the book.

The good thing about HTML coding programs is that they work. The bad thing is that they don't always work perfectly. You might end up spending a lot of time trying to figure out how the heck the coding program works.

On the other hand, you could take the time to learn HTML. This method takes a little longer, but after a week or so you'll be coding like a pro.

Writing your Web pages directly in HTML costs less because you won't need an expensive software tool. Once you become familiar with the ins and outs of HTML, you'll also be able to debug and fix problems faster.

HTML Basics

There are two things you need to know about Hypertext Markup Language (HTML). First, it's simple. The commands are easy to understand, and it won't take you more than a week or so to learn it. Second, you don't really need to learn HTML. There are lots and lots of programs out there that will write HTML code for you. Programmers and purists will argue that these programs write ugly code, but if you're a beginner or a non-programmer, who cares? Still, it's a good idea to understand how HTML works.

Good Reasons to Use an HTML Code Generating Program

1. You don't have to learn HTML.
2. It can handle tables and lists easily.
3. It is as easy as a word processor.

Problems with HTML Code Generating Programs

1. They can give you a false sense of security—pages don't really look like that in browsers.
2. They can be buggy and generate strange HTML code.
3. You won't understand HTML and won't know how to fix problems.

Let's show you how it works first rather than explaining every-thing. Here's a very small, simple, and fairly useless Web page:

```
<HTML>
<HEAD>
<TITLE>This is the first example</TITLE>
</HEAD>
<BODY>
<H1>This is my web page</H1>
<P>
I'm just a beginner, so I don't quite know what
to put here.
I could put my biography, or a story about how
my cat played with yarn...
</P>
</BODY>
</HTML>
```

Just by looking at the tags in this Web page, you can begin to figure out how it works.

- HTML commands (known as tags) are always bracketed by less than (<) and greater than (>) signs.
- Tags typically enclose the part that they affect. The first tag indicates the start of a function. For most HTML tags, a second, concluding tag echoes the first but begins with a slash (/). For example, all HTML documents must begin with <HTML> and end with </HTML>. Everything in between is the Web page.
- The <HEAD> and </HEAD> commands surround the heading.
- The <BODY> and </BODY> commands surround the body of the page.
- The <P> command tells the browser to begin a new para-graph. It's like a carriage return. You don't need a closing </P> command, but it doesn't hurt.

All Web pages contain a header and a body. The headers give the browser information about the Web page, like its title, how big

HTML stands for Hypertext Markup Language. HTML files are text files that tell your browser how to format the Web page on your screen. Coding is what computer program-mers do when they type in computer programs. An HTML generator is a piece of software that writes HTML for you. This can both save time, and create some strange-looking code.

the page will display, default fonts or background colors, and so on. The body contains all of the text and references to images that are visible on the screen. The body may also contain links to other Web sites, as well as special tags to access multimedia.

While HTML tags can be typed in uppercase or lowercase (or both), by convention the tags are capitalized to distinguish them from the surrounding text. This is what the page looks like in Internet Explorer.

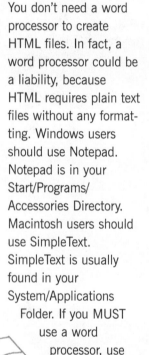

You don't need a word processor to create HTML files. In fact, a word processor could be a liability, because HTML requires plain text files without any formatting. Windows users should use Notepad. Notepad is in your Start/Programs/Accessories Directory. Macintosh users should use SimpleText. SimpleText is usually found in your System/Applications Folder. If you MUST use a word processor, use the "Save As Text" option.

> ## This is my web page
>
> I'm just a beginner, so I don't quite know what to put here. I could put my biography, or a story about how my cat played with yarn...

Here's the same page in Netscape:

> ## This is my web page

Right away you'll notice two things: (1) How the page looks in each browser is *radically* different, and (2) the line break between the two sentences vanished when the page was viewed in the browsers.

The line break problem is easier to fix than the first. To insert a line break, simply type <BR>:

```
<P>I'm just a beginner, so I don't quite know
what to put here.<BR>
I could put my biography, or a story about how
my cat played with yarn...</P>
```

That will create a line break without any white space between the two sentences.

If you use <P></P> then the browser will create a new paragraph with white space between the two lines.

```
<P>I'm just a beginner, so I don't quite know
what to put here.</P>
<P>I could put my biography, or a story about
how my cat played with yarn...</P>
```

Lesson 1—A Basic Page

In this lesson you'll learn how easy it is to place basic text and images in a Web page.

Case Study: Granny Goose's Family Circle

Our guinea pig for this lesson will be Granny Goose. Granny Goose doesn't get out much any more. She loves her family and friends and wishes that there was a way to stay in better touch. Her youngest son, Jacob, gave her a new computer, and she's just learning how to use it.

In this lesson, Granny Goose has decided to create her very first Web page. She doesn't like complicated programs, so she's decided to type everything herself.

For her first attempt, all she wants to do is explain what the purpose of her Web page is and to proudly display a picture of her newborn great-grandson, Joey. Here's what she needs to know:

1. Every HTML document needs to begin with the <HTML> tag and end with the </HTML> tag.
2. The header of her document needs to begin with the <HEAD> tag and end with the </HEAD> tag.
3. Her document's title must begin with the <TITLE> tag and end with the </TITLE> tag.
4. Any text paragraphs must begin with <P>.
5. To insert an image on the simple page, she must remember where that image is stored on her Web site. In

How to Use These Lessons and Tutorials

1. Skip and skim; take frequent breaks. Don't try to absorb everything all at once.
2. IMPORTANT: Use a simple word processing tool. These tools will save your HTML texts without any extra formatting. They won't use smart quotes or unusual keys. They won't add strange formatting commands. Programs like Word and WordPerfect add hundreds of extra bits and pieces to document files, including things like creation date and where a window opens on the screen. You don't want any of that garbage in your HTML files.
3. View your work in any browser. Occasionally take a look at the same work in another browser.
4. Every time you save a different version of the HTML file, you'll need to click on the "Reload" or "Refresh" page button in your browser.

this case, her great-grandson has helped her by uploading the picture "joey.jpg" to the subdirectory "images."

6. The tag to place an image on a Web page is <IMG SRC="images/joey.jpg">.

Here's what Granny Goose typed in:

```
<HTML>
<HEAD>
<TITLE>Granny Goose's Family Page</TITLE>
</HEAD>
<BODY>
<P>My grandson, Joel, said that I should really
get started on this home page. So here goes.
<P>I love my family, and I want to show them off
to the entire world!
<P>Eventually, I'd like to have pictures of
everybody online, and maybe even one of those
family trees. Wouldn't that be wonderful?
<P>Oh, here's a picture of my newest great-
grandson, Joey.
<IMG SRC="images/joey.jpg">
<P>Isn't he cute?
</BODY>
</HTML>
```

This is what her first Web page looks like:

My grandson, Joel, said that I should really get started on this home page. So here goes.

I love my family, and I want to show them off to the entire world!

Eventually, I'd like to have pictures of everybody online, and maybe even one of those family trees. Wouldn't that be wonderful?

Oh, here's a picture of my newest great-grandson, Joey.

Isn't he cute?

Problems with Granny Goose's Page

1. The background is a boring shade of gray.
2. The picture is squeezed over to the right of the page, and there's a big gap of space around it.
3. The text size is big, but Granny Goose doesn't really know why. (And she doesn't really mind, because she's far-sighted anyway.)

Granny Goose was amazed! It only took her 15 minutes to get her Web page online, and it contained everything she'd put into it.

She did an excellent job making sure that all the important elements were included. She did leave out the quotation marks around her image name, but in this case, it didn't matter.

We, however, as Webmasters-in-Training, are going to be a bit more critical.

Lesson 2—Improving upon the Basic Page: Headers, Text Colors, and Background Colors

After Granny Goose posted her first Web page, she called her grandson, Joel, who took a look at her source code and clucked softly to himself. Then he offered some suggestions.

"Why not give your page a background color, or a background image?" he said. "Also, it's very easy to set up text headings to give the page a stronger sense of purpose."

Granny thought it over and decided to try Joel's suggestions. She tried two changes:

```
<BODY TEXT = BLUE BGCOLOR = LIME>
<H1>Welcome to Granny Goose's Family</H1>
```

After viewing the results in her browser, she decided that she liked the new header and the blue text but hated the lime green color for the background. Fortunately, her grandson sent her a background image, which she put in her images subdirectory. So, she tried giving her page a background image:

```
<BODY TEXT = BLUE BACKGROUND = "images/back-
ground.jpg" BGCOLOR = LIME >
```

That worked, sort of. She got the background she wanted, but the screen flashed lime green for a moment before loading the background image. So she took out the BGCOLOR.

Tags Used

`<HTML></HTML>`
This tag tells your browser that the file is an HTML file.

`<HEAD></HEAD>`
Identifies the header part of your HTML file. This part usually contains <TITLE> tags as well as <META> tags.

`<TITLE></TITLE>`
The document's title is enclosed between the <TITLE> and </TITLE> tags. This is the information that shows up in search engine displays, as well as at the top of browser windows.

`<BODY></BODY>`
Defines the beginning and end of the body of the HTML document

`<P>`
Signals the beginning of a new paragraph. Does not require a </P> to conclude.

`<IMG SRC="theimage-locationandname">`
This tag tells Web browsers to display an image. Images may be stored in GIF, JPEG, X Bitmap, or PNG format.

Color Names and Numbers

You can make Web colors as simple or as complicated as you like. HTML 4 recommends the use of sRGB (standard Red Green Blue) values for color designations, but you can also use names for a limited list of colors (See below).

Color names and sRGB values:

Black = "#000000"
Silver = "#C0C0C0"
Gray = "#808080"
White = "#FFFFFF"
Maroon = "#800000"
Red = "#FF0000"
Purple = "#800080"
Fuchsia = "#FF00FF"
Green = "#008000"
Lime = "#00FF00"
Olive = "#808000"
Yellow = "#FFFF00"
Navy = "#000080"
Blue = "#0000FF"
Teal = "#008080"
Aqua = "#00FFFF"

Lesson 3—Better, Cooler Images

Now Granny Goose was starting to have fun. She'd visited other Web pages and knew that the picture of Joey looked crude. She asked Joel what suggestions he had to make it look better.

The first image correction Joel Goose suggested was that his grandmother add alternative text to the image. He strongly recommended that she make a habit of using ALT labels for every image.

"Some people," he explained, "don't have browsers that display images while others don't like to wait for images to download, so they turn off the images in their browsers. The ALT

HTML Word Processor Tip

Be sure to turn off the "Smart Quotes" feature (it creates curly quote marks as shown here) in your word processor if you use it to write your HTML code. HTML only recognizes the dumb quotes as delimiters for attributes. For example, if you use smart quotes in <IMG SRC="image.jpg">, your image won't load.

A tag is another word for an HTML command.

Eyeballs are a webbie way of saying customers, viewers, or audience members.

attribute is a way of letting those people know exactly what they're missing."

He also suggested that she put a border around the picture using the BORDER attribute. Finally, he said that by aligning the picture relative to the text she'd have a much nicer looking page.

Granny played around for a while and realized that when she put the picture on the left with a 2 pixel border the text scrunched too close, so she looked up another attribute, HSPACE, which gave the picture a left/right space border.

Here's the code Granny Goose wrote and the results in the browser:

```
<IMG SRC="images/joey.jpg" ALT="Joey!" BORDER=2
ALIGN=LEFT HSPACE=3>
```

Welcome to Granny Goose's Family

I love my family, and I want to show them off to the entire world!

Eventually, I'd like to have pictures of everybody online, and maybe even one of those family trees. Wouldn't that be wonderful?

Oh, here's a picture of my newest great-grandson, Joey.

Isn't he cute?

That was enough for one day. Granny uploaded the new file and sent an e-mail to all her friends that her great-grandson was now officially "online."

Image alignment options

Images may be aligned TOP, BOTTOM, or CENTER to text. In other words, the first line of text will be displayed at the top, bottom, or center of the image.

Tags and Attributes Used

`<H1></H1>;`
`<H2></H2>` through
`<H6></H6>`
Heading tags are used to distinguish between headlines of differing importance.

`BGCOLOR=COLOR`
Sets the background color of the element. In this example, we'll be using

`BACKGROUND="back-groundimage"`
Sets the background image of the element.

`TEXT=COLOR`
Sets the color of the text that is displayed on the page.

Tags and Attributes Used

ALT
The text description of images displayed in nonimage browsers and while images are loading.

ALIGN
Aligns the image relative to the text.

BORDER
Sets the size of the border surrounding the image. Be sure to set this value to zero (0) if you don't want a border.

HSPACE
Specifies the amount of space the browser puts on the left and right sides of the image (in pixels).

This is an image with TOP alignment.

This is an image with MIDDLE alignment.

This is an image with BOTTOM alignment.

```
<HTML>
<HEAD>
<TITLE>Aligning Image Sample Number 1</TITLE>
</HEAD>
<BODY BGCOLOR="#FFFFFF">
<P>This is an image with TOP alignment. <IMG
SRC="images/dogbone.gif" ALT="dogbone"
ALIGN=TOP>
<P>This is an image with MIDDLE alignment. <IMG
SRC="images/dogbone.gif" ALT="dogbone"
ALIGN=MIDDLE>
<P>This is an image with BOTTOM alignment. <IMG
SRC="images/dogbone.gif" ALT="dogbone"
ALIGN=BOTTOM>
</BODY>
</HTML>
```

Web Page Design Methods and Problems

1. Use simple HTML. Avoid tags that can cause conflicts or that aren't supported by browsers. And preview your work in as many different browsers as possible. This method works. The problem is that basic HTML limits the "cool" factor on your Web site.

2. Use frames. Frames can help you control the design and the navigation of your Web site. Unfortunately, the proportions of frames can vary widely from browser to browser and even from monitor to monitor. Different DPIs change the proportions of frames radically.

3. Use tables. Like frames, tables can help you control the design and the navigation of your Web site. Unfortunately, the proportions of tables can vary widely from browser to browser and even from monitor to monitor. Different DPIs change the proportions of tables radically. Working with tables can be an effective way to create a "rough" design. Be sure to preview in different browsers and at different monitor resolutions.

4. Use a program like Flash to design your Web pages. This works wonders. You'll be able to set graphics precisely and show off some very cool effects. But Flash and other multimedia do have drawbacks—users with older browsers won't ever see what you're up to, and search engines will be completely lost. In other words, it may look cool, but you're losing potential audience.

Images may also be aligned LEFT or RIGHT in relation to text. These attributes will not only push the image to the left or right side of the screen, but will allow text to wrap around the image.

> This is an image with LEFT alignment. Keep an eye on how the text wraps in one direction or another. When you put images that have LEFT or RIGHT alignment on the same page, some strange things can happen, especially if the text isn't long enough to prevent overlapping.
>
> On "LEFT" alignment, the text wraps around to the right of the image. It's exactly the opposite on "RIGHT" alignment."
>
> This is an image with RIGHT alignment. Keep an eye on how the text wraps in one direction or another. When you put images that have LEFT or RIGHT alignment on the same page, some strange things can happen, especially if the text isn't long enough to prevent overlapping.
>
> On "LEFT" alignment, the text wraps around to the right of the image. It's exactly the opposite on "RIGHT" alignment."

```
<HTML>
<HEAD>
<TITLE>Aligning Image Samples—Left and
Right</TITLE>
</HEAD>
<BODY BGCOLOR="#FFFFFF">
<IMG SRC="images/dogbone.gif" ALT="dogbone"
ALIGN=LEFT>
<P>This is an image with LEFT alignment. Keep an
eye on how the text wraps in one direction or
another. When you put images that have LEFT or
RIGHT alignment on the same page, some strange
things can happen, especially if the text isn't
long enough to prevent overlapping.
<P>On LEFT alignment, the text wraps around to
the right of the image. It's exactly the oppo-
site on RIGHT alignment.
<HR>
<IMG SRC="images/dogbone.gif" ALT="dogbone"
ALIGN=RIGHT>
<P>This is an image with RIGHT alignment. Keep
an eye on how the text wraps in one direction or
another. When you put images that have LEFT or
RIGHT alignment on the same page, some strange
things can happen, especially if the text isn't
long enough to prevent overlapping.
<P>On "LEFT" alignment, the text wraps around to
the right of the image. It's exactly the oppo-
site on "RIGHT" alignment.
</BODY>
</HTML>
```

The Problem with Web Design—Not All Web Browsers Are Equal

"Here's the big problem with designing a Web page," said John Speck, the public relations director for MediaSpaceBank.Com. "You can't control how the page looks on your viewer's browser. You just can't."

That is the problem that has plagued Web designers since the first graphical browser was invented. After all, even with a single browser, users had different-sized monitors and different monitor resolutions. Now that there are a number of different browsers on the market the problems multiply.

The same Web page can look radically different in different Web browsers. This fact is one of the most challenging aspects of Web page and Web site design.

The problem that you will have as you design your Web pages and your Web site is how do you make your site look the way you want it—most of the time? The fact is, you can't—not without beginning to lose potential eyeballs. And, as a general rule, the simpler you keep your Web pages, the more likely they are to view decently on any browser.

A Simple Way to Check for Browser Conflicts

Try the Web Page Backward Compatibility Viewer by DJ Delorie that allows you to view your Web site through the eyes of others. Here's how it works.

1. Point your browser to www.delorie.com/web/wpbcv.html.

2. Type in the URL you want to view.

3. Click on the check boxes to select the features you want the Viewer to show or hide.

4. Click the "view page" button.

CHAPTER 6

Moving from Web Page to Web Site

OPEN

Photo Album

OUR TRIP

RECIPES

BIRTHDAY'S

ANNIVERSARIES

W e're moving quickly now. You've created your first Web page, and now we're going to extend that into a Web site. We'll start by talking a bit about what makes up a home page and then look at what else goes into a Web site. In the next chapter we'll start creating links and formatting the text.

The Home Page

The home page is the first page that your Web visitors see when they visit your site. It's the front door to your Web site. It's the most important Web page in your site because you never get a second chance to make a first impression. When someone types in your URL or clicks on a link, this is the page you want them to see.

What makes up a good home page?

Links to other major areas of the site
Strong images that create a sense of the Web site
Good design
Fast loading
Clear user interface that makes it easy to find what you want

Remember, your Web site consists of many pages, so you don't need to get everything onto the home page.

When someone enters your Web domain, they can either type in the whole address (which usually ends in .htm or .html) or they can simply type in the domain name.

Typically, the automatic default page is your "Home Page." Depending on your operating system, this page should be named index.htm or index.html, home.htm or home.html.

If there is no default page, users will see an automatically generated index of pages in the directory. Check with your Web host to find out which convention they support.

There are a whole bunch of theories about the best kind of home page. They range from simple to ornate, low multimedia to high multimedia, lots of buttons to just one button.

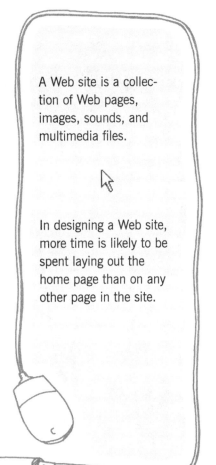

A Web site is a collection of Web pages, images, sounds, and multimedia files.

In designing a Web site, more time is likely to be spent laying out the home page than on any other page in the site.

Our biggest tip is to make sure that the home page loads fast. It's the very first page people see when they come to your site, and you don't want them to click away before you're done inviting them in.

Professional Advice: A Step-by-Step Process for Designing Your Web Site

Eric Holter is the President and Creative Director of Newfangled Graphics (www.newfangled.com). His company makes useful Web sites. They designed the ultra-cool Etonic shoes Web site and the incredibly informative Rhode Island Public Transit Authority Web site, which includes quick access to every bus schedule in the biggest little state.

Even though Holter works with big companies, many of his ideas work brilliantly for individuals with smaller sites. Keep in mind that you won't be doing everything he suggests in this order, but this should give you a good idea of the process you can go through to design a high-quality site.

The Strategy Phase—Determining Goals

Your first step in designing a site is to understand your goals. Do you have marketing goals? Who is your audience? What are you trying to accomplish? You need to define your strategy. That will take a little bit of time. You want to have clear examples of other sites that are similar to what you want.

The Concept Phase—Trying Out Ideas

Once you know what you're trying to accomplish, then you go into the Concept phase. You can sketch the sample pages on a piece of paper, or work in a graphics program like Adobe Photoshop, Illustrator, or Freehand. After you have a number of designs, see which ones you like best.

What to Include in Your Web Site

All Web sites include (Well, almost all Web sites…)
Links to other pages in your site
Text
Images
Links to other sites

Business Web Sites Include
Product descriptions
Detailed information
Directions on how to get to your location
Prices
Catalog
Privacy Policies

Cool Things to Include
Calendars
E-mail Lists
FAQs (Frequently Asked Questions)

Advanced Things to Include
Databases
Multimedia
Sound Files
Guest Books
Chat Rooms

The Interface Design Phase—
Working It Out in HTML

Once you've picked a design, it's time to turn it into HTML. (That's where learning HTML comes in handy.)

If you're creating a complex layout, consider using tables to place graphics and text on the pages. Leave your graphics in Photoshop and break them up into smaller pieces.

For example, you can copy and paste navigation graphics and break them up into smaller GIFs or JPEGS and create background graphics from the same layered file.

You can then piece those things together in HTML until you've built a prototype of your site. The links will work but the copy and images will be stand-ins.

The Production Phase—
Putting It All Together

Now it's time to go into production phase. That's when the actual images and text are added and you're working on getting the entire site completed.

By now you have created a template—a basic layout for almost every page in the site. Once you've gotten that far and you've gotten the template done, the rest of the site doesn't have to take a lot of time to complete. Unfortunately, most people rarely take into account how long it will take to collect or edit or create content for their Web site.

One of the problems that people have is realizing that maintaining a Web site is a job. If you're in a business, this is often a new task that's not part of the employee's job description. They don't realize that it's going to take a couple of weeks to do this work, so those weeks can turn into months.

The Testing and Posting Phase—
Putting It Up

Throughout the process, check on how the Web site looks in various Web browsers. Once the whole site is completed, you need to test it both on your computer and on the server.

You'll probably want to make sure it works before you start a nationwide ad campaign—or before you tell your family and friends.

Marketing Phase—Out in the World

Now it's time to go public. You will register with search engines. You'll start recording and analyzing traffic. If you're trying to make money, you'll create banner ads and start running banner ads to drive people to the site. You should also begin a link campaign—try to find appropriate places to set up link relationships with other sites—to help market the site online.

Ongoing Maintenance

Continuing to maintain and update the site is an ongoing process. We recommend that you update the site as frequently as possible. Some sites we update every month, some are quarterly, some are daily—it all depends on what the purpose of the site is.

There are a few ways for you to update the content. Some of the tools you can use are programs like FrontPage or Dreamweaver. Alternatively, you can write some scripts to update your stuff on the Web instantaneously. That can be useful if you're changing your site frequently.

Problems Faced by Beginning Designers

Content is one of the biggest problems for beginners. People who build their own sites get the shell up pretty quickly. They build their main sections but then you click through and find a lot of "Under Construction" areas that never seem to go away. Content is a big issue, even when you're doing it yourself.

Design is also something you can't get from reading a book. It's half talent and half good solid training and practice. I would highly recommend that people doing Web sites themselves keep it as simple as possible. When someone who's not a designer tries to get fancy with their graphics it's always a nightmare. It's always apparent that it's not a professional site. You're always better off keeping it simple.

I would recommend going to some of the major sites and seeing how they've set up their structure. Then mimic it, and without using a lot of graphics, create some type of graphic buttons for your sections. By and large stick to straight HTML and keep it clean and consistent. If you use a certain font size and color to represent headings, always use the same color and size and font

Databases

If you're interested in developing databases on the Web, one of the simplest ways to do so is with a combination of Microsoft Access and Microsoft FrontPage (www.microsoft.com) on a Windows NT server. Alternatively, you could use FileMaker Pro (www.filemakerpro.com) on a machine that has a FileMaker Pro server. Both of these methods avoid long, complex CGI programming because somebody else has already done the work. You'll also have the advantage of being able to use the databases on your own machine.

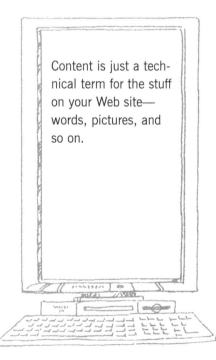

style. Try to organize your information clearly. Organization is one aspect of design that can be attained by thinking about it clearly. It's not a visual design, so a non-designer can think about how to structure the organization efficiently. That will help it a lot.

One of the most horrible new things is that some of the recent browsers have allowed background graphics to animate. That's really bad. It's horrible when you have an animated background graphic. I also hate the animated e-mail letter box graphic that opens. It is used on every single amateur site. It screams, "This is an amateur site."

Consistent navigation is another thing. When you go from one page to another, try to maintain a consistent navigation feel. Clearly identify your main sections, and distinguish what are subpages to certain main sections. Often people keep their navigation buttons all in one big list and they don't differentiate the links in their site. Don't just throw all the links into one list, but do have the navigation be the same on every page.

Content is just a technical term for the stuff on your Web site—words, pictures, and so on.

CHAPTER 7

Making Even Cooler Web Pages

The World Wide Web wouldn't be a Web without links. It would just be a bunch of pages, each floating in its own private space.

Making links in HTML is easy. In fact, it often takes less time to write a link in HTML than it does in some of the commercial HTML generation programs. The amazing thing about HTML is that one single tag is used to link nearly every other page on the Web. After you've got your links in order, then you can start making the text on your Web pages look cleaner.

How to Manage Files on Your Web Site

As you create your Web site, you'll need to keep track of where you put your files. There are two ways to manage your Web site:

1. The junk method. Throw everything in the same directory. It'll be a mess, but then you won't have to deal with subdirectories.
2. The file cabinet method. Create subdirectories for all (or most) important Web site categories. For example, most Web sites store their images in a subdirectory called /images/. You could have subdirectories called /sounds/ or /multimedia/ or /dogstuff/.

Our recommendation: Use the file cabinet method, but don't go overboard. Keep all images in a single image subdirectory rather than creating multiple image subdirectories.

What is a root directory?

A root directory is the folder or directory on the Web server that contains all your other directories. If you don't create any subdirectories, then this is the place where all your files are stored. Imagine a file cabinet. That's your root directory. Subdirectories will be the drawers in the file cabinet. When someone types in your home page URL, they will typically be taken to your root directory.

Creating subdirectories

Use your FTP program to create subdirectories. In some cases, when you drag a folder or directory into the FTP program, the subdirectory will be created automatically.

Pathnames

In order to get from one directory to another, you need to be careful with pathnames. A pathname is the path that a browser takes to get to a file. There are two kinds of pathnames: relative and absolute. The quick distinction between relative and absolute pathnames is that a relative pathname points to a file location that is relative to the currently open file. Absolute pathnames don't depend on the current file. They contain all the information that the browser needs to find the linked file.

Absolute pathnames

Absolute pathnames are easy to identify. They begin with the type of link:

http	a file on a World Wide Web Server
ftp	a file on an anonymous FTP server
file	a file on your local server/system
gopher	a file on a Gopher server
WAIS	a file on a WAIS server
news	a Usenet newsgroup
telnet	a connection to a Telnet service
mailto	an e-mail address

The format of an absolute pathname is

```
typeoflink://host.domain[:port]/path/
filename
```

According to the NSCA's *Beginner's Guide to HTML*, the "port" can usually be omitted—unless someone tells you it's necessary.

Here's a tag that uses the absolute pathname link to the Adams Media Web site:

```
<A HREF="http://www.adamsmedia.com/">Adams Media
Corporation</A>
```

Relative pathnames

A relative pathname points to a file within your local Web server. When you use local pathnames, you don't need to include

---

Reasons to Use Relative Paths

1. Less typing.
2. A little faster loading since the names aren't as long.
3. The connection remains with your local server rather than going out into the Web and coming back.
4. If you move an entire batch of pages to another directory, the links within that directory (and most other links) will still work.

the type of link, host, domain, or port. A relative pathname points to a location relative to the current file.

For example, the link to the file "granny_links.htm" from Granny Goose's home page could look like:

```
<A HREF="granny_links.htm">Granny Goose's
Links</A>
```

This link would look in the current directory for the file "granny_links.htm".

Relative links can also easily access files in other directories within your server. A typical Web site will have a number of directories and subdirectories. Standard directories include /images and /cgi_bin. But of course you can have whatever directories you like.

If Granny Goose decided to put her photo album into a subdirectory called "album," then the path to the index page could be written as either "/album/" or "/album/index.htm."

A link from the album index page back to the links page would look like this:

```
"../granny_links.htm"
```

The syntax for linking to a parent directory is ".."

If you have more than one level of subdirectories, your link might look like this:

```
"../../granny_links.htm"
```

In general, you'll be using relative pathnames to navigate within your own Web site. To point a browser to a subdirectory, write the pathname like this:

```
pathname/page.htm
```

If the current file is in a subdirectory and you want to point the browser to the root directory, then write the pathname like this:

```
../page.htm
```

If the current file is one subdirectory and you want to link to another subdirectory on the same level, then write the pathname like this:

```
../subdirectory2/page.htm
```

In practice, this stuff is much easier than it looks on the page.

Creating links to images and pages in subdirectories

Let's assume you've put all your images into a subdirectory called "images." Let's say you want to have a picture of a pizza on your home page. From your root directory, your links look like this:

```
<IMG SRC="images/pizza.gif">
```

If you have your recipes in a subdirectory called recipes and want to show a picture of a pizza on the page "mycooldomain.com/recipes/pizza.htm" then the image link would be written:

```
<IMG SRC="../images/pizza.gif">
```

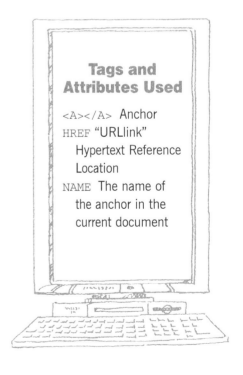

Tags and Attributes Used

`<A></A>` Anchor
`HREF` "URLlink" Hypertext Reference Location
`NAME` The name of the anchor in the current document

To create a link to the pizza page in the recipes subdirectory, you'd write this code:

```
<A HREF="recipes/pizza.htm">Click here to see my
pizza recipe</A>
```

To write a link to get back to the home page from that pizza page, then you'd write:

```
<A HREF="../index.htm">Click here to go back to
my home page.</A>
```

Site management tools

If you're using an HTML markup program, chances are that it's got some basic or advanced site management built in. Programs like FileMaker Home Page and Adobe PageMill will keep track of subdirectories automatically and write the code accordingly. They will also allow you to upload portions of the site and rename files into and out of subdirectories without losing the links.

Programs like Macromedia Dreamweaver and Adobe GoLive have extensive site management tools. You'll be able to take a look at what the site looks like visually.

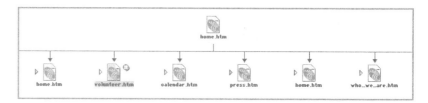

Lesson 4—Links, Anchors, and Simple Image Links

To insert a simple link in a document, just follow these easy steps:

1. Start with the anchor tag, plus a space after the A.

   `"<A "`

2. Use the parameter HREF = "filename" to identify the document you're pointing to. Follow this with the ">"

   ```
   <A HREF = "filename.htm">
   ```

3. Type the text that will be displayed by the browser as the link from the current page. Finish with the closing anchor tag "</A>"

   ```
   <A HREF = "filename.htm">Click here to go
   to filename.htm</A>
   ```

That's it!

Here's how Granny Goose can link her Web page to her son's business's Web page:

```
<A HREF = "http://www.joelgoose.com/
index.htm"> My son Joel's Web Page!</A>
```

These are some of my links on the web

My son, Joel's Web Page!

On the Web, you can link to:

- Other Web pages within your site. These are known as internal links.
- Web pages in other people's sites. These are known as external links and must use the full URL of the linked site.
- Parts of other pages in your sites. These are called anchors.
- Files on your site and other sites. These are accessed through FTP or File Transfer Protocol.
- Images. Images may be displayed within Web pages or on their own.
- Sounds.
- Newsgroups.

Link Formatting

With billions of links, the way that links are typed is absolutely vital. On UNIX servers, a mistake with upper and lower case will yield the dreaded error message:

```
Not Found
The requested URL / was not found on this server.
```

The upper/lowercase snafu is most apparent on UNIX servers. Users of Windows NT or Macintosh servers don't have to worry. Theoretically they can use any upper or lowercase naming convention they want. A problem arises, however, if you (or someone else) choose to move the Web site to a UNIX server. Many links

---

Index Pages

If no filename is specified along a certain path, the server will look for the index page. Depending on the server, this page may be named index.htm, index.html, home.htm, home.html, default.htm, or default.html.

If no index page is found in a path, the browser will usually display a list of files in that directory.

When you are setting up your Web site, be sure to learn which format your server uses for index pages.

won't work. As a rule of thumb, most Web designers name their files in all lowercase letters, for example: image.jpg or link.htm.

Mailto Links

If you want somebody to send you e-mail, it's incredibly easy to create a link on your site that will direct a message to you.

```
<A HREF="mailto:emailname@host">Send me
e-mail</A>
```

For example, Granny Goose might use:

```
<A HREF="mailto:granny@goose.com">Send me email
to tell me how cute my grandkids are!</A>
```

When the user clicks on the link, the user's email program opens with a message addressed to Granny.

Anchors

When you link to a Web page, you are typically taken to the top of that Web page. When you link to an anchor, you are taken directly to a particular spot on a Web page.

Anchors are particularly useful on long pages to take users directly to the information they're interested in, skipping over the boring or irrelevant bits in between. For example, in a company's contact list of addresses, the user may want to go straight to the personnel department's address.

Creating Anchors

To create an anchor within a document use the NAME= attribute for the anchor tag:

```
<A NAME="anchorname">
```

For example, in the document "addresses.htm" you might have the tag:

```
<A NAME="personnel">Personnel Department
```

Webmaster's Trick: Including the Subject in the E-mail.

To paste a subject into the e-mail, use the following format:

```
<A HREF= "mailto:
emailname@host?
subject=Vital
email">Send me
e-mail</A>
```

Or in Granny Goose's version:

```
<A HREF=
"mailto:granny@
goose.com?subject=
Cute kids">Send me
e-mail to tell me
how cute my
grandkids are!</A>
```

Note: This feature is undocumented and won't work on all browsers, but it is worth a try.

Linking to Anchors

You can link to anchors with either relative or absolute path-names. The # sign is used to indicate an anchor.

- To link to an anchor within the same document, simply reference "#anchorname"

  ```
  <A HREF="#personnel">Personnel Department</A>
  ```

- To link to an anchor within another document in the same directory (a relative path), simply use "documentname/#anchorname"

  ```
  <A HREF="addresses.htm/#personnel">
  Personnel Department</A>
  ```

- To link to an anchor in a document on another Web site or to use an absolute path, simply use "http://server/directory/addresses.htm/#anchorname"

  ```
  <A HREF= "http://www.bigcompany.com/
  addresses.htm/#personnel">Personnel
  Department</A>
  ```

Simple Image Links

Now that you've learned how easy it is to set up a link, it's time to set up a simple image link. The format for an image link is identical to the format for a regular link, except instead of using text for the link you use an <IMG> tag. Here's how it works.

```
<A HREF="test.htm"><IMG SRC="linkimage.gif"></A>
```

If Granny Goose wanted to make the picture of her grandson into a link to a page all about Joey, she'd just write:

```
<A HREF="joey.htm"><IMG SRC="images/joey.jpg"></A>
```

Pretty easy!

Lesson 5—Basic Text Formatting

Basic HTML text formatting is boring. Boring boring boring. Still, as a blossoming Webmaster, it's something you need to know. Once you understand it, you can use it easily, and ignore it when necessary. First a bit of theory.

HTML Formatting Theory

The guys who designed HTML were scientists, not graphic designers. They were interested in coming up with a mark-up format that allowed them to post their papers on the Internet. They really didn't care what stuff looked like on the page, as long as everything looked similar.

The idea was that they could take one piece of code and just paste different text into it. Every time somebody wrote a new paper, all she would have to do would be plug in the titles, headers, and citations.

This technology was very useful for the scientific community. It is also incredibly boring to look at. We'll get into some of the many other ways to make your page look cool later on.

Line Breaks—The
 Tag

Using the paragraph tag <P>, HTML browsers always display space between paragraphs. It's like a word processor that always adds a gap between paragraphs. The <BR> tag allows users to start a new line without that extra space.

Like the Paragraph <P> tag, you do not need a close tag to use the <BR> tag. With the <BR> tag, the designers of HTML had things like addresses in mind. For example, the next two pieces of code look quite different when viewed in a browser.

```
<P> John and Jane Doe
<P> 333 Lilac Lane
<P> Anytown, USA


<P> John and Jane Doe
<BR> 333 Lilac Lane
<BR> Anytown, USA
```

```
John and Jane Doe

333 Lilac Lane

Anytown, USA
```

```
John and Jane Doe
333 Lilac Lane
Anytown, USA
```

Headings

There are six levels of headings in HTML. Heading number one is the most important and heading number six is the least important. Headings are used to delineate between sections of your document. Level one headings are frequently document titles. Level two and three headings are usually used for section headings and subheadings.

Headings five and six tend to be very small font sizes and could be used for information like copyright notices and other legal disclaimers.

All headings begin with the heading tag and end with a close heading tag. For example:

```
<H1>This is the most important thing I have to
say.</H1>
<H6>This is the least important thing I have to
say.</H6>
```

Here's a look at all six headings:

Tags and Attributes Used

`<BR>`
Break line (forced line break)
`<H1>` Heading 1
`<H2>` Heading 2
`<H3>` Heading 3
`<H4>` Heading 4
`<H5>` Heading 5
`<H6>` Heading 6
`<PRE>` Preformatted Text

This is what a Level One Heading looks like.

This is what a Level Two Heading looks like.

This is what a Level Three Heading looks like.

This is what a Level Four Heading looks like.

This is what a Level Five Heading looks like.

This is what a Level Six Heading looks like.

```
<HTML>
<HEAD>
<TITLE>Basic Text Formatting — Headers</TITLE>
</HEAD>

<BODY BGCOLOR="#FFFFFF">

<H1>Here's what Heading level one looks
like</H1>
<H2>Here's what Heading level two looks
like</H2>
<H3>Here's what Heading level three looks
like</H3>
<H4>Here's what Heading level four looks
like</H4>
<H5>Here's what Heading level five looks
like</H5>
<H6>Here's what Heading level six looks
like</H6>

</BODY>
</HTML>
```

There is one big problem with headers—different browsers display headers differently. In other words, as with every other element in HTML, when you use headers, you can't guarantee exactly what your viewer will see.

(Image note: Open BTF_headers.htm in Netscape and Explorer.)

Compare these two images. The differences are subtle. Also, when your user adjusts the text size in her browser, the size of the headers also changes.

(Image note: Open BTF_headers.htm in browser normal, large, and smallest text size.)

Recommended style versus *your* style

The HTML purists have very strong opinions on the use of headings. For example, they recommend that you always nest headings. Start with a level one heading, then a level two, level three, level four, and then go back out with a level three, level two, etc. They also recommend that you not skip from heading level one to heading level three.

For formal Web pages, such as papers and other "official" documents, these are both excellent rules to follow. But for ordinary Web pages, we recommend breaking the rules as you see fit.

For example, we like the level three header <H3> a lot. It just seems to have the right level of emphasis over ordinary text. So we'll often start a page off with an <H3> rather than an <H1>.

We do, however, recommend that you be consistent about the rules you break within any given area of your Web site. If you've got a series of four articles that start with <H3>, starting number five with an <H2> will be jarring to a viewer.

Preformatted Text <PRE>

You may not remember, but in the old days when people still used typewriters they put two spaces at the end of a sentence after a period. That stylistic choice has largely vanished in the computer era. HTML is no exception. HTML browsers automatically delete all extra spaces from sentences before showing them.

```
<H3> Regular text</H3>
<P>In a browser,
<BR>this line looks the same as
<BR>this  line looks the same  as
<BR>this line looks the   same as
<BR> and so on.
```

Preformatted text is an old-fashioned way of handling this problem and solving others. Here's how the <PRE> tag works.

Text enclosed by the <PRE> and </PRE> tags is displayed in the browser exactly as typed in the HTML document. This includes carriage returns. Extra spaces are not deleted. It is important to remember, though, that HTML does NOT recognize tabs in its documents. Use spaces instead of tabs in the <PRE> tag.

Also, a monotype font is used instead of a proportional type font. In a monotype font, any word with four letters takes up the same space as any other word with four letters. In a proportional font, the letter W takes up more space on the screen or page than the letter i.

This is what happens to the same lines when we use the <PRE> tag:

Tip

The folks who like standardized HTML don't encourage the use of the <BR> tag. They like things broken up in an orderly way. We, however, disagree. Use the <BR> tag whenever you want! One perfect type of Web page for playing with the <BR> tag is in poetry.

If you are writing poetry, put the <BR> tags at the end of the previous line so that when you look at your raw HTML code, it will look better.

```
<P>
Roses are red<BR>
Violets are
blue<BR>
Computers are
swell<BR>
And so are you!
```

looks the same as

```
<P>Roses are red
<BR>Violets are
blue
<BR>Computers are
swell
<BR>And so are you!
```

```
<H3> Preformatted text:</H3>
<PRE>In a browser,
this line looks the same as
this line looks the same as
this line looks the same as
and so on.</PRE>
```

Regular text

In a browser,
this line looks the same as
this line looks the same as
this line looks the same as
and so on.

Preformatted text:

In a browser,
this line looks the same as
this   line   looks the same   as
this line looks the   same as
 and so on.

You can use preformatted text for things like lists:

```
<H3>Here is a list of states and speed-dial
codes</H3>
<PRE>
State   Code
MA   12
RI   13
NY   17</PRE>
```

Or if you're going to quote bits of HTML code, it's useful to make it look different:

```
<H3>Or maybe some HTML code...</H3>

<PRE>&lt;H3&gt; This is Level Three Heading
&lt;/H3&gt;
&lt;P&gt;This line starts a new paragraph.
&lt;P&gt;This line starts another new paragraph.
</PRE>
```

```
Here is a list of states and speed-dial codes

State      Code
MA         12
RI         13
NY         17


Or maybe some HTML code...

<H3> This is Level Three Heading </H3>
<P>This line starts a new paragraph.
<P>This line starts another new paragraph.
```

Why you will probably never use the <PRE> tag:

1. It's old-fashioned.
2. Most of you won't be putting stuff that looks like raw code on your Web pages.
3. Tables do a better job of keeping columns of information in lines.
4. The   (see below) is a better way of adding an extra space to a line.

Lesson 6—Spacing and Alignment

Although Web pages don't really work like word processors or page layout programs such as PageMaker, you do have some control over how pages are formatted.

The ALIGN tag is used to set paragraph (or page) justification.

The non-breaking space is used to add extra spaces between words.

Aligning paragraphs and other elements with the ALIGN attribute and the <CENTER>

The ALIGN attribute is used to align paragraphs and other elements in a page. So is the <CENTER> tag. Obviously, the <CENTER> tag is only used to center something. The ALIGN attribute can force left, right, or centered justification.

Important Note

The <, >, and & characters are used as part of HTML's coding, so if you want to use them in your document, you must use their "escape sequences" to display the characters.

To display a
Less Than Sign (<) use:
<

To display a
Greater Than Sign (<)
use:
>

To display an
Ampersand (&) use:
&

The `<CENTER>` tag must be used with a `</CENTER>` tag. It will center all text and elements between the `<CENTER>` and `</CENTER>` tags. Unlike the `<CENTER>` tag, the ALIGN attribute must be used within a tag. For text manipulation, the ALIGN attribute can be used inside `<P>`, `<H1...H6>`, and `<PRE>` tags. The ALIGN attribute can't be used inside a `<BR>` tag. The ALIGN attribute can also be used inside an image, as we've seen earlier.

Here's an example of how the `<CENTER>` tag and ALIGN attributes work.

This is a centered heading

This paragraph is also centered

This is an aligned-centered heading

This is an unaligned paragraph

This paragraph is right aligned.
Notice how the jagged-margin is on the left side now.

The alignment resets at a new paragraph break.

This paragraph and image are aligned center.

```
<HTML>
<HEAD>
<TITLE>Aligning Text and other elements</TITLE>
</HEAD>
<BODY BGCOLOR="#FFFFFF">
<CENTER><H1> This is a centered heading</H1>
<P>This paragraph is also centered</CENTER>
<H1 ALIGN=CENTER>This is an aligned-centered
heading</H1>
<P>This is an unaligned paragraph
<P ALIGN=RIGHT>This paragraph is right aligned.
<BR>Notice how the jagged margin is on the left
side now.
<P>The alignment resets at a new paragraph
break.
<P ALIGN=CENTER>This paragraph and image are
aligned center.<IMG SRC="images/dogbone.gif"
ALT="dogbone">
</BODY>
</HTML>
```

Non-Breaking Space—

HTML strips out extra spaces and carriage returns. "Here I   am" will appear on the screen as "Here I am."

So, how could you add extra spaces into a line without using preformatted text? The escape sequence, " " is the easiest way to force the browser to show a space in the middle of a line. For example, if you're a poet and you want to display a few lines that look like this:

```
computer screen glare
   I have radiation burns
        Please let me shut down
```

The code would look like this:

```
<P>computer screen glare
<BR>   I have radiation burns
<BR>      Please
let me shut down
```

One of the most useful ways to use a non-breaking space is to keep an empty table cell from collapsing. When you create a table in HTML, browsers frequently mush together cells that contain no data. This can make your table look pretty ugly. The solution: insert a non-breaking space into every cell. The table will look like a standard spreadsheet.

Lesson 7—Playing with Fonts (Part One)

If you want to make a point in a word processor, you use bold type or you blow up the font size. Here's the first lesson on how to manipulate fonts in HTML.

Two types of formatting

According to the folks who make HTML standards, there are two types of font formatting or "styles" for documents.

The first group are "physical" styles; they adjust the display of the font in a physical way. This group includes the <B>, <I>, <TT>, and <STRIKE> tags. We'd also make the argument that the <FONT SIZE> tag is a physical style adjustment.

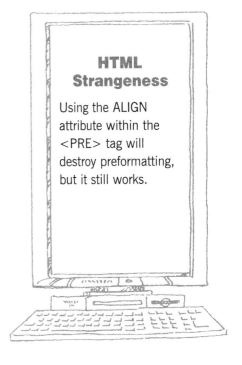

HTML Strangeness

Using the ALIGN attribute within the <PRE> tag will destroy preformatting, but it still works.

Font Sizes

(Notice that using <B> tags within a header has no effect.)

This is normal, untagged, type.

This is Font Size 1 type.

This is Font Size 2 type.

This is Font Size 3 type.

This is Font Size 4 type.

This is Font Size 5 type.

This is Font Size 6 type.

This is Font Size 7 type.

Font Sizes

(Notice that using <B> tags within a header has no effect.)

This is normal, untagged, type.

This is Font Size 1 type.

This is Font Size 2 type.

This is Font Size 3 type.

This is Font Size 4 type.

This is Font Size 5 type.

This is Font Size 6 type.

The other method of adding font style to documents is by using "logical" styles. By labeling text <STRONG> or <CITATION>, you're defining what that labeled text is. Text enclosed by the <CODE> and </CODE> tags is meant to be computer code.

Got it? OK. Now, unless you're an academic, forget all about logical styles. Nobody uses them.

Physical Style Font Manipulation

Using tags like <B></B> for **boldface** text and <I></I> for *italics* mirrors the way your word processor works. The <FONT SIZE = > tag is a bit trickier. There are two ways to define font size, either by number or relative to the base size. Numerical fonts range from 1 (the smallest) to 7 (the largest). The base size starts by assuming a font of 3 and then adding or subtracting from that.

The problem with the <FONT SIZE> tag (aside from the fact that it doesn't work in older browsers) is that the font size is relative to the font size the user has chosen for his browser. If the user has rotten eyesight and sets her regular font viewing size to be large, and you use a <FONT SIZE = "+1," the type could be absolutely gigantic.

```
<HTML>
<HEAD>
<TITLE>Font Styles</TITLE>
</HEAD>
<BODY BGCOLOR="#FFFFFF">
<H3><B>Font Sizes</B></H3>
<P>(Notice that using &lt;B&gt; tags within a
header has no effect.)</P>
<P>This is normal, untagged, type.</P>
<P><FONT SIZE=1>This is Font Size 1
type.</FONT></P>
<P><FONT SIZE=2>This is Font Size 2
type.</FONT></P>
<P><FONT SIZE=3>This is Font Size 3
type.</FONT></P>
<P><FONT SIZE=4>This is Font Size 4
type.</FONT></P>
<P><FONT SIZE=5>This is Font Size 5
type.</FONT></P>
<P><FONT SIZE=6>This is Font Size 6
type.</FONT></P>
<P><FONT SIZE=7>This is Font Size 7
type.</FONT></P>
<HR>
<P><B>This text is Bold</B></P>
<P><I>This text is italicized.</I></P>
<P>Part of this text is <SUP>superscript.</SUP>
Part of this text is
<SUB>subscript.</SUB> Notice how the type size
changes!</P>
<P><U>This text is underlined. Note: This can be
confusing because links are frequently under-
scored.</U></P>
<P><TT>This is what typewriter text looks
like.</TT></P>
<P>When you make a <STRIKE>mistake</STRIKE>
error, you can make it look like this.</P>
<P></P>
</BODY>
</HTML>
```

Webmaster Notes

- The ALIGN attribute resets at the next paragraph, heading, or preformatted text tag.
- Alignment always defaults to left. If you do not use the <CENTER> tag or the ALIGN attribute, the paragraph or header will be left aligned.
- Images without alignment line up with the paragraph they are inside. However, an image alignment overrides a paragraph alignment. <IMAGE ALIGN=LEFT> will override a <P ALIGN = RIGHT>.

Physical Styles

`<FONT SIZE></FONT SIZE>`
Set font size. Can be relative to browser default (i.e., <FONT SIZE="+4"> or defined specifically as <FONT SIZE=?> where ? is a number between 1-7)
NOTE: FONT SIZE is not supported in all browsers.

`<B></B>`
Bold text

`<I></I>`
Italicize text

`<U></U>`
Underscore text

`<TT></TT>`
Typewriter text

`<STRIKE></STRIKE>`
Strikethrough text

`<SUP></SUP>`
Superscript text

`<SUB></SUB>`
Subscript text

Logical Styles

`<STRONG></STRONG>`
Strong emphasis. Usually displayed in bold face.

`<EM></EM>`
Emphasize text. Usually displayed in Italics.

`<DFN></DFN>`
Definition text

`<CITE></CITE>`
Citation text (ex. used for book title). Usually displayed in italics.

`<VAR></VAR>`
Variable name. Usually displayed in italics.

`<CODE></CODE>`
Computer code. Usually displayed in monotype font.

`<KBD></KBD>`
Keyboard entry. Usually displayed in monotype font bold.

Logical Style Font Manipulation

If you're writing an academic paper, or posting research on the Web, play by the rules. Use the conventions established within the scientific community. The reason for using logical rather than physical style manipulations is that the style choices add meaning to the document rather than just look good.

Using a <CITE></CITE> tag tells an academician that the text enclosed between the tags is a citation. If they're searching for your sources, this is an easy way to find information. Additionally, some browsers may be configured to display information like citations in different fonts or colors.

Logical Style Elements

This indicates an abbreviation

THIS INDICATES AN ACRONYM

Citation

Computer Code

A Definition

Emphasize this!

This text should be inputed from a Keyboard

This is sample output

Strong Emphasis!

Put variable names here

```
<HTML>
<HEAD>
<TITLE>Logical Style Elements</TITLE>
</HEAD>
<BODY BGCOLOR="#FFFFFF">
<H3>Logical Style Elements</H3>
<P><ABBR>This indicates an abbreviation</ABBR>
<P><ACRONYM>This indicates an acronym</ACRONYM>
<P><CITE>Citation</CITE>
<P><CODE>Computer Code</CODE>
<P><DFN>A Definition</DFN>
<P><EM>Emphasize this!</EM>
<P><KBD>This text should be typed in from a
Keyboard</KBD>
<P><SAMP>This is sample output</SAMP>
<P><STRONG>Strong Emphasis!</STRONG>
<P><VAR>Put variable names here</VAR>
</BODY>
</HTML>
```

Text Formatting Tutorial

Now we're going to create a basic Web page template that's going to rock! Feel free to change any of the text between the tags to keep yourself amused. Just make sure you close all your tags.

1. Create your empty Web page. Include <HTML>, <HEAD>, and <BODY> tags.

```
<HTML>
<HEAD>
<TITLE>My Cool Tutorial</TITLE>
</HEAD>
<BODY BGCOLOR="WHITE">
```

2. Give your document a level one header.

```
<H1>I'm the best HTML programmer on
page!</H1>
```

3. Write some text.

```
<P>Ok, now it's time to get serious. I
believe that we need to end hunger as a
problem on the planet. I'd like to figure
out something to do about it.
<P>There are all kinds of things I could
do. I could donate to charity. I could vol-
unteer at a soup kitchen. I could organize
a canned foods drive.
<P>All excellent ideas.
<P>But I've known about those things for a
while.
<P>So, why don't I do anything about it?
```

4. Heavy stuff. First let's close out the </BODY> and </HTML> tags.

```
</BODY>
</HTML>
```

5. Save the file as hunger1.htm

6. Open your favorite Web browser and use the "Open" choice from the File menu to open the file and see what it looks like.

7. Now, let's change some of the emphasis. Put a couplet of <B> tags around the word "serious." Put a couplet of <I> tags before and after the sentence, "So, why don't I do anything about it?"

8. Save the changes. Click the "Reload" button in Netscape or the "Refresh" button in Explorer.

9. Hmm, it's still a little funky. Change the title to "Hunger Idea Diary." Change the <H1> text to "Ending Hunger." Delete the line, "Ok, now it's time to get serious."

10. Save and refresh/reload. Almost.

11. Now we're going to make your ideas into a bullet list. We'll get around to the nitty gritty-details of how that works in the next chapter.

12. Put a <P> before the words: "There are all kinds of things I could do."

13. Create the bullet list by typing the tag <UL> (<UL> stands for unnumbered.)

14. Type the tag <LI> before the next three instances of the words "I could." Type </LI> at the end of each line.

15. Close the list with the </UL> tag after the words "food drive."

16. Click "Save As" and rename the file "hunger2.htm" (Hint: when you begin to make drastic changes to a base document it's a good idea to save a copy of the original.)

17. Take a look at the new document in your browser (refresh/reload).

18. Not bad. Now it's time to put the Web to work.

19. Before the </BODY> tag, type the tag <HR>. (<HR> adds a "Horizontal Rule." It's a quick way to break up a page.)

20. Type the following:

```
<P>I heard about this Web site called <A
HREF="http://www.thehungersite.com">
The Hunger Site.</A> They're getting spon-
sors to donate food to the hungry every
```

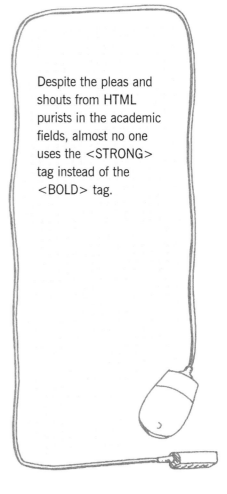

Despite the pleas and shouts from HTML purists in the academic fields, almost no one uses the <STRONG> tag instead of the <BOLD> tag.

time somebody clicks on the site's button. All you have to do is go to the site and click. One click per day per person around the world could make a huge difference. <P>Click here: <A HREF="http://www. thehungersite.com">The Hunger Site.</A>

21. Save and preview.

Ending Hunger

I believe that we need to end hunger as a problem on the planet. I'd like to figure out something to do about it.

There are all kinds of things I could do.

- I could donate to charity.
- I could volunteer at a soup kitchen.
- I could organize a canned foods drive.

All excellent ideas.

But I've known about those things for a while.

So, why don't I do anything about it?

I heard about this web site called The Hunger Site. They're getting sponsors to donate food to the hungry every time somebody clicks on the site's button. All you have to do is go to the site and click. One click per day per person around the world could make a huge difference.

Click here: The Hunger Site.

Notice that you've created a link to another site on the Web. We've actually created the same link twice. This sort of redundancy is common but useful. At the first instance of the words "The Hunger Site," the reader has the immediate opportunity to click through to the next site. At the end of the document, that invitation is made even more specific.

Here's what your finished document should look like:

```
<HTML>
<HEAD>
<TITLE>Hunger Idea Diary</TITLE>
</HEAD>
<BODY BGCOLOR="#FFFFFF">
<H1>Ending Hunger</H1>
<P>I believe that we need to end hunger as a
problem on the planet.
I'd like to figure out something to do about it.
<P>There are all kinds of things I could do.
<UL>
<LI>I could donate to charity.</LI>
<LI>I could volunteer at a soup kitchen.</LI>
<LI>I could organize a canned foods drive.</LI>
</UL>
<P>All excellent ideas.
```

```
<P>But I've known about those things for a
while.
<P><I>So, why don't I do anything about it? </I>
<HR>
<P>I heard about this web site called <A
HREF="http://www.thehungersite.com">The Hunger
Site.</A> They're getting sponsors to donate
food to the hungry every time somebody clicks on
the site's button. All you have to do is go to
the site and click. One click per day per person
around the world could make a huge difference.
<P>Click here: <A HREF="http://www.thehunger-
site.com">The Hunger Site.</A>
</BODY>
</HTML>
```

Lesson 8—Horizontal Rules

Horizontal rules are a simple and quick way to divide a page. Essentially, they draw a line across the page, dividing it into two parts. Beginners tend to overuse horizontal rules, choosing to break the page with their lines rather than using headings or subheadings. Advanced HTML designers tend to underuse horizontal rules, preferring to do pretty things with tables or graphics. Used with judicious restraint, the <HR> tag can be exceptionally useful in creating clear breaks in a page's content.

To insert a horizontal tag, breaking up a pair of paragraphs, simply type:

```
<P>This is the top part of the page
<HR>
<P>This is the bottom part of the page.
```

If you'd like to adjust the alignment width or thickness of the rule, simply use the attributes.

```
<P>This is the top part of the page
<HR WIDTH="50%" ALIGN = "CENTER">
<P>This is the bottom part of the page.
```

Ordinary Horizontal Rule

50 Pixel Horizontal Rule Default Alignment (Center)

50 percent horizontal rule, size 5 aligned left

50 percent horizontal rule with no shading, size 10 aligned right

This little HTML page gives you a good idea what various horizontal rules look like.

```
<HTML>
<HEAD>
<TITLE>Horizontal Rules</title>
</HEAD>
<BODY BGCOLOR="#FFFFFF">
<P>Ordinary Horizontal Rule</P>
<HR>
50 Pixel Horizontal Rule Default Alignment
(Center)
<HR WIDTH="50">
<P>50 percent horizontal rule, size 5 aligned
left</P>
<HR WIDTH="50%" ALIGN="LEFT" SIZE="5">
50 percent horizontal rule with no shading, size
10 aligned right
<HR NOSHADE SIZE="10" WIDTH="50%" ALIGN="RIGHT">
</BODY>
</HTML>
```

CHAPTER 8

Adding Images and Pictures

We've spent a lot of time discussing the guts and bones of the site, now we're going to take a little time to talk about one of the most important parts of the site—the graphical content.

What Kinds of Images Are Used on the Web?

GIFs and JPEGs are the most common graphics file formats by far on the Web.

GIF (Graphics Interchange Format) files end in ".gif" and can range from 256 colors to monochrome. GIFs are used often in logos, banner ads, and computer-generated art. JPEG images, a compressed graphics format created by the Joint Photographic Experts Group, have a filename ending in ".jpg" or ".jpeg" and are often used for photographs and complex images.

PNG or Portable Network Graphic is a third, up and coming, graphics format. It has just been recently supported by the major browsers. The major limitation to PNG is that it is only supported by Netscape version 4.04 or better and Internet Explorer 4.0 or better. Furthermore, some of the functionality of PNG (such as transparency) is not supported even by these early adopters. In a few years, when most people are using browsers that support PNG, it may be the best format to use because it is patent-free. (See "The GIF Licensing Surprise" on p. 122.) Because of the reliability of JPEG and GIF and the unreliability of PNG graphics, we don't recommend using that format.

You'll often see tiny images, called thumbnails, which you can click to see a full-screen image. This can be quite striking if it's a beautiful artwork or scenic photograph. Image maps are images that are broken down into sections, each of which you can click to see a particular section. For example, you'll often see a map of the United States and be able to click on a certain state, region, or city.

GIF Advantages and Disadvantages

For cool graphic effects on the Web, GIF wins out over JPEG. There are three ways of handling GIFs that give it an edge over JPEG.

GIF Without Transparency.......GIF With Transparency

1. Transparent backgrounds. On the Web, all graphics are treated as rectangles. By altering a GIF so one of its colors is transparent, users can place an odd-shaped GIF any-where on a Web page and the page's back-ground color or image will bleed through.
2. Interlacing. There are two ways to load a GIF: the standard method, which loads the image from top to bottom until it's all done, and interlacing. Interlaced GIFs load a little like a venetian blind. The whole shape of the image will load quickly but in a lower resolution— leaving out parts. The image then starts at the top and fills in the missing bits. This allows the general image to load very quickly and reduces viewer impatience.
3. Animated GIFs. If you've surfed the Web, you've seen ani-mated GIFs. The much maligned "Send Us Email" icon showing an envelope opening or the "Under Construction" icon showing a stick-figure worker shoveling are both ani-mated GIFs. Essentially, you take one image, modify it slightly, and bundle the images, like an animated cartoon.

Sounds great, right? Unfortunately, on a graphical level, GIFs just don't have the kind of photographic image quality as JPEGs. For simple images with limited colors, GIFs work wonderfully. For a detailed photograph, a GIF image will be a larger file with worse res-olution than a JPEG.

JPEG Advantages and Disadvantages

JPEGs are superior for photographs and high-quality images. They offer varying degrees of compression so that you easily choose whether to sacrifice image quality in favor of a faster download, or get a high-resolution image that takes longer to download.

The drawback to JPEGs is that smaller JPEG images take up more space than GIFs. They also don't have the transparent background, interlacing, or animation features.

How Can I Get Images for My Web Site?

There are five basic ways to get images for your Web site.

1. Scanning in photos or other images. Fairly high-quality scanners have become incredibly inexpensive these days. A scanner can take any flat object and turn it into a digital image. You can then take that image and alter it with any photo or graphics editing program.
2. Printing your photo film to CD-ROM or diskette. You may have noticed that your local film developer can have your film printed both on paper and to CD-ROM or diskette. Kodak Picture CDs offer digital images at a very high resolution. When your pictures are printed to floppy disk, the resolution will be considerably lower, but that is usually sufficient if you are interested in posting those images on the Web.
3. Clip art CD-ROMs or clip art Web sites. A great many artists have realized that they can try to sell their work to one or two clients, or they can create digital albums that they then license to individual users. Before you buy a clip art CD-ROM, you should read the licensing agreement carefully. Specifically, you should find out whether this purchase allows you to reproduce the work for sale.

    There are many commercial clip art CD-ROMs available at computer and office supply stores (we even saw one at the local supermarket!). One of our favorites, Web Explosion, comes from Nova Development (www.novadevelopment.com/). We like it because it includes a variety of clip art, rulers, buttons, and animations, but not too many. After all, if there are 1 million images to check out, how are you going to find the one you want? Be sure the CD-ROM is compatible with your computer and that it has a catalog program for quick viewing bundled with it.

Many Web creation programs come with clip-art. Chances are, if you own a new computer you've got a cache of clip art somewhere.

On the Web there is a wealth of free clip art available. Try not to steal art that isn't free. Even though it will be almost impossible for someone to track you down, you wouldn't want them stealing from your site, would you?

4. Drawing or painting programs. If your computer has a drawing or painting program, you can create a digital picture and upload it to the Web. The quality of this art work will, of course, depend on your talents and abilities. Use the "Save As" feature to save it as a JPEG or GIF.

5. Digital cameras. Follow the directions on your digital camera to download the photos onto floppy disk or directly into your computer.

Image Handling Software

In other sections of this book, we recommend that our readers spend some time learning HTML to augment or replace the use of HTML page generation programs. When it comes to images, though, software rules. Most of the WYSIWYG HTML page generation programs allow you to scale graphics, draw image maps, and set image transparencies.

Five Rules of Image Management Software

1. The more expensive the image management software, the more it can do and the harder it will be to learn.
2. It's a lot easier to scale an image within a software program than to use a calculator to maintain the proportions.

Use GIFs for simple graphics with limited colors and in situations where transparent backgrounds are necessary.

Use JPEG for photos and high-quality images.

The GIF Licensing Surprise

In the fall of 1999, Unisys, the huge computer corporation, announced that it owned the patent on the GIF format and that it was going to start enforcing its license. According to the Unisys Web site, "In all cases, a written license agreement or statement signed by an authorized Unisys representative is required from Unisys for all use, sale or distribution of any software (including so-called 'freeware') and/or hardware providing LZW conversion capability (for example, downloaded software used for creating/displaying GIF images).... For example, the typical Unisys license for standalone software does NOT permit copying, modification, resale, use on a server or in a network, or use for Internet/Intranet/Extranet or Web site operation. Other limitations may also be applicable. Upon request, Unisys will, in most instances, be able to advise you whether a specific software vendor is licensed by Unisys and the scope of this license." (www.unisys.com—http://corp2.unisys.com/LeadStory/lzwfaq.html)

Essentially, that means that if you create a GIF, you may be liable for a licensing fee of up to $5,000. Furthermore, according to Unisys, more than 2,000 corporations have already paid their licensing fees, so if you use one of their products to create GIFs you may be exempt. Some of these companies are Microsoft, Macromedia, Corel, Adobe, NetObjects, Visio, Eastman Software, Claris, Deneba Systems, and Scansoft/Visioneer.

Bottom line: If you're planning on making a pile of money using GIFs, spend some time researching whether you need a license.

In other words, when you alter the height of a 4 x 5 image, most image management programs can automatically adjust the width. While scaling a 4 x 5 image to 2 x 2.5 is simple, reducing a 7.69 x 8.42 image by one-third takes a little thinking (5.08 x 5.56).

3. Setting GIF transparency and interlacing is usually a one- or two-click process.

4. Nearly all the top image management programs have compression utilities. In other words, you can reduce the amount of disk space and download size for any image.

5. Image management software allows you to add lots of cool effects to your images. Some are as simple as taking the red-eye out of a photo. Others are essential, like brightening up a dark image.

How do I make a GIF transparent or interlaced?

The easiest way to make a GIF transparent is to use a page generation program or image management software. For a list of image management software, see Appendix A: Links.

Setting Transparency in FileMaker Home Page (Windows, Mac)

1. Double-click or right click on an image.
2. Click on the Transparency and Interlacing "Set" button.
3. Choose the Transparency tool and select which color to make transparent.
4. Click the Interlace button.
5. Save the altered image.

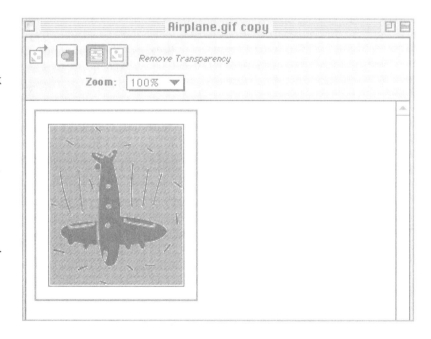

Setting Transparency in Adobe PageMill (Windows, Mac)

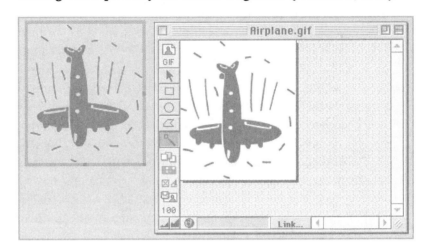

1. Right click or double-click on an image. Select "Open Image Window." (Or just select "Open Image Window" from the Edit/Images menu.)
2. Use the transparency wand to select which color to make transparent.
3. Click on the Interlace button.
4. Save the altered image.

Setting Transparency in Adobe ImageReady

1. Open the image.
2. Click Transparency.
3. Click Interlaced.
4. Save the image.

What if I don't have any software to do that?

If you don't have any page layout or image management software, you can surf on the Net for shareware. Try Shareware.Com (www.shareware.com) or CNET Download.com (www.download.com). Special for Macintosh owners: Look for the freeware GIFConverter and GIF Builder.

Putting Images on Your Web Pages

We've already gone over some of this, but putting it all in one place makes sense. For the following examples, we're assuming that all images have been placed in a subdirectory called "images."

Setting a Background Image

Choose your background image with care. Background images tile. In other words, if you have a one-inch square image, it will repeat itself five or six times across and five or six times down when viewed in a typical Web browser. Consider using clip art or shareware background images for wallpaper or texture backgrounds.

Although both GIFs and JPEGs may be used for background images, if you're using a more literal image, consider using a transparent GIF and fading the image way into the background, like a watermark.

Be considerate of your viewers. If you use a dark blue background image, then black type isn't going to show up well. If you use the same background image throughout your site, the viewer will only have to load it on the first page.

To create a sidebar, you can create a rather nice effect by using a narrow strip image, say 20 pixels high by 800 pixels wide. If you put a stripe on the left side of the image, then the image will effectively only tile down on the browser.

Placing Images on the Page

To place an image onto a page, use the following code:

```
<IMG SRC="coolpicture.gif">
```

This image will default to the actual size of the image.

Changing image size

To make the image larger or smaller, use the HEIGHT and WIDTH attributes. As a rule, reducing an image's size works better than increasing it, because resolution is lost in the expansion. Try to keep images proportional to their original size, or else you'll see some really weird distortions.

Setting a border

To set a border around an image, use the BORDER attribute. The default border for an IMG tag is zero. The default for an image used in a link is 1.

Tips for Managing Images

1. Put all your images in a subdirectory called images. From your root directory, your image source code will look like this:
   `<IMG SRC= "images/ imagename.gif">`
2. If you're creating a photo album, make all the images the same height.
3. Use clip art that looks similar to create a similar look and feel.
4. Don't use ultra-high resolution images. Web experts agree that 72 dpi (dots per inch) resolution is sufficient for most images.

Alternative descriptions

To give the image an alternative description, use the ALT="name" attribute. Use of the ALT attribute is recommended to help people with slow browsers pass the time, and to give more information to people who can't see images.

Aligning an image relative to text

The ALIGN attribute is used to set the relationship of an image to the text immediately following it.

ALIGN=RIGHT will place the image on the right margin and wrap all text to the left of the image.

ALIGN=LEFT will place the image on the left margin and wrap text to the right of the image.

The TOP, CENTER, and BOTTOM alignments take a single line of text and align that title with the top, middle, or bottom of the picture.

Using multiple attributes

You may use any or all of the above attributes within an IMG tag. Here's an example:

```
<HTML>
<HEAD>
<TITLE>Basic Image Manipulation</TITLE>
</HEAD>
<BODY BGCOLOR="#FFFFFF">
<IMG SRC="images/coolimage.gif" BORDER=1 ALIGN=
RIGHT ALT="Auntie Gonzo" HEIGHT=300 WIDTH=350>
<H1>Auntie Gonzo</H1>
<P>Hi y'all. Yep, I'm Auntie Gonzo. <BR>
When Uncle Gonzo and I went to Niagara Falls, we
had a cartoonist draw me, and I think he did a
swell job. <BR>
Anyway, if you folks want to swap recipes, you
just let me know. OK?
</BODY>
</HTML>
```

Making an entire image into a link

Making an entire image into a link is incredibly simple; just enclose the image in an anchor tag.

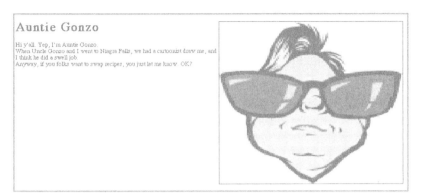

```
<A HREF="more_about_auntie.htm">
<IMG SRC="images/coolimage.gif"></A>
```

The IMG tag within the link may be modified with any or all of the attributes listed above.

Note: When an image is turned into a link, it is automatically given a 1-pixel border. To eliminate the border, use the BORDER=0 attribute.

Image Maps—More than one link on a single image

Would you like to have more than one link within the same image, in other words, create some "hot spots" in an image? Our advice is to get an HTML generation program and use it to create these client-side image maps.

Creating an image map in FileMaker Home Page

1. Double-click on the image or open the Object Editor from the Window menu.
2. Click the Behavior tab.
3. Click the Image Map radio button. Click Edit.
4. Select the circular or rectangular image map button.
5. Drag and drop to select the area of the image you want to map.
6. Type the URL in the Link Editor Window.
7. Repeat steps 4–6 as many times as you'd like.

To put a background image into an entire Web page, use the following HTML code.

```
<BODY BACKGROUND=
"images/background.gif">
```

To put a background image into a table or table cell, use the following HTML code.

```
<TABLE BACKGROUND=
"images/background.gif">
```

or for a single cell:

```
<TD BACKGROUND=
"images/background.gif">
```

8. If you want to include a default URL, type the URL into the Default URL box.
9. Close the box.

Creating an image map in Adobe PageMill

1. Double-click on the image to select it.
2. From the Edit/Image menu select either Rectangle Hotspot, Circle Hotspot, or Polygon Hotspot.
3. Define the hot spot within the image.
4. Click in the Link To box and type the URL link.
5. Repeat 3 and 4 as many times as you'd like.

Creating an image map in Macromedia Dreamweaver

1. Click on the image to select it.
2. Click the Map button on the properties inspector.
3. Select the Rectangle, Circle, or Polygon button
4. Define the hot spot within the image.
5. Click in the Link box and type the URL link.
6. Repeat steps 3–5 as many times as you'd like.
7. Give the map a name in the Map Name box, and click OK.

Creating image maps with HTML

Here's why it's difficult to create an image map by yourself.

1. Use the <MAP> tag to give the map a name. <MAP name="imagemap">
2. Define the shape and the hot spot within the <AREA> tag. Area shapes can be a CIRCLE, RECT (rectangle), or POLY (polygon). <AREA SHAPE=CIRCLE>
3. Use the CORDS attribute to define the coordinates of the circle relative to the upper left corner of the image in pixels. THIS IS THE HARD PART! If the shape is a CIRCLE, then the COORDS are X-axis location, Y-axis location, and radius. CORDS="X,Y,R"

    If the shape is a RECT, then the COORDS are upper left corner location and lower right corner location. RECT="X-top,Y-top,X-bottom,Y-Bottom"

If the shape is a POLY, then the COORDS are X1,Y1, X2,Y2... Don't worry about closing the polygon, the computer will do it for you.

4. Give the AREA a URL link, for instance HREF= "link1.htm".

5. Give each AREA an ALT name, for instance "Left hot spot."

6. Repeat steps 2 through 5 for each hot spot.

7. Close the map with a </MAP> tag.

8. Use the map by assigning the USEMAP attribute within an IMG tag.

By now you're probably wondering what the heck does all that mean? Let's use a very simple example.

If we have an image that's 400 pixels high by 400 pixels wide and we want to divide it in half, with a hot spot on either side, then this is our map and our image code:

```
<MAP NAME="hotspotmap">
<AREA SHAPE="RECT" COORDS="0,0,200,400"
HREF=left.htm ALT="Left side link">
<-The left side starts at 0,0 and goes down to
200,400->
<AREA SHAPE="RECT" COORDS="200,0,400,400"
HREF=right.htm ALT="Right side link">
<-The right side starts at 200,0 and goes down
to 400,400->
</MAP>
<IMG SRC="images/dogbone.gif"
USEMAP="#hotspotmap" WIDTH=400 Height=400>
<-Note, to tell the browser that the map is in
the current page, use the # sign before the
map's name.->
```

As soon as you start to get more complex, you're far better off working with a page generation program that will keep track of all the coordinates for you. (For instance, what happens if you want to resize your image? How do you figure out the shape of the polygon?)

Historical Note

Early-model Web browsers were unable to process image maps, so hot spots were created using server-side image maps. In other words, the image map was on the server. Since client-side maps have been available since version 2 of most browsers, almost nobody uses server-side maps any more.

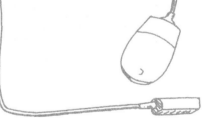

Image Compression

Image compression is vital on the Web. Most users have slow modem connections, and waiting ten minutes to see a picture of Granny Goose's dog is going to bore them.

As a general rule, 72 dpi is more than sufficient for Web photos. So when you scan in high-quality images or get photos back from AOL or Kodak, be sure to save them at a lower resolution.

Most image manipulation programs will allow you to adjust the quality of your images. The faster the image, the lower the quality. This isn't necessarily bad. A faster loading image is probably better than a gorgeous slower loading image.

To adjust image quality, you'll almost certainly need an image manipulation program.

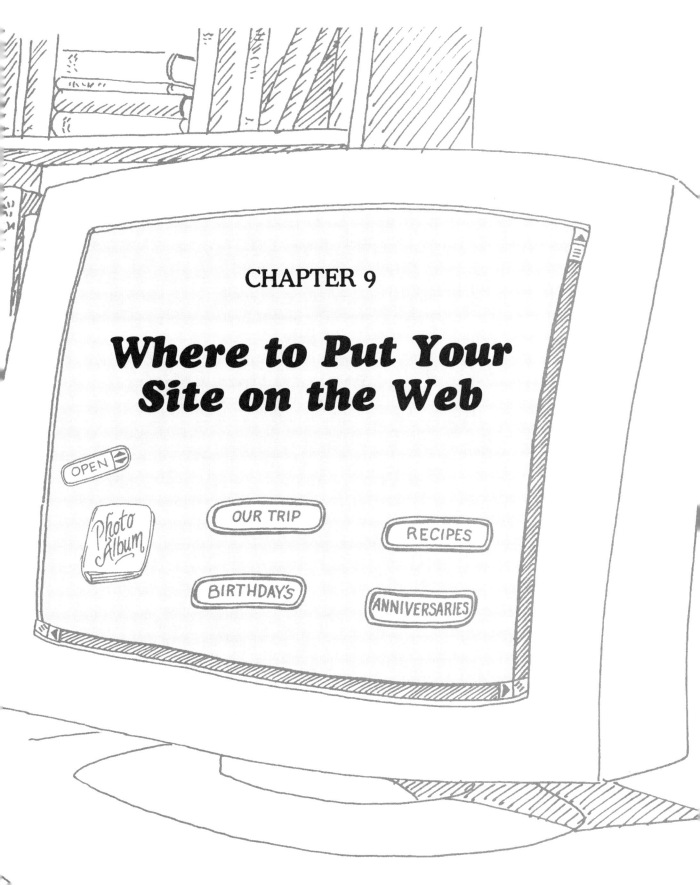

N ow that you're beginning to develop your Web site, it's time to think about where to put your site on the Web.

Choosing Your Web Host

What is a Web host? In order for your Web site to be online 24 hours a day, you need to have a connection to the Internet 24 hours a day, right? Well, that's true if you plan on hosting your own Web site, but unless you're a computer geek or part of a large corporation, chances are that you won't be interested in doing that.

Instead, most of us use other people's Web servers to host our sites. A Web host differs from an Internet service provider in a number of fundamental ways.

THE DIFFERENCE BETWEEN A WEB HOST AND AN INTERNET SERVICE PROVIDER

INTERNET SERVICE PROVIDER	WEB HOST
Your connection to the Internet. The ISP is how you get online.	You use your modem to connect to their server. Probably doesn't offer a connection to the Web.
Typical cost: $10–$25 for dial-up modem connection, $40–60 for cable modem connection.	Cost starts at $20 per month and goes up based on services, Web space, Web traffic, etc.
Offers limited disk space.	Specializes in Web hosting.
Typically 2–10 megabytes.	Minimal Web hosting will start at 10–50 megabytes. The more you pay, the more space on the Web you'll get.
Does not offer domain hosting. You'll have a web site, but usually with a convoluted URL name	Offers domain hosting. You'll have your own .com, .org, or .net address. Multiple domain hosting is typically available for an additional fee.

INTERNET SERVICE PROVIDER	WEB HOST
Does not offer domain registration.	Offers domain registration. For a fee, they will help you register your domain and have it assigned to your space on their server.
Offers email at their address. (example: youraddress@ispname.com)	Offers email at your domain's address. (Example: youraddress@yourdomain.com)
Offers limited number of email addresses	Multiple email addresses likely. May offer unlimited email addresses.
Email forwarding and vacation messages are rarely offered	Additional email services typically include email forwarding, vacation messages.
May have limited traffic.	Higher levels of Web traffic. Allows your Web site to have more hits. May cost more for increased traffic.
May offer CGI scripts	Offers CGI scripts
No Web site statistics	Offers Web site statistics
FTP downloads unlikely	Offers FTP downloads
eCommerce unlikely	ECommerce an option (usually at an extra cost)
Secure forms processing unlikely.	Secure forms processing an option (usually at an extra cost).
Database hosting service unavailable	Database hosting an option at an extra cost.
Multimedia hosting unavailable	Multimedia hosting available.
Streaming Video and audio available. Usually at an extra cost.	

Domain Registration

There are hundreds of other domain registration services available. You can view the Internet Corporation for Assigned Names and Numbers List of Accreditation-Qualified Registrars at:

www.icann.org/ registrars/ accredited-list.html

Free Web Hosting

Nearly every single Internet service provider (ISP) offers between 5 and 10 megabytes of online storage space included for free with your account. Even America Online offers 2 megabytes of space per screen name for a total of 10 megabytes per account. This amount goes up by another 12 megabytes if you register on America Online's Hometown.

Free home pages are also available from some community-building sites on the Web, such as GeoCities (now owned by Yahoo!), Tripod, and theglobe.com. You'll be given free, easy-to-use tools and instructions to design your own Web site (without knowledge of HTML, if you choose). You can select images, background, and text colors, or upload those you already have from your hard drive. You can create and edit text, and create links within or outside your site. The community online service or ISP will then publish your site, which will be hosted on its server, and your site's URL will include its domain name.

If you want to see what other people's home pages look like for inspiration, check out GeoCities, Tripod, and theglobe.com. All offer additional storage space if you are planning a more elaborate Web site and other extra features, if you are willing to pay a small amount for premium services.

These services are quick and easy to set up, and the price is right. For example, GeoCities (www.geocities.yahoo.com), the biggest such community on the Web, features over one million home pages in over 40 neighborhoods centered around shared interests such as arts, family, sports, travel, and music. "Bourbon Street" is for fans of jazz, Cajun food, and Southern culture, while "Athens" is devoted to literature, writing, philosophy, and education. GeoCities will register your site, based on the keywords you select, within its community and in online directories of personal Web pages, which are segmented by geography and topic, so you can be found. GeoCities, a Santa Monica company, which has grown enormously since its launch in mid-1995, will throw in a free e-mail account to anyone who signs up for a home page.

Members, called homesteaders, must be willing to accept banner ads, which may promote an interest area or specific site in

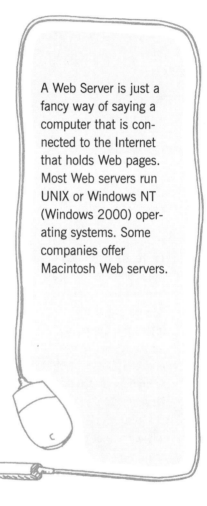

A Web Server is just a fancy way of saying a computer that is connected to the Internet that holds Web pages. Most Web servers run UNIX or Windows NT (Windows 2000) operating systems. Some companies offer Macintosh Web servers.

GeoCities or a sponsor. If they wish, they can have forum, search, and e-mail functions on their sites. To encourage communication and cross-fertilization, descriptions and links to cool sites in GeoCities are featured daily. An exhibit of desert photos, classical piano solos, and a Cajun food site are among those that are offered.

Tripod (www.tripod.com), a community site geared mostly to people in their twenties and thirties, has over 800,000 members in over 30 communities of interest (or pods) such as "Media" for movies, books, music, and television or "Funny Bone" for humor. Tripod members also get free e-mail accounts so they can pick up and send mail from its Web site.

Tripod has a number of features that make it an attractive option:

- CGI and JavaScript library—FREE scripts for your site
- Add CGI to your site—Write your own Perl scripts.
- Build with FrontPage 2000—Tripod supports FrontPage extensions.
- Builder Bucks—If your page meets or exceeds 1,000 add impressions per day, you will earn $1 for every 1,000. Otherwise, you'll earn $.50 per 1,000.
- Domain Registration—Get your own .com! (Costs $25 to set up plus a one-year service fee of $24.95)

Theglobe.com (www.theglobe.com) is a community site with over one million members, about half under the age of 30. There is a strong emphasis on meeting people through chat and bulletin boards. Interest groups, called cities, range from arts & entertainment, life, infobahn (Internet and computers) to romance, and members also get free Web-based e-mail accounts.

WebJump—25 Megs for Free!

How would you like 25 megabytes of free Web hosting without annoying pop-up ads? How would you like to assign your domain name to that space? Run CGIs?

Recently acquired by theglobe.com, WebJump (www.webjump.com) offers all that plus 24/7 tech support—for free.

Resolution Tips

- Be sure to save the original higher-quality image and then SAVE AS the lower-quality image so that you can go back and work on the better image.
- Preview your image in different browsers at different resolutions. If you can't tell the difference, go with the faster image.

Adobe ImageReady began its life as a stand-alone program and is now bundled as part of Adobe PhotoShop. It is designed to excel as a Web preparation and image compression tool. You can choose which formats (GIF, JPEG, PNG) and compression levels, and then view the changed image in comparison to the original.

Even better, once you've decided what format, effects, and compression you want, you can create a "Droplet." The droplet is a batch processing tool that allows you to drag half a dozen images onto it and have the exact same process applied to all of them.

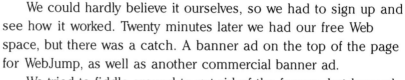

We could hardly believe it ourselves, so we had to sign up and see how it worked. Twenty minutes later we had our free Web space, but there was a catch. A banner ad on the top of the page for WebJump, as well as another commercial banner ad.

We tried to fiddle around to get rid of the frames, but learned that WebJump rewrites code that tries to bypass its frames. So much for the free lunch. (You might put a note to click or right-click on the page and tell the browser to "open frame in new window.")

Another drawback to WebJump is that they don't allow FTP downloading. That means if you want to move your Web site somewhere else later, you'd better maintain a copy on your own computer. Otherwise you'll have to download it page by page.

Still, WebJump is an excellent space, and for someone who wants a professional-looking, robust site with lots of space, it's easy enough to set up and won't cost anything.

Registering with WebJump

1. Go to www.webjump.com.
2. Choose between setting up your Web site as a subset of WebJump (www.everything.webjump.com) or as www.everythingwebsite.com. The domain registration will cost you $70 from InterNIC, but everything else will be free. You can also transfer your existing domain to WebJump for free!
3. Click "Sign Up."
4. Click "Create a New... Account."
5. Fill out the information on the form. You'll need to give them your e-mail address to receive the FTP log-in instructions.
6. Click "Let's Create The Web Site Name."
7. Choose the domain you'd like to have your site registered under. WebJump offers more than 20 different domain name options, ranging from jumpautos.com and jumpcomputers.com to jumpfun.com, jumpfood.com, or even jumptunes.com. We decided to go with "everything.jumpfun.com."

8. Decide whether you want to add a profession or geo-graphical classification to your site. This is optional.

9. Click "Submit."

10. Oops, our everything.jumpfun.com wasn't available.

11. We clicked "Back" and then tried everything.webjump.com, but that didn't pan out.

12. Finally, we tried "website.jumpfun.com" and got it!

13. Fill out the search engine information. This is where you get to define your site a little bit. Don't worry if you don't have all the answers. You can always change them later.

14. Click the button "Register and Create Your WebJump Web Site Now."

15. Within 15 to 20 minutes you'll receive your account and password by e-mail. (While you're waiting, read a chapter in this book!)

16. Check your e-mail. You should have received an e-mail from support@webjump.com with a URL. Either click on that URL or copy it and paste it into your Web browser to go to that page.

17. In a few minutes you'll get yet another e-mail with your new site address! You'll also get instructions on how to post your pages through FTP and your personal user name and password for your File Transfer Protocol access.

18. If you have any questions about FTP uploading to WebJump, go to www.webjump.com/support/info_ftp.html.

> Co-located hosting is when you purchase your own Web server computer on which you can host multiple domains, but the server resides with the hosting company. They plug it into their high-speed line. This is not a typical choice for individuals or small businesses.

Do I Need a Professional Web Host?

Most people won't need to spend the money on a professional Web hosting service. But if you envision a large site, or if you're in business, chances are that you'll want to use a professional Web hosting service.

Web hosting services are designed to serve your Web site professionally. That means they're "up" 24 hours a day, seven days a week. They have fast connections to the Internet. They offer technical support.

Why do Web hosts charge money? You're paying for reliability, speed, options, and service. Most Web hosting services rent you a portion of their computer's disk space and a slice of their connection to the Internet. If you were going to host your own site, chances are it would cost you significantly more than you'll pay your Web host.

You should use a professional Web host if:

- You've got a big Web site (more than 10 megabytes).
- You want extended domain name access (i.e. www.everythingwebsite.com/morestuff).
- You want to set up a store on the Web.
- You plan on putting a database online.
- You're going to have streaming audio, video, or multimedia on your Web site.

What to Look for in a Professional Web Host

1. Longevity. How long has this company been in business? It's very easy for someone with a Windows NT machine to connect to the Web and offer to rent a portion of his or her computer to the world. You'll be hosting sensitive information online, and you'd like to know that the company is honest, secure, and will be around for a while.
2. Do they offer 24-hour toll-free technical support? If you call them at 2 A.M., do they answer?
3. Do they reply to emails quickly?
4. Do they offer free Web tracking software? Will you be able to easily tell how many hits, page views, and downloads your site is getting on a regular basis?
5. Do they offer e-commerce and multimedia options? Can the services they offer grow with you?
6. What type of hosting hardware do they offer? When you shop around for servers, shop by what you need, by reliability, and by price. You may not even have a

choice of operating systems. If you choose to go with a particular Web hosting service, they may only offer one type of server.

7. What kind of connection to the Net do they offer? Look for at least a T1 connection.
8. Do they have regular backups? Uninterruptible power supplies?
9. Are they going to oversell you? Resist pushy salespeople. Are they going to try and get the most money from you right now or allow you time to grow?
10. Do they offer discounts for long-term contracts?
11. Can they help you set up your Internet e-commerce store?
12. Do they offer database hosting?
13. Can they help you with bugs, problems, or Web site design problems?

Finding a Web Host

The Internet List (www.InternetList.com) brings together a number of sites that allow you to find a Web host, an Internet service provider, and even a Web design firm.

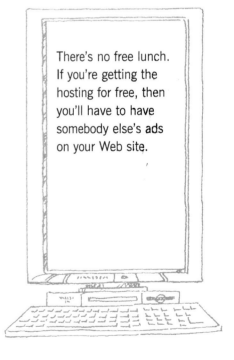

There's no free lunch. If you're getting the hosting for free, then you'll have to have somebody else's ads on your Web site.

1. Click on "Find a Web Host."
2. Choose which category you'd like to search: Budget, Personal, Small Business, Corporate or Adult.
3. Select the hosting options you need, such as e-mail forwarding or database support.
4. Click "Search!"
5. As you narrow your search, add the hosts to your shopping cart for a complete list of options when you're done.

Case Study: Northeast Aikikai— Business on the Web Success Story

When Beth offered to do the Web site for Northeast Aikikai, an Aikido dojo in Chelmsford, MA, seventh degree black belt Lou Perriello raised an eyebrow.

"Sure," Lou said. "How much is it going to cost me?"

At the time, there was no inexpensive way to get root domain name access. The minimum cost for that was $50 a month. That was too much money, so for the first year and a half, Northeast Aikikai's Web address was something like: www.chelmsford.com/home/aikido.

Perriello went ahead with the Web site. After results began to show up (and everyone got tired of trying to explain the whole long name), he spent the money for the Web hosting.

Was it a good investment?

"Everybody who looks at northeastaikikai.com seems to think it's one of the best Web sites they've seen," Perriello said. "I would say that it's increased my enrollment probably 30 percent since it's been in existence. People are not just coming in to try on a whim and leave. They have researched what Aikido is, and they're interested in learning it. They're impressed with the Web site, my credentials, and all the articles.

"It also answers an awful lot of questions that I'd normally have to answer myself verbally in a telephone call. Virtually every single call that comes into the dojo, I ask if they have access to the Web, and if they do I say they should check our Web page. Ninety-five percent of the people who call say that they have access, and they weren't aware that we had a Web site. I've gotten many calls back from people who take a look at the Web site and they're very impressed.

"I've also been invited to teach seminars in other parts of the country based on the Web site. It's broadened our horizons with other Aikido people around the world.

"We had one instance where somebody in Sweden was trying to find out information about Sekiya Sensei. Our site is the only one on the whole Web that had any information about him. I recently had an e-mail from somebody who trains in Chelmsford, England. He was really excited to see Northeast Aikikai in Chelmsford, MA. Plus, our links to other sites give our students a connection to other Aikido schools while they're traveling.

"I haven't sold any tee shirts, but I just sold a couple of videos from our anniversary celebration to people in Brazil, Argentina, and Puerto Rico. And Lowell, MA.

"It's totally positive and it's working for us."

Are there any downsides?

"I can't hide anything from Big Brother anymore," Perriello laughs. "All he has to do is put my name in the Web and click on it. He's going to know who I am, where my school is, and what I do."

How Do I Get My Own Domain for Free (Almost)?

It used to cost a lot of money to get your own top-level domain name. There were companies out there that charged hundreds of dollars for the "service" and additional monthly fees to host your domain.

Not any more. Mydomain (www.mydomain.com) offers a free registration and URL forwarding service. That's right, FREE! In other words, you'll be able to keep your current Web site on whatever Internet service provider you've signed with—even on America Online—and give it a prestigious .com, .org, or .net address. *Note:* You'll still have to pay the $70 registration fee to Network Services for two year's registration.

So what does mydomain.com do? First of all, they don't provide you with Web space. They will provide a single marker page that will tell people your domain is coming before you set it up.

Mydomain.com registers your domain name and then establishes a URL forwarding to whatever location you specify. In other words, if you have a Web site on AOL, GeoCities, Netcom, or wherever, when somebody types in "www.mycooldomain.com" their browser will be forwarded to your site.

Do I get e-mail forwarding? Yep. If you want to have people send e-mail to "itsme@mycooldomain.com," you can. That's one of the supreme benefits of having your own domain. No longer will you be at the whim of your Internet service provider or saddled with an @yahoo or @hotmail address. Whenever you move, you'll be able to keep the same address.

Here's how you register at mydomain.

1. Open your Web browser and go to www.mydomain.com.
2. Enter the domain you'd like and click on "Free Domain Search."

How to Find Other Free Web Hosting Options

For lists of free Web hosting options, go to:

- www.TotallyFreeStuff .com/pages/
- dir.yahoo.com/ Business_and_ Economy/Companies/ Internet_Services/ Web_Services/ Web site_Hosting/ Free_Web_Pages/

3. If the domain name is taken, try another one. If you're very attached to a particular name, try the .net or .org version. *Note:* mydomain only registers the top-level domains available in the United States: .com, .net, and .org.

4. When you find one that you like, click on "Register This Domain and Become a mydomain.com Member."

5. Read the "Terms of Agreement" and click on "I Agree." (*Note:* This just says that you own the domain, mydomain doesn't allow pornography or spam domains, and you'll have to pay the $70 registration fee to InterNIC.

6. Fill out the customer information form with your name or company name, address, phone number, and e-mail address. Click "Continue."

7. Click your customer type: Individual or Company/Other Organization. Click "Continue."

8. Review your information, and click "Submit."

9. You'll receive a flurry of e-mails about your domain. Within 6 to 24 hours, your new domain will be available!

10. You'll have to write a check to Network Services for $70 within two months; otherwise your domain will be turned off. The $70 covers two years, registration, so it's not a bad deal.

    Note: If you messed up, and picked a domain name that you're not happy with, don't worry! Pick a new domain name and don't pay Network Services for the bad name. It's all computerized, so you're not hurting anyone.

11. Log into the mydomain.com member service area. (Your registration name and password will have arrived by e-mail. Be sure to save this information!). Click on Domain Manager.

12. Set up the URL to which you'd like your domain to be forwarded. Decide whether you want them to "Stealth" the old URL. Stealth the URL means that when somebody goes to the new Web address, they'll only see www.mycooldomain.com in the address box. The advantage is that it makes your Web site look professional. The disadvantage to stealth is that it creates a frame around

the Web site, eliminating its viewing by people with old browsers. Also, some browsers may have difficulty with the "refresh" button.

13. Set up any e-mail forwarding you'd like. Mydomain.com allows you to redirect e-mail to up to 5 addresses. Additionally, any e-mail sent to any e-mail address at your domain can be forwarded to a catchall e-mail address. Essentially that means that you can receive e-mail from itsme@mycooldomain.com on your AOL account.

    Note: Most ISPs allow you to send e-mail under a different name, but AOL does not. If you're using AOL, you'll have to send it out under your AOL screen name.

14. You're done!

Advantages to mydomain.com:

1. Free and simple domain registration. The only cost is the $70 InterNIC fee.
2. URL forwarding.
3. E-mail forwarding.

Disadvantages to mydomain.com:

1. You can't use addresses like www.mycooldomain.com/pictures/index.htm.
2. No firm guarantee of service. In other words, you're not paying for this, and they could vanish.
3. Service outages. When the mydomain.com computer is down, so is your domain name. We wouldn't even mention this, except when we were in the process of writing this chapter the system went down for about six hours. If their computers go down, so does your forwarding.

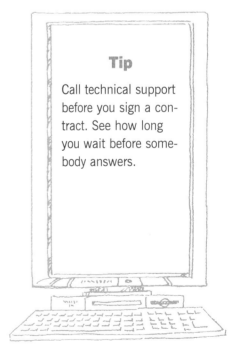

Tip

Call technical support before you sign a contract. See how long you wait before somebody answers.

Our recommendation? Use this service. The price is right and the reliability is good. However, if you're building a large Web site, want to use subdirectories, or are running a business that requires more reliability, then go with a commercial Web host.

What Is the Web Host Guild?

The Web Host Guild is dedicated to setting industry standards and protecting consumers. For a list of Web Host Guild certified members, go to www.whg.org/certified/. Some members include:

AboveNet Communications (www.above.net)

Concentric Network (www.cncx.com)

Datarealm Internet Services (www.serve.com)

INETU (www.inetu.com)

Interland Inc. (www.interland.net)

Interliant (www.interliant.com

Media3 Technologies (www.media3.net)

9NetAvenue (www.9netave.net)

Online Marketing (www.OLM.net)

Rackspace.com (www.rackspace.com)

SiteHosting.Net (www.Sitehosting.net)

Superb Internet Corp. (www.superb.net)

Teleport Internet Devices (www.teleport.com)

TierraNet (www.tierranet.com)

Verio (www.verio.com)

Webhosting.com (www.webhosting.com)

Serving Your Site on Your Own Computer

Did you know that you can serve your Web site on your own computer? You don't need to pay somebody else, you can do it yourself. You'll need:

1. A computer. Any computer will do. In fact, many computer geeks use their old computers for exactly that purpose. The more powerful the computer, the faster it will be able to serve multimedia or graphics. For text files, however, you don't need a very fast computer.

   You'll probably also want to get an uninterruptible power supply with a rebootable system, in case the power goes out so that your server can get back online without your waking up at three in the morning.

2. A continuous connection to the Internet with a "static IP address." This is where the problem starts, and where it can get a lot more expensive to serve your own Web site. In order to serve your Web site reliably, you'll need to be connected to the net 24/7 (24 hours a day, 7 days a week). That means you'll need a permanent connection through an Internet service provider of some kind, whether it's a dial-up, ISDN, T1, or cable provider. That starts to cost money. Serious money. Inexpensive dial-up services don't want you to be logged on all the time, so they knock you off after a certain amount of time. You could write a program that simulates net usage even when you're not online, but you're still tying up a telephone line at however many dollars a month that costs you.

   Furthermore, every top-level domain on the Web has an IP address. Actually, every computer on the Web has an IP address. The difference between the two is that the domain IP addresses are "static." That means that the Domain Name Servers always know what address to forward your viewer's Web browser to. With a static address, your computer can be just as effective (if not as powerful) as a top-of-the-line Web server.

International Domain Names

To find a registrar for an international domain name, visit CORE, the Internet Council of Registrars, at http://corenic.org/langcomnetorg.htm. A complete list of countries, as well as how to contact them about domains, is available at www.iana.org/.

**A Few Books on
Web Hosting**

*Building Professional Web
Sites with the Right
Tools*, Jeff Greenberg and
J. R. Lakeland, Prentice
Hall, 1999

*Building Net Sites with
Windows NT: An Internet
Services Handbook*, Jim
Buyens, Addison Wesley,
1996

*Internet Server Construction
Kit for Windows*, Greg
Bean, John Wiley and
Sons, 1995

Linux Web Server Toolkit,
Nicholas D. Wells, IDG
Books Worldwide

*Mac OS 8 Web Server
Cookbook*, David L. Hart
and Philip E. Bourne,
Prentice Hall, 1998

*Planning and Managing
Web Sites on the
Macintosh: The Complete
Guide to Webstar and
MacHttp*, Jon Wiederspan
and Chuck Shotton,
Peachpit Press, 1996

*Openlinux Web Publishing
Toolkit and System
Administrator's Guide*,
Second Edition, Caldera
and Komarinski, Prentice
Hall, 1998

The problem is that, unless you pay extra, most Internet service providers won't guarantee your IP address. Every time you dial up, you'll get a different address.

3. Web-ready operating system and server software. There are lots of Web server programs out there. Some of the best and most stable are written for UNIX and can be run on a personal computer configured with Linux.
   - Windows NT is designed to work as a Web server.
   - Macintosh Server G4 with AppleShare IP 6.2 is also configured as a high-level server.
   - Any machine with Linux (a version of UNIX) can be configured as a server.
   - All Macintosh computers, including the iMac, and all Windows 98 systems have limited Web serving capabilities.

4. The knowledge and ability to run the operating system and server software.

There's more to running a Web server than just building a Web page. It's time to start looking for another book.

UNIX, Windows NT, and Macintosh Hosting

Most Web hosting is done on computers running a form of UNIX or Windows NT. Macintosh hosting, while powerful and easy to configure, is even smaller than their market share in desktops. In a nutshell, here are the differences between the three options:

- UNIX is considered the most stable operating system. That means it doesn't crash, which means your Web site will stay up and available. Anyone who's surfed the Web knows that when a Web site isn't available, you don't come back, so stability is a definite selling point. UNIX has been around for 30 years, and most of the bugs have been worked out of the operating system. On the downside, if you want to do anything other than basic HTML, you'll

have to learn all about CGIs and PERL. Creating forms in HTML is easy, but having those forms do what you want is more difficult,
especially when you're dealing with a programming language. If you want to run a database, for instance, you may find yourself turning to professional help.

- Windows NT is considered by many to be Microsoft's most stable operating system to date. Windows 2000 is actually a version of Windows NT. The main advantage of going with a Windows server is the level of plug-and-play software support Windows offers. On a Windows server, you'll be able to take full advantage of software like FrontPage 2000, use ActiveX extensions, and serve your Microsoft Access databases with ease. If you do go with a Windows server, check your site from time to time to make sure it's working.

- Macintosh servers are probably the simplest kind of server to set up and operate. They are very stable—as long as they're not being used for other functions. For instance, if you're planning on serving up a Web site in your home, a Macintosh may be the way to go, but use an old Mac as the server and don't play any games on it. Macintosh servers can do anything a UNIX server can do. They don't run ActiveX or Front Page 2000 extensions. You can get software that will let you serve your FileMaker Pro databases incredibly easily. In fact, the latest versions of FileMaker Pro (bundled with FileMaker Home Page) are ready to run on the Web right out of the box. Unfortunately, in a world ruled by numbers, Macintosh servers are a small minority.

If you're trying to serve a database on a budget and planning on using your own Macintosh to serve FileMaker Pro, go with an older version. The basic FileMaker Pro 5 ($249) limits your Web publishing to 10 IP addresses per day. In other words, only 10 people can view your database daily. The Unlimited version costs $999.

Cable Modems for Web Hosting

We'd recommend using a cable modem as a method of hosting your site, but buried deep in the fine print of your service agreement, many cable services specifically say,

> "Customer shall not use the Equipment or the Service directly or indirectly to... operate a Web, http, FTP, email, chat, nntp, game, Gateway or proxy server from home."

(Source: Cox@home. www.cox.com)

Uploading Your Web Site

Uploading means getting your Web site from your computer onto the Internet. Now that Granny Goose has a Web page, she'll want to upload it onto the Internet.

FTP—File Transfer Protocol

FTP means File Transfer Protocol. It is client-server protocol that allows a user to transfer files from one computer to and from another computer over a TCP/IP network. An FTP client is a fancy name for the software that lets you FTP.

FTP software

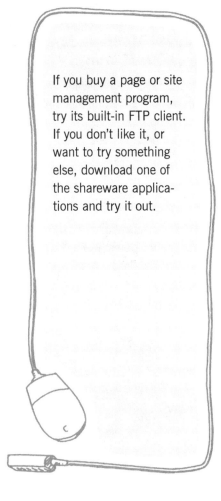

If you buy a page or site management program, try its built-in FTP client. If you don't like it, or want to try something else, download one of the shareware applications and try it out.

FTP software is used to upload and download programs, HTML pages, image files—whatever—to and from a server. You'll find that your browser is capable of downloading files from the Web but not uploading them onto the Web. When you sign up, your ISP may have given you an FTP program. America Online, for example, has its own FTP procedure.

Built-In FTP programs

Many of the commercial Web site and home page–building programs have FTP built in. Aside from the fact that they're free, the advantage to using one of these packages is that you'll probably have some site management capabilities. In other words, instead of just uploading one page at a time, you'll be able to upload the entire Web site, or only those pages you've changed.

The disadvantage to using the built-in FTP programs is that they seem to run slower than most commercial single-purpose FTP programs. Additionally, you may bump into problems if you modify your HTML outside of the page-building program. Also, you may have trouble uploading multimedia, CGI, or other files that aren't typical.

FTP programs you can download

This is a partial list of FTP shareware programs available as shareware or freeware on the Internet. Shareware means you have to pay for it after an evaluation period. These programs cost about $30.

Windows shareware:
- FTP Voyager is available at www.ftpvoyager.com/
- WS_FTP Pro is available at www.ipswitch.com/
  Products/WS_FTP/index.html
- Cute FTP is 30-day shareware available at www.cuteftp.com/

Shareware for Macintosh:
- Fetch is available at www.dartmouth.edu/pages/softdev/
  fetch.html

What you need to know before you can FTP

You'll need to get the specific information to FTP from your Web host. After you set up your FTP program the first time, be sure to save the shortcut so you can quickly get back to your site without having to remember all the details. Here's what you'll need to know:

- Host name. The host name is the name of the server where the bits and bites reside. This often, but not always, starts with the letters ftp. If you have your own domain, it is usually something like ftp.mycooldomain.com or simply mycooldomain.com. (For instance, the site: ftp.ncsa.uiuuc.edu has copies of the original Web browser Mosaic for both Mac and Windows.)
- User ID. The User ID is your identification. Ask your host what this is. Frequently it's your primary e-mail account name.
- Password. This is usually preset by your Web host, and it may be the password for your primary e-mail account. Be sure to change your password from the default soon after you set up your account.
- Directory. If this is left blank, you'll be taken to the root directory in your FTP space. As you develop your Web site, you'll begin to develop subdirectories. These directories can be used to store images (/images) or CGI scripts (/cgi-bin), or you can use it as you would use folders or subdirectories on your computer. For instance, you might want to put your resume in a separate directory: mycooldomain.com/resume. When you want to go straight to the subdirectory, type its name in the directory box.

Password Backup Recommendation

We highly recommend printing out or writing down your FTP and e-mail information and passwords and keeping them in a secure location. While you'll probably be able to recover this information if your computer crashes, it may take a while for you to remember where everything is stored. If you're worried about security, keep the password in your memory.

Uploading Your Site To America Online

Select which screen name you want your Web site to be filed under. Each AOL screen name gets 2 megabytes of disk space. You can use all 10 megabytes and link the sites to each other. AOL calls your Web site MyPlace.

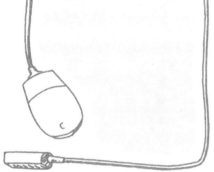

Downloading from Other Sites

When you use an FTP program to log onto an FTP server that isn't yours (for download purposes) the User ID should be "Anonymous" and the password should be your e-mail address (me@mycooldomain.com).

1. Type in Keyword "MyFTPspace." You'll see two subdirectories, "myhomepage" and "private."
2. Double-click on "myhomepage."
3. Click the "Upload" button to begin uploading.
4. Give the file you're uploading the name you want to appear in your home page directory. Be sure to use the proper extension (.html, .htm, .gif, .jpeg, and so on).

   Note: This is one of AOL's more annoying features. Rather than just assuming you're going to keep the same name for the file you're uploading, they make you type the names in. If you're doing a lot of changes or file uploading, you're going to get very tired of this.
5. Click which kind of file you're uploading. HTML files are ASCII and everything else is binary.
6. Click "Continue."
7. Select the file you want to upload and click "Add."
8. Click "Attach."
9. Repeat steps 4–8 until your site is uploaded.

To delete or rename a file on AOL's FTP space:

1. Select the file.
2. Click the "Utilities" button.
3. Click "Delete" or "Rename"; type in the new name.
4. Click "OK."

To create a subdirectory on AOL's FTP space:

1. Click "Directory."
2. Type in the new directory name. For example, "images."
3. Click "Continue."
4. Click "Ok."

What is my AOL URL?

Your typical AOL URL will be: http://members.aol.com/
~YOURSCREENNAME/myhomepage/. Just remember to replace the
word YOURSCREENNAME with your screen name.

To shorten your AOL URL and to make your Web site more
interesting, we recommend that you set up an index file in your
root myFTPspace called "index.htm."

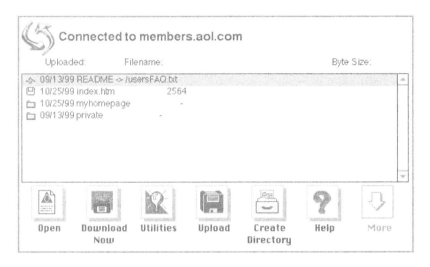

1. Create your home page.
2. Make all links on this home page relative to the subdirectory "myhomepage/." For example, rather than creating a link to recipes at:

   ```
   <A HREF="recipes.htm">Click Here for
   Recipes</A>
   ```

   you'd type:

   ```
   <A HREF="myhomepage/recipes.htm">Click Here
   for Recipes</A>
   ```

   If you keep images in an image subdirectory of myhomepage, then you'd use this code to place an image:

   ```
   <IMG SRC"=myhomepage/images/
   coolimage.gif">
   ```

You can download software via FTP from your Web browser by using ftp://sitename.com instead of http://sitename.com

3. Upload this page with the name "index.htm" into the root directory.

4. If you want to link back to the index page, your links should read,

```
"../index.htm"
```

Your new AOL home page URL will be http://members.aol.com/~YOURSCREENNAME. Web browsers will now see your default index.htm page, but any links will be forwarded to the myhomepage subdirectory.

CHAPTER 10

Laying Out Pages with Lists and Tables

In this chapter we'll look at tables and lists. You'll find numbered or bullet lists scattered throughout most Web pages. Definition lists are used for dictionary-like indentation. Tables are trickier and far more useful for designers. With borders, they can look a lot like entries into a spreadsheet. Without borders, they are a vital page design and layout tool.

Lists

Lists are actually very simple to do in HTML. The only reason we've categorized them as slightly more advanced is that nesting lists takes a bit of practice.

There are two kinds of lists: ordered lists or unordered lists. Ordered lists are standard numbered lists. They can be used for any itemized list, including outlines. Unordered lists are bullet lists. They make quick points.

Both types of lists use the same format: they must begin with a list tag and finish with an end of list tag.

All list items are delineated by a list item tag <LI>. In other words, a numbered list looks like this:

```
<OL>
<LI>      The first item
<LI>      The second item
<LI>      The third item
</OL>
```

A bullet list looks like this:

```
<UL>
<LI>      The first item
<LI>      The second item
<LI>      The third item
</UL>
```

You'll notice that by changing the <OL> tag into an <UL> tag, the numbers turn into bullets. Simple!

In other words, a numbered list looks like this:

1. The first item
2. The second item
3. The third item

A bullet list looks like this:

- The first item
- The second item
- The third item

Nesting Lists and List Attributes

The easiest way to understand nesting lists and list attributes is to try them out. Any time you insert one list inside another it's called "nesting." The second list will be indented from the first. The only trick to nesting is to remember to close out the nest with the appropriate </UL> or </OL> tags. And, yes, you can nest ordered lists inside unordered lists and vice versa.

For example, using a combination of nesting and TYPE attributes is an easy way to make an outline-style list.

```
<OL TYPE="I">
<LI> First Outline Level
<OL TYPE="A">
<LI> Topic A
<LI> Topic B
<OL TYPE="1">
<LI> First item
<LI> Second item
</OL>
<LI> Topic C
</OL>
<LI> Second Outline Level
</OL>
```

```
 I.  First Outline Level
       A.  Topic A
       B.  Topic B
             1.  First item
             2.  Second item
       C.  Topic C
 II.  Second Outline Level

Nested Unordered List

   ■  First Outline Level
        ■  Topic A
        ■  Topic B
             •  First item
             •  Second item
        ■  Topic C
   ■  Second Outline Level
```

Naturally, using the START= attribute will restart the numbering at a different point. This is useful when creating two lists on the same page, because ordinarily the second list would start with the default of 1. The START attribute can be set to either restart the entire list, or at a particular entry.

Using the <LI VALUE=> attribute is not recommended, mostly because it defeats the purpose of using a numbered list in the first place. *Note:* Even when using letters or Roman numerals, the START and VALUE attribute values are written in Arabic numerals.

```
<UL>
<LI>First Outline Level
<UL type=I>
```

```
<LI>Topic A</LI>
<LI>Topic B
<UL>
<LI>First item</LI>
<LI>Second item</LI>
</UL>
</LI>
<LI>Topic C</LI>
</UL>
</LI>
<LI>Second Outline Level</LI>
</UL>
```

Notice that nesting unordered lists automatically changes the TYPE of the indented bullets. To maintain the same type of bullet, use the <UL TYPE=DISC> attribute in each new tag.

Case Study: Examples from Northeast Aikikai

On the Northeast Aikikai page describing Lou Perriello, the chief instructor, an unordered list was used to call out Perriello Sensei's accomplishments. (Sensei means teacher in Japanese.)

"Then there is Lou Perriello. His art is Aikido. His technique is like stones rolling together That's how strong his Aikido is."
--Philip Porter, 9th Dan Judo, in *World of Martial Arts*, March/April 1998.

Profile of Lou Perriello Sensei

- Shidoin, Go Dan (Fifth Degree Black Belt) in Aikido IAF, Hombu Dojo
- Shichidan/Senior Teacher's Rank (Seventh Degree Black Belt) by the United States Judo Association and the United States Martial Arts Association.
- Chairman of the Aikido Divisions of the United States Judo Association and the United States Martial Arts Association
- Shihandai, assistant to the Shihan and Member of the teaching committee of the Aikido Association of America.
- Shodan USJA and USMA Judo.
- Certified by the United States Department of The Interior to teach Aikido for Law Enforcement.
- Coordinating Instructor of the Association for Tactical Application, an organization established to teach defensive tactics, applied Aikido and other martial arts for law enforcement.
- Perriello Sensei has taught seminars in Traditional Aikido, Aikido for Law Enforcement, and defensive tactics throughout the U.S., Canada, and Central America.

Early years

Perriello Sensei began his martial arts career in 1958 with the study of Kodokan Judo and Shotokan Karate. After experiencing Aikido in 1962, Mr. Perriello became a student of Hatanaka Sensei, practicing Aikido and Judo until 1964. In 1964, he became a full time Aikido student under Hatanaka Sensei, and practiced with him until 1966.

If we'd continued using the bullet list for the rest of the biography, the emphasis that the initial bullet items generated would be lost.

```
<H1>Profile of Lou Perriello Sensei</H1>
<UL>
<LI>Shidoin, Go Dan (Fifth Degree Black Belt) in Aikido IAF, Hombu Dojo</LI>
<LI>Shichidan/Senior Teacher's Rank (Seventh Degree Black Belt) by the
<AHREF="http://www.csprings.com/usja/">United States Judo Association</A> and
the <AHREF="http://www.mararts.org/">United States Martial Arts
Association</A>.</LI>
<LI>Chairman of the Aikido Divisions of the United States Judo Association and
the United States Martial Arts Association</LI>
<LI>Shihandai, assistant to the Shihan and Member of the teaching committee of
the <A HREF="http://www.aaa-aikido.com/">AikidoAssociation of America</A>.</LI>
<LI>Shodan USJA and USMA Judo.</LI>
<LI>Certified by the United States Department of the Interior to teach Aikido
for Law Enforcement.</LI>
<LI>Coordinating Instructor of the Association for Tactical Application, an
organization established to teach defensive tactics, applied Aikido and other
martial arts for law enforcement.</LI>
<LI>Perriello Sensei has taught seminars in Traditional Aikido, Aikido for Law
Enforcement, and defensive tactics throughout the U.S., Canada, and Central
America.</LI>
</UL>
</TD>
</TR>
</TABLE>
<A NAME=anchor1451010></A>Early years</H3>
<P>Perriello Sensei began his martial arts career in 1958 with the study of
Kodokan Judo and Shotokan Karate. After experiencing Aikido in 1962, Mr.
Perriello became a student of Hatanaka Sensei, practicing Aikido and Judo
until 1964. In 1964, he became a full time Aikido student under Hatanaka
Sensei, and practiced with him until 1966.</P>
<P>In 1966, before returning to Japan, Hatanaka Sensei wrote a letter of
introduction to the newly arrived Kanai Sensei, recommending Mr.Perriello as a
student.</P>
<P>As one of the original students of New England Aikikai, Mr. Perriello prac-
ticed almost exclusively with Kanai Sensei from 1966 through 1978. During this
period, he worked with several of the Founder's original students, helping to
establish the United States Aikido Federation. He also studied with Yamada
Sensei, Chiba Sensei, Tohei Sensei and most of the other Hombu Dojo Shihan.</P>
```

Tags and Attributes Used

`<OL></OL>`   Ordered list. A numerical list.

            START   Starts your list from something other than the default of 1.

            TYPE   What kind of numbering do you want?

                = A   uppercase letters

                = a   lowercase letters

                = I   uppercase Roman numerals

                = i   lowercase Roman numerals

                = 1   Arabic numbers (default)

`<UL></UL>`   Unordered list. A bullet-style list.

            TYPE   Changes the type of bullet.

                = "CIRCLE"   a circle bullet

                = "DISC"   a filled-in circle bullet (default)

                = "SQUARE"   a square bullet

`<LI>`   List Item. Used to designate the start of a new item in a list. Does not need an `</LI>` tag

            VALUE   Assigns a new starting value for this and subsequent items in a list. Allows ordered lists to have mixed-up order.

            TYPE   Changes the kind of numbering in an ordered list or the type of bullet in an unordered list.

                = A   uppercase letters

                = a   lowercase letters

                = I   uppercase Roman numerals

                = i   lowercase Roman numerals

                = 1   Arabic numbers (default)

                = "CIRCLE"   a circle bullet

                = "DISC"   a filled-in circle bullet

                = "SQUARE"   a square bullet

Definition Lists

A definition list is very similar to any dictionary entry. It begins with the definition list start tag <DL>, includes a definition term <DT> followed by a definition description <DD>, followed by any number of terms and descriptions, and closes with a definition list close tag </DL>. The definition description is indented from the definition term and on the line immediately below. The next Definition Term starts outdented to the left, and on the line immediately below.

Here's an example:

```
<DL>
<DT>Definition List
<DD>This is what a definition list and its
description look like.
<DT>The Definition—DFN tag
<DD>The DFN tag is not necessary to take advan-
tage of Definition Lists.
</DL>
```

Tables—Useful Advanced HTML

Tables are excellent. They are currently the most popular way for graphic designers to impose their wills on Web pages.

How can HTML tables, which can look an awful lot like boring spreadsheet grids, make a Web page's graphics look phenomenal? Simple, by using the BORDERS=0 attribute.

Still not following us? Let's start at the beginning. One of the problems that Web designers have is in placing graphic elements and text on the page. Aligning photos left and right only gets you so much variety. So, some bright designer realized that she could put graphics into a table and guarantee that they would appear in certain areas of the page.

Let's pick an easy example. We're going to explain the process first before we get into the HTML.

Tutorial: Ida's Eye Clinic

Let's say that Ida is building a Web page for her eye clinic. She knows exactly what she wants: the name of the clinic on top, an eyeball in the middle, all her services surrounding the eyeball.

HTML generators aren't always the wrong choice. One of the best uses for an HTML generation program like Home Page or FrontPage is for tedious tasks like formatting lists. As you look at the code of any formatted list, your eyes will start to glaze over. Imagine trying to type in every single <LI> and </LI> tag. HTML generators will automatically make sure that all the tags are accounted for.

WebTV Note

Unordered lists with a TYPE = CIRCLE display a triangle when viewed on WebTV because the small hollow circle image of a bullet doesn't show up well on television.

Tip

To start a new line without starting a new item in a list use the <BR> tag. The new line will be indented in line with the previous line. This holds true for ordered, unordered, and definition lists:

<UL>
<LI> The first item

 More info on the first item.
<LI> The second item
<LI> The third item
</UL>

The only way to accomplish this in HTML is to create a 3 x 3 grid, put the eyeball in the middle, and surround it with the other elements.

Name of the company Service Eyeball Service

A simple way to create this table would be in a page design program that creates WYSIWYG tables. The least expensive software choices for this task would be Adobe PageMill.

High-end users could use Macromedia Dreamweaver, or Adobe GoLive. In fact, GoLive uses a page-generation trick that allows users to place elements on a grid and then converts everything into tables.

Creating the table in Adobe PageMill

1. Open Adobe PageMill and type "Ida's Eye Clinic" in the title box.
2. Click the table icon.
3. Set the Rows to 3 and Columns to 3. Set the Border to 0.
4. Set the Table Width to 100 Percent.
5. Click OK.
6. Tab to the second cell and type, "Ida's Eye Clinic." Click the Center Align button.
7. Tab to the first cell in the second row and type "Eye Glasses." Click the Right Align button.
8. Tab to the middle cell and click the Insert Image Button. Insert the image "eye.gif." Click the Center Align button.
9. Tab to the third cell in the second row and type "Contact Lenses."
10. Tab to the middle cell in the third row and type "Eye Exams." Click the Center Align button.

DONE! Save and preview.

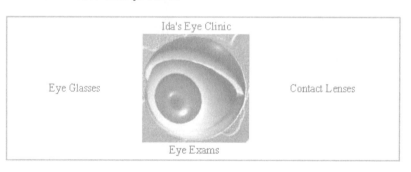

Creating Tables in HTML Code

Writing the code for a table in HTML is very similar to the process of writing a nested list.

1. Start a table with the <TABLE> tag.
2. Give it an optional <CAPTION> </CAPTION> tags.
3. Start a row using the <TR> tag.
4. Give the row or column a header with the <TH></TH> tags (optional).
5. Add data using the <TD></TD> tags.
6. Add more <TD> tags. Each new <TD></TD> sequence creates a new column. Repeat until you have the number of columns you want.
7. Close the row with a </TR> tag.
8. Start a new row with a new <TR> tag.
9. Repeat creating cells and rows until you're done.
10. Close the table with a </TABLE> tag.

Here's what Ida's Eye Clinic's page looks like. Notice that we've set the column widths to 33 percent and put a non-breaking space ( ) in all the empty cells. (See Table Tips and Tricks on the next page.)

```
<HTML>
<HEAD>
<TITLE>Ida's Eye Clinic</TITLE>
</HEAD>
<BODY>
<P><CENTER><TABLE WIDTH="100%" BORDER="0"
CELLSPACING="2" CELLPADDING="0">
<TR>
<TD WIDTH="33%"> </TD>
<TD WIDTH="33%">
<P><CENTER> Ida's Eye Clinic</CENTER></TD>
<TD WIDTH="34%"> </TD>
</TR>
<TR>
<TD WIDTH="33%">
<P ALIGN=RIGHT> Eye Glasses</TD>
<TD WIDTH="33%">
<P><CENTER> <IMG SRC="images/eye.gif"
```

Definition lists may be nested, and will indent, but the results are particularly ugly. We don't recommend it.

```
ALIGN="CENTER" BORDER="0"></CENTER></TD>
<TD WIDTH="34%">Contact Lenses</TD>
</TR>
<TR>
<TD WIDTH="33%"> </TD>
<TD WIDTH="33%">
<P><CENTER>Eye Exams</CENTER></TD>
<TD WIDTH="34%"> </TD>
</TR>
</TABLE></CENTER>
</BODY>
</HTML>
```

Table Tips and Tricks

- Be sure to have the same number of columns in each row. That means if you've got three <TD></TD> sequences in the first row, you'd better have three in each row. If you add an extra <TD>, then you'll get an extra column with a lot of strange space around it.

- If you don't specify the width of a table column or cell, then the width will default one of two ways.
    1. If there are images, the width will default to the width of the widest image in that column.
    2. If there are no images, then the width will get funky. If the text in the first column is short, then the width will be the width of the longest sentence in the first column. If the text in the first column is long, then the first column will get wider and the remaining columns will get narrower. The best way to be certain about the column width with text in tables is to specify the width of that column or cell.

- When you're working with images, set the VALIGN of all rows or cells. If you don't, then you might end up with a centered image and the text to its right at the top or bottom of a nearby cell.

- For any graphic placement table, set the BORDER of the table to 0 (zero). Unless you're working in a spreadsheet, or have a specific reason to show them, nobody wants to see those borders.

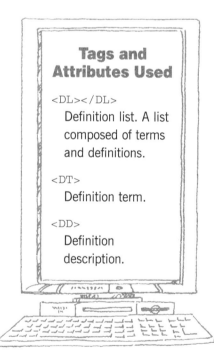

Tags and Attributes Used

<DL></DL>
  Definition list. A list composed of terms and definitions.

<DT>
  Definition term.

<DD>
  Definition description.

Tags and Attributes Used

\<TABLE>\</TABLE>	Tag defines the table.
ALIGN	Aligns the entire table LEFT, RIGHT, or CENTER. (Default is LEFT).
BACKGROUND	Defines a background image for the entire table. For example: BACKGROUND="images/background.gif"
BGCOLOR	Defines the background color for the table.
BORDER	Defines the table's border widths.
BORDERCOLOR	Defines the table's border color. This has no effect if BORDER is set to zero (in Internet Explorer only).
CELLPADDING	Defines the space between the stuff in the cell and the cell's border. Either a percentage or pixel value.
FRAME	Sets what part of the table's border will be visible. Options include: ABOVE, BELOW, BORDER, HSIDES (left and right border), VSIDES (top and bottom border), LHS (left hand side), RHS (right hand side), and VOID (no borders around the outside but borders in between cells to create a tic-tac-toe effect). Not valid in Netscape.
HEIGHT	Sets the table's height.
WIDTH	Sets the table's width either in pixels or as a percentage of the remaining width.
\<TR>\</TR>	Table row. Tables must have at least one row. Rows contain table data \<TD> and may have a table header \<TH>.
ALIGN	Defines the alignment of all the cells in this row (LEFT, RIGHT, or CENTER plus JUSTIFY or CHAR). The ALIGN=CHAR will create alignment around the decimal point allowing lists of numbers to line up. To use an alternative character, use the CHAR= attribute.
BACKGROUND	Sets the background image for the entire column.
BGCOLOR	Defines the background color for the entire column.
CHAR	Defines an alternative alignment character when ALIGN=CHAR.
VALIGN	Defines the vertical alignment. Options include: TOP, MIDDLE, BOTTOM, and BASELINE.

<TD></TD>	Table data. Put the text and/or images for each table cell in between the <TD> and </TD> tags.
ALIGN	Specifies the cell's alignment.
BACKGROUND	Specifies the cell's background image.
BGCOLOR	Specifies the cell's background color.
COLSPAN	Allows a cell to cross more than one column. The default is 1. A COLSPAN=0 allows a header to continue across all remaining cells to the end of the table.
HEIGHT	Defines the cell's height.
NOWRAP	Turns off automatic wrapping. Warning: May make cells very wide.
ROWSPAN	Allows a cell to cross more than one row. The default is 1. A COLSPAN=0 allows a header to continue down all remaining rows to the bottom of the table.
VALIGN	Defines the cell's vertical alignment: TOP, MIDDLE, BOTTOM, or BASELINE.
WIDTH	Sets the cell's width. *Note:* To set a cell's width, you must set the table's width.
<TH></TH>	Table header. Defines table heading text.
ALIGN	Defines the header's alignment (LEFT, RIGHT, or CENTER plus JUSTIFY or CHAR).
BACKGROUND	Defines the header cell's background image.
BGCOLOR	Defines the header cell's background color.
COLSPAN	Allows a header to span more than one column.
HEIGHT	Defines the cell's height.
NOWRAP	Turns off the automatic wrapping feature.
ROWSPAN	Sets the number of rows the header cell spans.
VALIGN	Defines the header's vertical alignment.
<CAPTION></CAPTION>	Defines a caption for a table. These tags only work within a TABLE.
ALIGN	Specifies where the caption will be placed: TOP, BOTTOM, LEFT, or RIGHT. (*Note:* Netscape does not support LEFT and RIGHT).

Tables Within Tables

Web designers can get really sneaky. Let's say you want to divide the Web page in two parts; one is 200 pixels wide and the rest of it extends to the right margin. On the left side you want a five-button button bar, and on the right side you want all the other text and images. How would you do it?

The simplest way is to define a one-row, two-column table, and put two more tables inside it. The left column would contain a one-column by five-row table, and the right column would contain whatever else you wanted to put on the right side of the page.

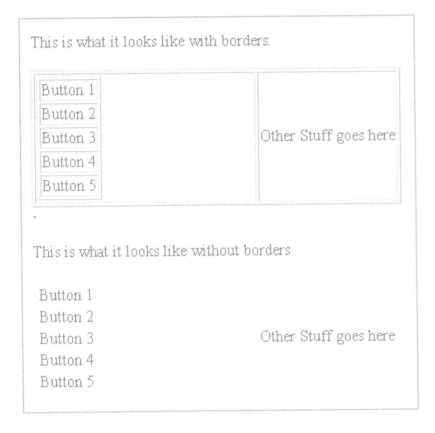

This is what it looks like with borders.

Button 1		
Button 2		Other Stuff goes here
Button 3		
Button 4		
Button 5		

This is what it looks like without borders

Button 1
Button 2
Button 3   Other Stuff goes here
Button 4
Button 5

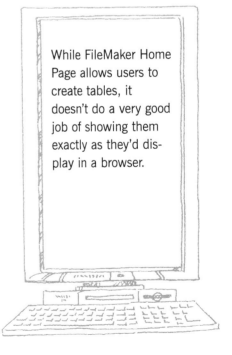

While FileMaker Home Page allows users to create tables, it doesn't do a very good job of showing them exactly as they'd display in a browser.

```
<P><TABLE BORDER=0>
<TR>
<TD VALIGN=top WIDTH=200>
<P><TABLE BORDER=0>
<TR>
```

```
<TD>
<CENTER>Button 1</CENTER>
</TD>
</TR>
<TR>
<TD>
<CENTER>Button 2</CENTER>
</TD>
</TR>
<TR>
<TD>
<CENTER>Button 3</CENTER>
</TD>
</TR>
<TR>
<TD>
<CENTER>Button 4</CENTER>
</TD>
</TR>
<TR>
<TD>
<CENTER>Button 5</CENTER>
</TD>
</TR>
</TABLE>
</P>
</TD>
<TD>
<P>Other Stuff goes here</P>
</TD>
</TR>
</TABLE>
</P>
```

As the World Wide Web moved away from the scientific community and into the hands of the designers, entrepreneurs, and entertainers, the limitations of the markup language began to become clear. Each new version of the official HTML standards has extended the boundaries of design and usability.

Two of the newer methods of laying out pages are frames and cascading style sheets. Cascading Style Sheets allow designers to control fonts, margins, and page placement of elements. With Frames, designers usually use a portion of the page for a banner, another portion as a menu, and a third portion for viewing the changing text accessed by the menu links.

Both methods of laying out pages have the usual advantages and disadvantages of Web design—they work (most of the time) and have problems (some of the time).

Forms are not as much a design option as a method of getting information back from your site's visitors.

Cascading Style Sheets (CSS)

Cascading style sheets aren't particularly difficult to use. They're a lot like the style sheets you probably use in your word processor every day. Of course, as soon as we move to the Web, things become a bit convoluted.

In an effort to have more control over the way Web pages are viewed, many designers are turning to cascading style sheets.

Essentially, a Cascading Style Sheet defines an alternative way that an HTML element is displayed. For example, every <H1> could be displayed as blue in a document without having to use the COLOR=BLUE in every tag. Cascading style sheets are a way of giving pages and sites an easily modifiable unified look and feel without too much work.

As with all new HTML developments, CSS doesn't work in early browsers; they are only supported in Netscape 4.x and higher and Internet Explorer 3.x and higher. Keep in mind that Web browsers also allow their users to turn off style sheets. So you've got no guarantee that the page will really look that way. However, since a page with cascading style sheets will still display with some accuracy even if the browser can't view them, CSS tend to be a better choice than frames.

For complete details on the Guidelines for Accessible Web Authoring, visit the World Wide Web Consortium at www.w3.org/.

There are a number of ways to use cascading style sheets:

- Internally—with the <STYLE> tag in a document header.
- Externally—referencing an external style page somewhere else on the Web.
- Imported—the style sheets are imported from another document but then modified within the calling page.
- Inline—inline styles are styles added within a tag. They override any pre-existing styles and go away at the end of that tag.
- Span and division styles—since styles can be applied to any tag, you can use <SPAN> and <DIV> tags to create subsections of documents with completely different styles from the rest of the document.

Internal Style Sheets

An internal style sheet is defined in the HTML page's head and modifies the entire page accordingly.

Here's a brief piece of code that uses cascading style sheets. Things to look for:

- The style sheets go in the header.
- You can define styles for any page element—headers, paragraphs, even <B> boldfaced fonts.
- If the browser doesn't support CSS, then the styles are ignored.

Style Sheets

The W3C Core Styles offer authors an easy way to start using style sheets without becoming designers. By adding a link in the head of your documents, a CSS browser will fetch one of eight style sheets from W3C's server when it encounters your document. A non-CSS browser will display the HTML document as usual. Go to www.w3.org/StyleSheets/Core/ for more details

```
<HTML>
<HEAD>
<TITLE>Cascading Style Sheets Number One</TITLE>
<STYLE>
H1 {font-size: 36pt; color: blue}
H2 {font-size: 22pt; color: red}
</STYLE>
</HEAD>
<BODY>
<H1> This is the Header 1</H1>
<H2> Here is Header 2</H2>
<H3> Here is Header 3</H3>
<H4> And another Header </H4>
</BODY>
</HTML>
```

External Style Sheets

The <LINK> tag is used to access an external style sheet. In other words, rather than typing a style sheet into the header of every document, Webmasters can define one style sheet, save that on their Web site (or any other Web site), and have that referenced by many different pages. If you want to change the way all those pages look, just change the single style sheet.

How the <LINK> Tag Works

1. Create a style sheet in a text editing program like Notepad or SimpleText. Don't include any tags in the style sheet document—that means no <HTML>, <HEAD>, or even <STYLE> tags. For example:

   P {margin: 20px}
   H1 {font-size: 36pt; color: blue}
   H2 {font-size: 22pt; color: red}

2. Save the document with the extension .css. For example, "stylesheetname.css."

3. In the <HEAD> of your HTML document, insert the tag:

   ```
   <LINK REL=StyleSheet HREF=
   "stylesheetname.css"TYPE="text/css"
   MEDIA=Screen>
   ```

   Note: You don't need to use the <STYLE> tag if you're using the <LINK> tag and vice versa.

4. Test the page in several browsers to be sure it works correctly.

Other Methods of Using Style Sheets

Importing a style sheet

A style sheet may be imported within a <STYLE> tag. This is a method of both using standardized externalized style sheets and modifying them for a particular document. Any styles specified in the <STYLE> tag override the imported style attributes. For example:

```
<HEAD>
<STYLE>
@import url(stylesheetname.css);
BODY {background: white}
</STYLE>
</HEAD>
```

Inline Styles

If you only want to use a style for one particular paragraph or heading, you may "inline" the style. This new style will override any previously defined styles. This sort of style manipulation isn't really recommended because it diminishes the usefulness of document-wide or site-wide style sheet use.

To use inline styles, you'll need to put a special META tag in the document's header:

```
<META HTTP-EQUIV="Content-Style-Type"
CONTENT="text/css">
```

Example:

```
<HTML>
<HEAD>
<TITLE>This is an inline style choice.</TITLE>
<META HTTP-EQUIV="Content-Style-Type"
CONTENT="text/css">
<HEAD>
<BODY>
<H1>No style sheet on this header.</H1>
<H1 STYLE="color:red">We've inlined the sheet on
this header.</H1>
</BODY>
</HTML>
```

<SPAN> and <DIV> tags

The <SPAN> and <DIV> tags are quite similar. The main difference is that the <DIV> tag is used to define an entire section of a document. It can contain paragraphs, headings, tables, and other divisions. A <SPAN> tag may also be used to encompass a number of elements, but it may also be used within a paragraph. <DIV>

Style Sheet Tip

When you first begin to work with style sheets, try working with an internal style sheet. Once you find a style that works, create an external style sheet that can control the entire look of your Web site. Keep in mind that style sheets will be invisible when pages are viewed by older browsers.

To set up a style sheet, you define the style either internally or externally and mark up the page as usual. The browser handles the rest.

Perhaps you want to set all your headers to a number of varying font sizes and colors. The next example sets anything defined as <H1> to size 36 font, blue. All text marked <H2> will be displayed at size 22 and in red. Headers of <H3> to <H6> will remain as they would by default.

Tags and Attributes Used

`<DIV></DIV>`
Defines a division or sub-section in the document
`CLASS=name`
The name of the span.
`STYLE="attribute: value"`
A style applied to this particular span.

`<SPAN></SPAN>`
Defines a span of text or images.
`CLASS=name`
The name of the span.
`STYLE="attribute: value"`
A style applied to this particular span.

and <SPAN> tags may be used with external style sheets, giving them even more flexibility.

The following example from an Aikido Web page colors the Beginners section of the page red and the Intermediate section blue. However, the names of techniques in both sections will be black because of the <SPAN> tag.

```
<HTML>
<HEAD>
<TITLE>How DIV and SPAN tags work.</TITLE>
<STYLE TYPE="text/css" MEDIA="screen, print,
projection">
.beginner {color:red}
.names {color:black}
.intermediate {color:blue}
</STYLE>
</HEAD>
<BODY>
<DIV CLASS=beginner>
<H1>Beginners</H1>
<P>Anyone who is a beginner needs to know the
definitions of these Aikido techniques:
<UL> <SPAN CLASS=names>
<LI>ikkyo</LI>
<LI>nikkyo</LI>
<LI>sankyo</LI>
<LI>yonkyo</LI>
<LI>gokyu</LI>
<LI>rokyu</SPAN></LI>
</UL>
</DIV>
<DIV CLASS=intermediate>
<H2>Intermediate</H2>
<P>Intermediate students should know everything
a beginner knows. And then some.
<UL> <SPAN CLASS=names>
<LI>shohonage</LI>
<LI>kokyuho</LI>
<LI>kokyunage</LI>
<LI>kotegaishi</LI>
<LI>jujunage</SPAN></LI>
</UL>
</DIV>
</BODY>
</HTML>
```

Attributes or Properties that May Be Defined in Cascading Style Sheets

Note: These aren't all the CSS attributes available. For a complete list, go to the World Wide Web Consortium's site at www.w3.org/Style/css/.

- {background:}
  The background attribute defines the background style applied to that particular element. Its possible values include:
  > background-color
  > background-image

  For example, you could use:
  > BODY { background: white url(images/background.gif) }
  > STRONG {background: black; font: white}

  The first style creates a body background taken from background.gif. In case the user isn't showing images, it defaults to white. The second style shows any <STRONG> text as white-on-black (see {font} below).

Borders

These style attributes are used to set borders around elements.

- {border-width:value}—Sets a border around an element. Values: thin, medium, thick, length.
- {border-color:value}—Values: color.
- {border-style:value}—Values: dashed, dotted, double, groove, inset, outset, ridge, solid.

Instead of defining each attribute separately, one border style may be defined using the {border:value value1 value2}.

```
<P> {border: blue dotted}
A:link {border: thick double green}
```

Note: With all specific border commands, more than one keyword may be specified. If only one is specified, for example {border-style:dashed}, then the whole border will be dashed. If two are specified, the first will apply to top and bottom and the second

Media

The MEDIA attribute is used to tell the browser how to display the page, depending on the type of media it is viewed on. MEDIA types include:

all—all output devices

aural—speech synthesizers

braille—for Braille readers

print—for output to a printer

projection—for projected presentations

screen—monitors (default)

tty—for teletype-style output

tv—televisions

to the right and left. If four are specified, the order will be top, right, bottom, left.

Alternate attributes {top-border:}, {bottom-border:}, {left-border:}, {right-border:}

- {font:}
  The font attribute may be used to include all the various font properties, including attributes like italics, font size, font style, and even line height. For example: <P> {font:bold, 12 pt, Palatino, serif} will create a boldfaced paragraph, 12 points tall, with Palatino or another serif font.

- {font-family: "font name", fontname..., family name}
  The font-family style is used to coax a browser to display text in a particular font. If that font doesn't exist on the user's computer, it will go to the next font. The final font in the list is not a font name but the font's family name. Sample family names are serif (such as Times New Roman or Palatino), sans serif (such as Arial or Helvetica), cursive, fantasy, or monospace (such as Courier). *Note:* if you want to use a font that has spaces in its name, be sure to enclose it in quotes ("Times New Roman").

- {font-size: sizevalue}
  The font-size style attribute may be absolute (such as 12 pt. or "Large") or it can be relative to the default font size and the subsequent choices that the user makes in the browser (such as "Larger"). In addition to the font size number, possible size values include: xx-small, x-small, small, medium, large, x-large, xx-large, larger, smaller.
  H1 {font-size:X-LARGE}
  <P> {font-size: larger}
  <H3> {font-size: 14pt}

- {line-height:value}
  Sets the height of a line, which is useful for double spacing!
  number—multiply the font's size by the number (i.e. 2)
  percentage—relative to that element's font size (i.e. 200%)
  Example: <P> {line-height: 200%}

Margins and Borders

- {margin:value}—the margin attribute allows you to set all margins with one command, or the specific margins can be set individually.

  {margin-bottom:value}

  {margin-left:value}

  {margin-right:value}

  {margin-top:value}

  Values: Length

  Percentage. *Note:* Percentage values are relative to the parent element's width. Negative margins may be used.

  When using the {margin:value} you may either specify a single margin for the entire element or use {margin:topbottom right eft} or {margin:top right bottom left}. For example:

  BODY {margin:20px} creates a 20 pixel margin for ALL elements in the body.

  P {margin: 20px 10px} creates a margin with top and bottom margins of 20 pixels, and left and right margins of 10 pixels relative to the BODY margin.

  P {margin: 5px 10px 7px 20px} has a top of 5, right of 10, bottom of 7, and left of 20—relative to the BODY margin.

  Other margin examples:

  DT { margin-bottom: 5% }

  ADDRESS { margin-left: 50% }

- {text-indent:value}

  The text-indent style attribute allows indentation of paragraphs!

  Possible values: length, percentage

  Example: P {text-indent: 5em}

- {text-transform:}

  Transforms the text cases.

  capitalize—Capitalizes The First Character Of Each Word

  uppercase—ALL LETTERS IN CAPITALS

  lowercase—all letters in lowercase.

  Examples:

  H1 { text-transform: uppercase }

  H3 { text-transform: capitalize }

There is a bug in Netscape Navigator 4.x that ignores all style sheets with any MEDIA except screen. Our suggestion: either use MEDIA="Screen" or leave the attribute blank.

Cascading Style Sheets Size or Length Units Explained

Percentages may be expressed either as a positive or negative percentage. This amount is a multiplier. In other words, +200% is twice as large as normal; -50% is half as large. You don't need to use the + sign, it is the default.

Height or width size units

These relative units are used as an alternative to percentages:

em—relative to the height of the element's font
ex—relative to the height of the letter "x" in that font.
px—the number of pixels, relative to the resolution

These absolute units may create problems in browsers that have font sizes modified, so sticking to relative units is recommended:

in—inches
cm—centimeters
mm—millimeters
pt—points
   (1 point is 1/72 inch)
pc—picas
   (1 pica is 12 points or
   1/6 of an inch)

Examples: 200%, 3pt, 2ex

```
<HTML>
<HEAD>
<TITLE>Cascading Style Sheets Number Two</TITLE>
<STYLE>
H1 {font-size: 36pt; color: blue; text-
transform:capitalize}
H2 {font-size:22;color: red}
P {border:black thick; text-indent:20px}
</STYLE>
</HEAD>
<BODY>
<H1>the declaration of independence 1</H1>
```

```
<P>When in the Course of human events, it
becomes necessary for one people to dissolve
the political bands which have connected them
with another, and to assume among the powers
of the earth, the separate and equal station
to which the Laws of Nature and of Nature's
God entitle them, a decent respect to the
opinions of mankind requires that they should
declare the causes which impel them to the
separation.
<P>We hold these truths to be self-evident, that
all men are created equal, that they are endowed
by their Creator with certain unalienable
Rights, that among these are Life, Liberty and
the pursuit of Happiness.
<P>That to secure these rights, Governments are
instituted among Men, deriving their just powers
from the consent of the governed, —That whenever
any Form of Government becomes destructive of
these ends, it is the Right of the People to
alter or to abolish it, and to institute new
Government, laying its foundation on such prin-
ciples and organizing its powers in such form,
as to them shall seem most likely to effect
their Safety and Happiness.
</BODY>
</HTML>
```

Frames

One of the problems with HTML pages is that every time a new one loads, you lose the previous page, right? The theory behind frames is that one or more parts of the page remain intact while new pages are loaded into a different part of the page. The frame page is a container for content that is found in other HTML pages. So far it sounds good, but hold on.

The Frames Dilemma

Frames are one of those great ideas that lots of people use. Frames are also a horrible idea that cause many problems for browsers.

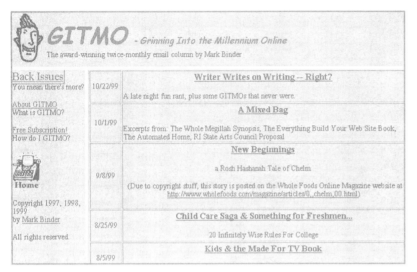

The first problem with frames is that some browsers don't recognize them. Old browsers and text-only browsers don't recognize frames. Instead, they'll see a blank page or a default image.

The second problem with frames is that many Web crawling search engines ignore frames. They don't see them at all. So if your entire site is set up as a frame, then only the home page will be cataloged.

The third problem with frames is that they get ugly at different monitor sizes and resolutions. What looks great on a 17-inch monitor at 832 x 624 resolution will look horrible on a 15-inch monitor at 640 x 480. Even worse, much of the important information you were trying to get across could be cut off or lost.

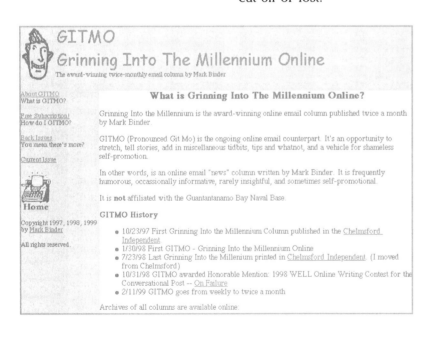

Frames Tutorial: How to Create and Use Frames

A typical use of frames is to create a page with three framed sections. A thin top section contains a banner or logo; a narrow left (or right) section contains a button list; and the changing content appears in the majority of the page to the right (or left) of the button list.

Despite their drawbacks, Mark used frames to create the Web page for his now-defunct e-mail newsletter, Grinning into the Millennium Online (GITMO).

Tags and Attributes Used

`<FRAMESET></FRAMESET>`	Defines an HTML document as a frames page. *Note:* Frames pages have no <BODY> tags. All content displayed from a frames page are contained within the <FRAME> or <NOFRAME> tags. <FRAMESET>s are defined with either rows or columns but may be nested to create more complex frames.
BORDER	Sets the width of frame borders. Can be set to zero.
BORDERCOLOR	Sets the color of the frame borders.
COLS	Sets the number of columns the <FRAMESET> will have. COLS are defined by a number of values separated by commas.
ROWS	Sets the number of rows the <FRAMESET> will have. ROWS are defined by a number of values separated by commas. Frames cannot have both COLS and ROWS attributes.
ROWS/COLS values	COLS or ROWS may have values set as either pixels, percentages, or stars. Using pixel-sized frames can be tricky, depending on the user's screen size. *Example:* COLS="138,74%" sets two columns, one with a width of 138 pixels, and the remainder set to 74% of the page. COLS="1*,2*" sets two columns. The first row will be one-third the width of the screen. The second will be two-thirds the width of the screen.
FRAMEBORDER	Sets the display of borders for the inside frames. Values are YES or NO.
FRAMESPACING	Sets the padding between frames in pixels.
`<FRAME>`	Determines the look and content of a particular frame, including what initially loads into that frame. The <FRAME> tag may only be used within a <FRAMESET>
BORDERCOLOR	Sets the border color of this frame. *Note:* No color will display if FRAMEBORDER is set to 0.
FRAMEBORDER	Determines whether a border is displayed between this frame and other frames. FRAMEBORDER values may be 1 or 0. Setting the FRAMEBORDER=0 hides the border between frames. The default is 1.
NAME	Defines the name of the frame. While defining a frame's name is optional, we recommend using this attribute because content is typically targeted into a frame by its name.
NORESIZE	Including this attribute prevents a user from resizing the frame. If you don't use the NORESIZE, HTML assumes that frames are resizeable by users.

SCROLLING	Including the SCROLLING attribute allows users to scroll around the frame. Values include:
	YES—Always displays a scroll bar.
	NO—Never displays a scroll bar.
	AUTO—Displays a scroll bar only when the frames content is larger than the FRAMESET's window's size. In other words, no scroll bar will appear if the frame's content fits in a window.
SRC	The URL that loads when the frame is initially loaded. If no SRC is defined, then the frame is displayed as blank.
<NOFRAME></NOFRAME>	Defines the content that will be displayed if the user has a browser that either can't show frames or is set to not display frames. Any browser that can view frames ignores content within the <NOFRAME> tags. <NOFRAME> is only used within a <FRAMESET> page. Treat a <NOFRAME> as a <BODY> command—all <BODY> elements may be included within a <NOFRAME>…</NOFRAME> tag set.
<BASE TARGET= >	Used within the <HEAD> of an HTML document that is framed. Sets the default target window or frame for a document. All links will open in the target window or frame. Useful for frames and for links pages. This default will be overridden by the use of a TARGET attribute in a link.
"targetname"	Targets may be defined as "targetname" to refer to a particular named frame window.
_blank	Link opens a new blank and unnamed window.
_parent	Link loads in the frame parent of the document. If there is no parent, the link opens in the current window.
_self	Link loads in the same window as the anchor that was clicked.
_top	Link loads in the entire window (eliminating any frames). If the document is already the top, then it defaults to _self.
<A TARGET=…>	Used within any HTML document, the TARGET attribute defines a target window or frame for a link. TARGET may be set as ="targetname," or _blank, _parent, _self, _top (as in BASE tag above). A target defined in a link overrides a <BASE> target.

Writing the code for the top border page

This page contains the GITMO logo (a grinning face) and the name of the column. It's a simple page that uses a table to align the images more precisely. *Note:* We gave the image a link to aboutgitmo.htm and a target frame of "stories." We'll save this file as grintop.htm.

```
<HTML>
<HEAD>
<BASE TARGET=stories>
<TITLE>Giggling Into the Millennium—a weekly
column by Mark Binder</TITLE>
</HEAD>
<BODY BGCOLOR="#FFFFFF" BACKGROUND="../
images/ringbinderblank.jpg">
<P><TABLE BORDER=0 HEIGHT=100>
<TR>
<TD VALIGN=top WIDTH=60>
<P><A HREF="aboutgitmo.htm"><FONT FACE=
"Comic Sans MS"><IMG SRC="../images/
grinning.gif" ALT="Grinning Guy" WIDTH=56
HEIGHT=89 BORDER=0 ALIGN=top></FONT>
</A></P>
</TD>
<TD>
<P><FONT SIZE="+4" FACE="Comic Sans MS"
COLOR="#CC0000"><B><I>GITMO</I></B><I>
</I></FONT><FONT SIZE="+1" FACE="Comic Sans MS"
COLOR="#CC0000"><I>-
Grinning Into the Millennium Online<BR>
</I></FONT>The award-winning twice-monthly email
column by Mark Binder</P>
</TD>
</TR>
</TABLE>
</P>
</BODY>
</HTML>
```

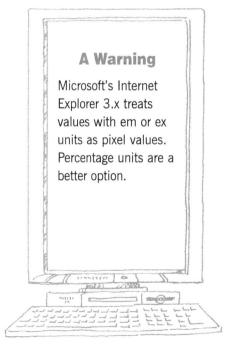

A Warning

Microsoft's Internet Explorer 3.x treats values with em or ex units as pixel values. Percentage units are a better option.

Step 1: Writing the code for the left column/links page

This page contains the links that will allow users to see past issues of GITMO, learn more about GITMO, get a free subscription,

and return to the home page. Notice the use of the <BASE TARGET=stories> tag. This will set the default for all the links in this window to open in the Frame named stories.

Note: The two links that don't have anything to do with GITMO—returning to the home page and finding out more about the author—use the attribute TARGET="_top." This will remove the frames. We'll save this file as grinmenu.htm

```
<HTML>
<HEAD>
<BASE TARGET=stories>
<—Sets the link default to open in the stories
frame —>
<TITLE>Grinning Into the Millennium—a weekly
column by Mark Binder</TITLE>
</HEAD>
<BODY BGCOLOR="#FFFFFF" LINK="#660000"
ALINK="#0099FF" VLINK="#006600"
BACKGROUND="../images/ringbinderblank.jpg">
<P><A HREF="contents.htm"><FONT SIZE="+2">Back
Issues</FONT></A><BR>
You mean there's more?</P>
<P><A HREF="aboutgitmo.htm">About GITMO</A><BR>
What is GITMO?</P>
<P><A HREF="aboutgitmo.htm#Subscribe">Free
Subscription!</A><BR>
How do I GITMO?</P>
<P><A HREF="thisweek.htm">The latest
GITMO</A></P>
<P><A HREF="../tableofcontents/index.htm"
TARGET="_top"><FONT COLOR="#0033FF"><IMG
SRC="../images/tableofcontents.gif" ALT="Table
of Contents" WIDTH=55 HEIGHT=70 BORDER=0
ALIGN=top></FONT></A></P>
<—By using the TARGET="_top" attribute, when the
user clicks on the home page, the frames will go
away.—>
<P>Copyright 1997, 1998, 1999<BR>
by <A
HREF="http://www.markbinder.com/contact.htm"
TARGET="_top">Mark Binder</A></P>
<P>All rights reserved.</P>
</BODY>
</HTML>
```

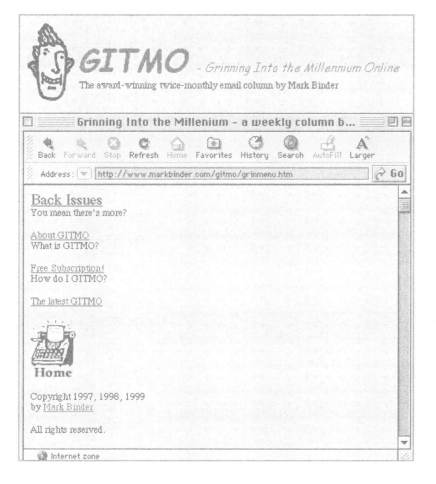

Page Generation Programs

Even though we suggest that you try out the HTML to create framed pages, we've found that using HTML generation programs such as FileMaker Home Page, Adobe PageMill, Macromedia Dreamweaver, and Adobe GoLive are the easiest ways for beginners to create framed pages.

Step 2: Writing the GITMO stories page

The GITMO stories default page will be called "thisweek.htm," and it will be changed every few weeks. It's a simple page with a white background and the text of the latest essay or story.

```
<HTML>
<HEAD>
<TITLE>Writer Writes on Writing—Right?</TITLE>
</HEAD>
<BODY BGCOLOR="#FFFFFF">
<H1>The End of GITMO?</H1>
<P>01/01/00</P>
<P>What will happen to GITMO after the turn of
the millennium? Will it disappear, as something
only relevant a thousand years ago, or will it
```

```
evolve, perhaps into Grinning In The
Millennium?</P>
<P>Tune in to find out.</P>
</BODY>
</HTML>
```

Step 3: Writing the code for the FRAMESET page

At last we're ready to write the FRAMESET page. This page will be saved in the GITMO subdirectory as index.htm so that anybody who types in "www.markbinder.com/gitmo" will see this page.

Remember: The top part of the GITMO page will contain the GITMO logo and banner. The left section below the banner will contain basic information about GITMO. The right section below the banner will contain the contents. It will default to "thisweek.htm."

1. Write the <HEAD> of the document.

    ```
    <HTML>
    <HEAD>
    <TITLE>GITMO—Grinning Into The Millennium
    Online</TITLE>
    </HEAD>
    ```

2. Define the top/bottom dividing FRAMESET. The top frame will contain the banner and needs to be only a little taller than the height of the images used. In this case, the table is 100 pixels high. The remainder of the frame will be set to 100%.

    ```
    <FRAMESET ROWS="100,100%">
    ```

3. Define the top of the page frame.

    ```
    <FRAME SRC="grintop.htm" NORESIZE
    SCROLLING=no MARGINWIDTH=0 MARGINHEIGHT=0
    FRAMEBORDER=0>
    ```

    This tells the browser to use the grintop.htm file we've created with no borders and no scroll bars.

4. Define the nested FRAMESET. This creates the left and right frames in the frame under the top of the page. *Note:* We set the first column width to 138 pixels mostly

because when we tried to set it as a percentage we had difficulty guaranteeing that people would see it correctly on oddly adjusted browsers.

```
<FRAMESET COLS="138,100%">
```

5. Define the left and right frames:

```
<FRAME SRC="grinmenu.htm" NORESIZE FRAME-
BORDER=0>
<FRAME SRC="thisweek.htm" NAME=stories
FRAMEBORDER=0>
```

Note: We set the name of the frame containing "Thisweek.htm" to "Stories."

6. Close the nested FRAMESETs.

```
</FRAMESET>
</FRAMESET>
```

7. Add the <NOFRAMES> page. This should go before the frameset so that it loads quickly into browsers for people who don't see frames. For GITMO, we just copied most of the HTML from grintop.htm and grinmenu.htm into the <NOFRAMES></NOFRAMES> area.

Here's what the whole page looks like in HTML, and on the screen.

The advantage to using a WYSIWYG page generator is that you can immediately see what the frame will look like. Then, when you adjust its borders in the page creation program, the HTML will adjust automatically. In other words, if you just drag it a bit, you'll get the perfect fit, rather than trying to figure out whether you need to set a frame's COL (column) width at 35 or 38 pixels.

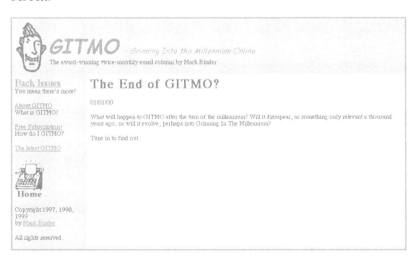

```
<HTML>
<HEAD>
<TITLE>GITMO—Grinning Into The Millennium
Online</TITLE>
</HEAD>
<—The NOFRAMES section tells non-frame browsers
what to display—>
<NOFRAMES><BODY BGCOLOR="#FFFFFF" BACK-
GROUND="../images/ringbinderblank.jpg">
<CENTER><TABLE BORDER=0>
<TR>
<TD VALIGN=top WIDTH=60>
<P><A HREF="aboutgitmo.htm"><FONT FACE="Comic
Sans MS"><IMG SRC="../images/grinning.gif"
ALT="Grinning Guy" WIDTH=56 HEIGHT=89 BORDER=0
ALIGN=top></FONT></A></P>
</TD>
<TD>
<P><A HREF="aboutgitmo.htm"><FONT FACE="Comic
Sans MS"><I><IMG SRC="../images/GITMO.gif"
WIDTH=489 HEIGHT=74 BORDER=0
ALIGN=top></I></FONT></A><FONT FACE="Comic Sans
MS"><I><BR>
</I></FONT>The award-winning twice-monthly email
column by
Mark Binder</P>
</TD>
</TR>
</TABLE>
<H3><A HREF="thisweek.htm">The Latest
GITMO</A></H3>
<P><A HREF="contents.htm">Back Issues</A><BR>
You mean there's more?</P>
<P><A HREF="aboutgitmo.htm">About GITMO</A><BR>
What is GITMO?</P>
<P><A HREF="aboutgitmo.htm#Subscribe">Free
Subscription!</A><BR>
How do I GITMO?</P>
<P><A HREF="../tableofcontents/index.htm"
TARGET="_top"><FONT COLOR="#0033FF"><IMG
SRC="../images/tableofcontents.gif" ALT="Table
of Contents" WIDTH=55 HEIGHT=70 BORDER=0
ALIGN=top></FONT></A></P>
<P>Copyright 1997, 1998, 1999<BR>
```

```
by <A
HREF="http://www.markbinder.com/contact.htm">
Mark Binder</A></P>
<P>All rights reserved.</P></CENTER>
</BODY>
</NOFRAMES>
<--This part defines the three frames-->
<FRAMESET ROWS="100,100%">
<FRAME SRC="grintop.htm" NORESIZE SCROLLING=no
FRAMEBORDER=0>
<FRAMESET COLS="138,100%">
<FRAME SRC="grinmenu.htm" NORESIZE FRAME-
BORDER=0>
<FRAME SRC="thisweektest.htm" NAME=stories
FRAMEBORDER=0>
</FRAMESET>
</FRAMESET>
</FRAMESET>
</HTML>
```

Step 4: What else needs to be done for GITMO?

Now the other pages need to be created, specifically the contents.htm page, which will contain a list of all the GITMO back issues. Initially we set a TARGET for the contents link, which would have replaced grinmenu.htm with the contents, but the stuff in the contents was too big. We decided to open contents in the stories frame. It makes one GITMO after another more difficult, but with frames there are always tradeoffs. Also, we made sure that the contents.htm page had a <BASE TARGET=stories>.

Forms With and Without CGI

Making a form in HTML is easy. Getting the form to do what you want isn't. In other words, we can teach you how to set up a form page for a guest book or an order form, but as far as getting the information posted into the guest book, or having the order form submit its results, all that depends on your Web host. Most forms are powered by CGI. Some are run in JavaScript. Others are handled by FrontPage extensions. Some can be structured as e-mail forms.

Frames Tips

1. Don't use too many frames on the page. They tend to crowd into each other.

2. View frames in lots of browsers and on different font sizes. We've said this before, but it's especially important with frames, which tend to get distorted easily.

3. Don't make your home page a frame page. Many search engines won't index it.

We're going to let ourselves off the hook by showing you how to create a form and then recommending that you speak with your Web host directly about how to manage the form's information.

What Is a CGI Script?

CGI, or Common Gateway Interface, is a specification that allows World Wide Web users to run programs on their computers. CGI isn't a programming language; it is a gateway that allows programs or scripts written in other languages to be run over the Internet.

CGI programs usually take input passed to it from a form on a Web page, process the information somehow, and then format the results in HTML. The result is a Web page that is generated on the fly.

The language of choice for CGI processing is Perl, or Practical Extraction and Reporting Language. Perl is used often because it is specifically designed to butcher multiple text files and format them nicely, making it exceptional for writing HTML. Other languages used occasionally for CGI scripts are (in descending order of popularity) C/C++, Visual Basic, AppleScript, UNIX Shell, and Tcl.

CGI scripts can do almost anything when they are cleverly written. Scripts exist that run search engines, manage chat rooms, and even control robotic arms remotely.

Several resources already exist to get you into CGI programming. One of my favorite places to start when I need inspiration is the CGI Resource Index (www.cgi-resources.com/), which has hundreds of scripts already written. You can look at the source code to see how the scripts are written.

If you want to write your own CGI programs in Perl, get a copy of either cgi-lib.pl (my personal preference) or CGI.pm. These libraries automate the process of getting form input from a Web page through CGI. They also provided a limited set of routines to begin building the framework of a resulting Web page.

For information on writing CGI scripts with Python, consult the Web topic guide at www.python.org for a comprehensive list of tools and documentation. Of course, if you are in need of programming help, the CGI Programming OpenFAQ is always available! ;) (*Note:* This description of CGI was excerpted from *CGI Programming OpenFAQ*, excerpt by JesseB jbarros@hcc.hawaii.edu and akuchling amk1@erols.com.)

Before You Start Creating a Form

Know what you want on your forms in advance. Be aware of the information you want before you start writing your form, rather than creating a form from scratch on the fly. In other words, take a piece of paper and a pencil and sketch it out. Before you even start working with forms:

1. Be sure that you can use CGI on your Web host. Some hosts are very particular. Most free Web hosts won't allow CGI. Tripod (www.tripod.com) is one notable exception.

2. Get the CGI and figure out how to use it. If you're not a programmer, this could take a while. Some CGIs come with detailed instructions, which can be fairly easy to follow. Others can be darned complex and might require an engineering degree.

Creating the Form in HTML

First we'll create the form in HTML; then we'll worry about how to make it work. The Apeiron Foundation wanted a guest book for their Web site. They wanted the following information: viewer's name, e-mail address, and snail mail address. They also wanted to know if the viewer was interested in volunteering.

Useful CGI Links

- Script Search.Com (www.scriptsearch. com/)—A huge script library that includes CGIs and JavaScripts
- Matt's Script Archive (www.worldwidemart. com/scripts/)
- CGI Authoring Newsgroup (comp.www. authoring.cgi)
- Perl Mongers (www.pm.org)

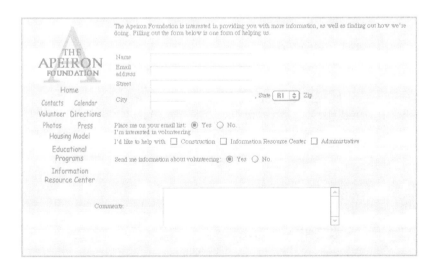

The HTML for Forms

`<FORM></FORM>`	Designates an area of the page as a form. Forms include at least one user input field.
ACTION	This attribute tells the browser where to send the data. It could be to the URL of the CGI that handles the information. It could be a simple mail command that goes to an e-mail address. (Naturally, this e-mail form, which would be the simplest for beginners to manage, won't work on some browsers—most notably Internet Explorer.) Example: <FORMACTION= "mailto:everyone@everythingbuildyourownhomepagebook.com"
METHOD	Tells how the data will be sent to the program. Options include GET or POST. Check with the CGI about which option is appropriate.
ONRESET	Designates the JavaScript to run when the user presses a "reset" field.
ONSUBMIT	Designates the JavaScript to run when the user presses a "submit" field.
TARGET	Designates the window in which the forms are opened.
INPUT	Creates an input control field for a <FORM>. Must be used within <FORM> tags.
TYPE	Tells what type of input this will be.
BUTTON	Creates a clickable button.
CHECKBOX	Creates a checkbox.
FILE	Allows a user to attach a file to the form.
HIDDEN	Information in this input is hidden from the user and not modifiable. Useful for letting you know what page someone is submitting from.
IMAGE	An image submit button rather than a text button.
PASSWORD	Information typed into this field will not be displayed on the screen.
RADIO	Creates a radio button. Every radio button in a group must have the same name, but they ought to have different values. Only one radio button in a group can be checked.
RESET	Resets the form.
SUBMIT	Submits the form.
TEXT	Creates a one-line text input field.
ALIGN	Aligns the INPUT field.
CHECKED	Automatically puts a check mark in the field when used with TYPE="RADIO" or TYPE="CHECKBOX."

MAXLENGTH	Sets the maximum number of characters of a TEXT or PASS WORD field.
NAME	Sets the name of the control field. This name will be part of the data sent to the server.
SRC	Sets the URL of the image used when TYPE="IMAGE."
VALUE	Sets the value of the element. The value has different results depending on the TYPE of input.
RADIO and CHECKBOX value	Sets the value that will be sent to the server if that radio or checkbox is checked.
BUTTON, RESET, and SUBMIT value	Sets the text of that button.
TEXT, PASSWORD, and HIDDEN value	Sets the default value of that field.
<SELECT></SELECT>	The <SELECT> tag defines a list of input control data from a list of <OPTION>s that may be selected. It is only valid in the FORM element. One example of a select box would allow the user to select the month from a list of 12 months.
MULTIPLE	Allows multiple items from the list to be selected.
NAME	Gives this input field a name that can be used by scripts.
SIZE	Sets the number of lines that are displayed at one time.
<OPTION></OPTION>	The option tag defines the value displayed in a <SELECT> input control list.
LABEL	The value that will be displayed in the list.
SELECTED	Sets this <OPTION> as a default value.
VALUE	Sets the value of the OPTION element.
<TEXTAREA></TEXTAREA>	Creates a text input field of more than one line.
COLS	Sets how many columns (characters) the text window will be.
NAME	Sets the name of the TEXTAREA field. This information will be submitted with the form.
ROWS	Sets the number of text lines shown on the screen.

Step 1. Define the form with the <FORM> tag. Since we don't really know how this form is going to be processed, we're going to fudge the <FORM> tag for now.

```
<HTML>
<HEAD></HEAD>
<BODY>
<FORM METHOD=POST ACTION=http://www.ape-
iron.org/cgi-bin/guestbook.cgi>
```

Step 2. Let's design the form. We start with a description and a number of text input fields.

```
<P> The Apeiron Foundation is interested in
providing you with more information, as
well as finding out how we're doing.
Filling out the form below is one form of
helping us.
<P>Name
<input type=text name="name" size=30>
<P>Email address
<input type=text name="email" size=30>
<P>Street
<input type=text name="street" size=30>
<P>City
<input type=text name="city"size=30>
```

For the state, we'll use a list option and assume that the viewer is someone local to the foundation to begin with.

```
<P> State
<select name="State">
<option value="RI" selected>RI</option>
<option value="MA">MA</option>
<option value="CT">CT</option>
</select>
<P>Zip
<input type=text name=name value=""
size=10>
```

Here are some radio boxes and check boxes. Notice that we've tried to manipulate the visitor into signing onto the mailing lists and volunteering.

```
<P>Place me on your email list:
<INPUT TYPE=radio NAME=emailist VALUE=yes
checked> Yes
<INPUT TYPE=radio NAME=emaillist VALUE=no>
No.
<br>
I'm interested in volunteering<BR>
I'd like to help with
<INPUT TYPE=checkbox NAME=Construction
VALUE=Construction> Construction
<INPUT TYPE=checkbox NAME=IRC VALUE=IRC>
Information Resource Center
<INPUT TYPE=checkbox NAME=Administrative
VALUE=Administrative> Administrative</P>
<P>Send me information about volunteering:
<INPUT TYPE=radio NAME=volunteerinfo
VALUE=yes checked> Yes
<INPUT TYPE=radio NAME=volunteerinfo
VALUE=no>No.</P>
```

Finally, we'll use a text area to collect any comments from visitors. We were forced to put the text and input area into a table to make it look good.

```
<CENTER>
<table width="75%" border="0">
<tr>
<td ALIGN=RIGHT> Comments:
</td>
<td> <textarea name="textfield" rows="5"
cols="50"></textarea>
</td>
</tr>
</table>
</CENTER>
</FORM>
</BODY>
```

This is what the screen looked like before we added graphics and more tables to make it look pretty.

The Apeiron Foundation is interested in providing you with more information, as well as finding out how we're doing.
Filling out the form below is one form of helping us.

Name

Email address

Street

City

State [RI ↕]

Zip

Place me on your email list: ● Yes ○ No.
I'm interested in volunteering
I'd like to help with ☐ Construction ☐ Information Resource Center ☐ Administrative

Send me information about volunteering: ● Yes ○ No.

Comments:

Using a Form Without a CGI— The Printer Method

At this point the automated system broke down. The Apeiron Foundation is a relatively new nonprofit. They didn't have a big budget for programming or Web hosting. So, instead of worrying about CGIs and trying to maintain the information on the computer, they finally decided to add this piece of text to the bottom.

```
<H2>Please Print and Fax this form to our
office!</H2>
```

A simple solution to a tricky problem. If they had wanted to include a submit button, the code would have read:

```
<INPUT TYPE=submit NAME=Submit VALUE=
"Submit">
```

An Easy E-mail Form—FormMail.pl CGI

As Mark was designing his Web site (www.chelmtales.com), he decided he needed to create a form that would allow visitors to receive a free trial subscription to his serialized novel.

He went to the Web and found a script called "FormMail" at Matt's Script Archive, Inc. (www.worldwidemart.com/scripts/). Here's how FormMail works:

1. Download the FormMail.pl CGI from the Web.
2. Follow the directions.
3. Change the "@referer" to allow forms to be located only on servers that are defined. (You'll need to know your domain's IP address.)
4. Upload the modified FormMail.pl to the cgi-bin subdirectory.
5. Tell the HTML subscription page that it should use the FormMail cgi, what e-mail address it should send the form to, and what the subject of the e-mail will be. Use the following code in the subscription form page:

```
<FORM ACTION="/cgi-bin/FormMail.pl"
METHOD=POST>
<INPUT TYPE=hidden NAME=recipient
VALUE="youremailaddress@domainname.com">
<INPUT TYPE=hidden NAME=subject VALUE="The
subject of the form email">
```

6. Upload the HTML page to the Web.
7. Test it out.

HTML page generators can do a pretty good job of creating forms. You type in the text and then modify it according to your whim. Unfortunately, these modifications usually require a lot of clicking, menu searching, and quite a bit of tabbing around within obscure dialog boxes. If you use a generator to lay out the page, consider going into HTML mode to modify it.

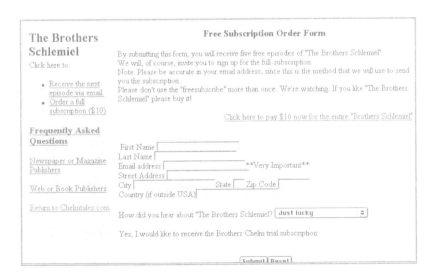

The Brothers Schlemiel
Click here to:

- Receive the next episode via email.
- Order a full subscription ($10)

Frequently Asked Questions

Newspaper or Magazine Publishers

Web or Book Publishers

Return to Chelmtales.com

Free Subscription Order Form

By submitting this form, you will receive five free episodes of "The Brothers Schlemiel" We will, of course, invite you to sign up for the full-subscription
Note: Please be accurate in your email address, since this is the method that we will use to send you the subscription.
Please don't use the "freesubscribe" more than once. We're watching. If you like "The Brothers Schlemiel" please buy it!

Click here to pay $10 now for the entire "Brothers Schlemiel"

First Name [ ]
Last Name [ ]
Email address [ ]   **Very Important**
Street Address [ ]
City [ ]   State [ ]   Zip Code [ ]
Country (if outside USA) [ ]

How did you hear about "The Brothers Schlemiel? [Just lucky ◆]

Yes, I would like to receive the Brothers Chelm trial subscription

[Submit] [Reset]

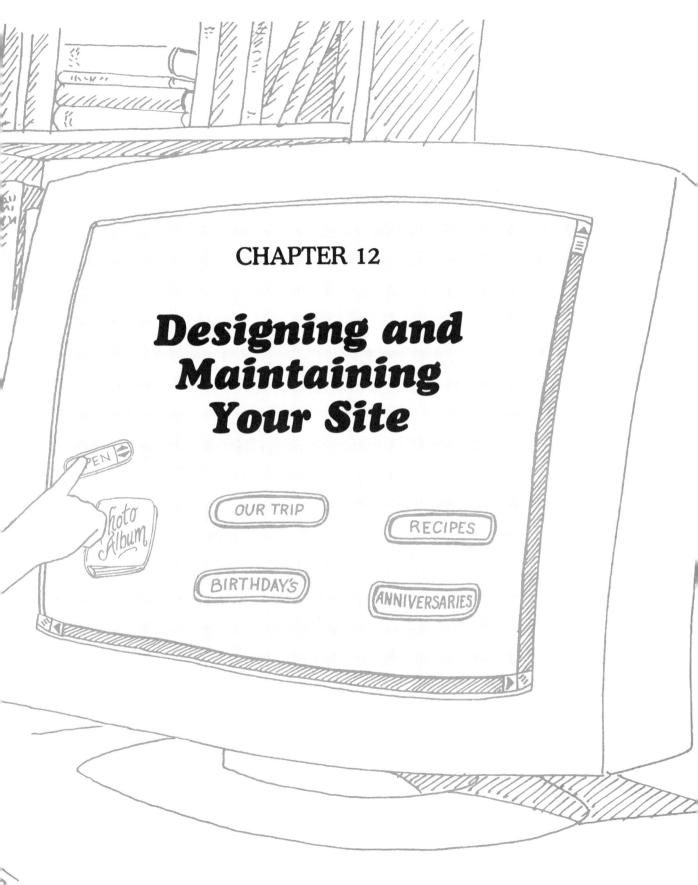

CHAPTER 12

Designing and Maintaining Your Site

B y now you've got a clearer sense of what goes into a Web page. You should have a sense of how to build one from scratch, or you've been using one of the HTML generation programs to lay your pages out for you. Either way, the next important phase in building your Web site is creating an overall design and navigational structure.

Case Studies

In this chapter we'll look at a number of Web sites and analyze some of the techniques they've used.

The Apeiron Foundation

Founded in 1994, the Apeiron Foundation is a nonprofit environmental organization working to promote sustainable living through education outreach and community building. It focuses on promoting things like ecologically friendly building, renewable energy sources, sustainable agriculture, and prevention and holistic-oriented health care. Their biggest project to date has been coordinating more than 75 organizations and over 500 individuals to build an environmental education center and sustainable housing model in Coventry, Rhode Island. The center is intended to be a valuable educational resource for thousands of students, homeowners, and builders in Southern New England to learn about more environmentally friendly ways of living.

> *Platform:* Windows, Mac
> *HTML editor:* Dreamweaver
> *Graphics:* Photoshop
> *FTP:* Fetch
> *Browser:* Navigator
> *URL:* www.apeiron.org

The Acme Clown Company and the Acme Miniature Flea Circus

Adam G. Gertsacov, the boss clown of the Acme Clown Company, first posted a few Web pages in 1996. Since then the site has evolved and grown into two sites, generating more than 50,000 page views of the home page. As of 1999, Gertsacov has generated between 15 and 20 percent of his performance gigs from the site—

including a standing-room only booking for his Acme Miniature Circus from the Mundao Festival in São Paolo, Brazil.

What Gertsacov wants to work on

"I've been thinking about animating my trained fleas home page. Right now the picture shows Midge and Madge [the fleas] after they've been shot out of the cannon. I'd like to show them in action.

"Something I've been planning on doing, but I haven't done it, is that I'm registering on Amazon.com as an associate bookstore. I'd like to do that, but it's time consuming.

"You can create your own store on the Internet. I forget where it was, but I haven't done that yet.

"There are a lot of little maintenance issues that I want to deal with, but it's low on my priority list. Eventually, I want to create the Flea Circus FAQ, and really get a good page of excellent links. But that all takes time. And it's not like I have anybody else doing it. I'm doing everything myself."

Platform: Macintosh

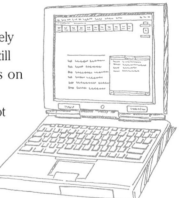

HTML editor: TexEdit ("I prefer to keep my Web sites relatively simple, so that even if you have an old/bad browser, you can still see my Web site. I'm not really interested in putting Java applets on my site. My brother has been talking with me about putting streaming video on my site, but I've been extremely hesitant. Not that I don't think it would be good or that people wouldn't be interested. I don't like pages that come up after a long period of time. Even my flea circus page comes up after a while because there are four pictures on it. I have a very slow modem right now, a 14.4 modem.")

Graphics: Deneba Canvas and freeware GIFConverter, GIFBuilder, and JPEGView

FTP: Fetch

Browser: Navigator 3.0

URLs: www.acmeclown.com and www.trainedfleas.com

Markbinder.com and Chelmtales.com— the home page for *The Brothers Schlemiel*

When Mark Binder began writing his serialized novel, *The Brothers Schlemiel*, one of the first things he did was register a home page. Brothers_Schlemiel.com was too long and confusing

and schlemiel.com was already taken. So, since he had written other tales of Chelm, he settled on www.chelmtales.com.

The initial home page was thrown up quickly. It had no graphics and little in the way of layout. Over the course of the next few months, he continued to look for just the right look and feel for the home page. Because "The Brothers Schlemiel" was meant to be a book, he decided on a book cover look and feel. He considered hiring a designer to illustrate and lay out the page for him, but budgetary constraints got in the way. Instead, he "borrowed" a Chagal he found on the Web and modified it using Flash. This made a very nice home page, but the rights from the estate of Chagal were not forthcoming. At the time this book was written, the cover page of chelmtales.com was still in transition.

Platform: Macintosh

HTML editor: HomePage, Dreamweaver

Graphics: Photoshop, Flash

FTP: Fetch

Browser: Internet Explorer 5

URLs: www.chelmtales.com and www.markbinder.com/chelmtales

First Priority: A Clear Navigational Structure

No matter what your Web site, you want people to be able to find what's inside. In a book, you know that if you open the book and turn the pages you'll find what you're looking for eventually. You can also read the table of contents or the index.

Web sites are different. They're webs. Each page links to other pages, and it's not always clear how to get there from here. Or back. Here are some tips and tricks:

- Button bars are cute, but make sure your buttons don't take too long to load.
- Keep a standardized navigational pattern throughout. Use the same buttons or links on every page.

- Make sure people can get back to your home.
- Try to keep top levels one click away from each other.
- If you have too many links, it may be difficult for visitors to find what they want. Then you'll find yourself in the situation where you have to organize your links, putting them into subcategories or on other pages.

Simple and to the Point

The first version of the Acme Clown Company Clown Links Page wasn't the prettiest links page on the Net, but it was specific, selective, and it loaded in seconds.

Notice the format. Each link is named with a little bit of explanation following some of them. After Adam Gertsacov learned that we were going to feature his page in the book, he decided to make it look better.

In the second version, Gertsacov uses tables to lay out the page. The banner at the top and sidebar to the left are the top row and the first column in a second row. The bulk of the page holding the links are divided into two columns. At the bottom of the new page is a nice text navigation bar to take users anywhere else in the Web site.

Some Highly Selective Pages You Might Enjoy

Theatre Central The definitive theatre resource page.

The Puppetry Home Page

Juggling Information Service

All Magic Guide

American Magic Lantern Theatre America's Only Authentic 1890's Magic Lantern Shows

The Contortion Home Page

Drew Richardson, Dramatic Fool. A very good clown from Chicago.

The Gesundheit! Institute, founded by the most spiritually advanced clown doctor that I've ever had the pleasure to meet, Patch Adams

Hello, Harold Lloyd

Buster Keaton

This page maintained by kafelown@well.com

First version

ACME CLOWN COMPANY

LINKS YOU MIGHT LIKE

Here are some highly selective links you might enjoy. This list is not meant to be complete. (Hey, the Web is huge!) but simply links that I find interesting or useful. If a link is outdated, please **email me** with the link and I will update it. Enjoy these sites!

NOTE: Some of the links listed are actually lists of links.

Acme Home

THEATRE REFERENCE

THEATRE CENTRAL

ARTSLYNX
Physical Theatre Links

PUPPETRY HOME PAGE

ALLMAGIC GUIDE

YAHOO THEATRE PAGE

AMERICAN THEATER WEB

YESAND.COM
Improv on the Web

'MAGIC THEATRE' LINKS
Theatres outside the mainstream

FEDERAL THEATRE PROJECT

CIRCUS & SIDESHOW

YAHOO CIRCUS PAGES

VAUDEVILLE MEMORIES

TRAPEZE.ORG

SIDESHOW.COM

NEW CIRCUS WEBRING

BINDLESTIFF FAMILY CIRKUS

PANTWILIGHT CIRCUS

NEW PICKLE CIRCUS

CONEY ISLAND USA

JOHN TOWSEN (author of CLOWNS)

NOUVEAU CIRCUS WEB RING!

Explore and Join The Theatre Idea, New Circus & Jugglers WebRing the Web Ring of Performing Art
[Next | Next 5 Sites | Award | Chat | Random Site | News | List Sites]

Second version

Nine Don'ts of Web Site Design

Here are nine don'ts of Web design, courtesy of Jeffrey M. Glover, a Web designer in Minneapolis and Webmaster of Glover.com. The "Sucky to Savvy" section of his dandy site (www.glover.com) offers clear, easy-to-follow instructions with a humorous touch on how NOT to design an effective site. Keep in mind that what one person hates another may like, and vice versa. His pet peeves are:

1. <BLINK> tag. You may love a page that is blinking, flashing, shimmying, rocking, and rolling, but others find this annoying and distracting.

2. Background music. Ever been greeted by a site that starts playing music or emitting sounds immediately? Just the thing to let your boss know you're hard at work preparing for today's meeting, right? Offering users a choice in playing music is good manners.

3. Loud backgrounds. Loud, neon, or overly fancy backgrounds overlaid with text can make it hard to read the words or make users' eyes hurt, which kind of defeats the purpose of your site. A light, easy-on-the-eyes background so your text stands out is better.

4. Gratuitous use of frames. Some browsers don't support frames. Frames also take longer to download. Many Web pages offer the choice of frame and no-frame versions.

5. Overuse of image maps. Big images, with many different spots to click that link to other pages, take a lot longer to download. If you're going to do an image map—for example, a map of a country with different regions to click—offer another way to access these links, such as a text-only menu at the bottom.

6. Construction signs. Those Site Under Construction signs are silly, Glover says, since all Web sites in theory are still under construction and should be updated, with dates noted, regularly.

7. Scrolling marquees. These rapidly moving lines of text, like a news ticker, can be hard to read and irritating. If the text is important, it should be stationary and easy to read. If it's not important, why include it at all?

8. Personalized alerts. These bulletins pop up on the screen during your visit or bid you farewell by name when you leave. Unnecessary and smart-alecky, in Glover's opinion.

9. Ticker tape status bars. These rapidly moving lines of text, like scrolling marquees, appear at the bottom of your screen and are annoying and unnecessary.

Glover also warns against link lunacy, or the foolishness of including too many links on the page and encouraging users to leave the page as soon as they enter it.

Creating a Site Template

Since the Web is nothing more than a huge collection of pages, how does somebody know if they're still in your Web site? Create a Web site with a consistent look and feel. You could retype all the same old stuff—the background image, the link colors, and so on—every time you write a new Web page, or you can create a site template.

You don't need a high-priced Web markup program or learn arcane HTML code to make all the pages in your Web site look similar. The easiest way to create pages is to create a basic template that you'll duplicate for each new Web page. This template will include:

```
<HTML>
<HEAD>
<TITLE>
<-Insert Title Here->
</TITLE>
</HEAD>
<BODY BGCOLOR="#FFFFFF" LINK="#000000"
BACKGROUND="images/backgroundimage.jpg">
<-Modify Background Color, Link Colors, and
Background Images to suit your site.->
<H1>
<-Insert Header Here->
</H1>
<- This is where you put everything
else ->
<-If you want to put a menu bar, put it here.->
</BODY>
</HTML>
```

A Case Study in Oops...

While we were writing this book, we wanted to look up something on the Chelmsford Online services site. So we went to http://www.chelmsford.com.

Unfortunately, that was the end of our Web journey. While they had the weather, a bookstore, and a link to Chelmsford, England, they'd forgotten to put in a link to information about the rest of their site. We let them know, and within a few days, they added the appropriate links.

Save this as a template file—template.htm. Every time you open up this template file, click "SAVE AS" and give it a new name. Then make the changes you want. Now, all your pages will have the same background image, the same link color, and the same basic look.

Opening Your Doors

After you've designed and put your site up on the Web, your job's not over. Once the site's ready to roll, we want you to be certain that everything is going to work—and that people are going to come and see you. That means testing, registering with search engines, and updating your Web site frequently.

Test, test, test

Does your Web site make sense? Can you get from the product to the order form, back to another product, and then checkout quickly? Does the ordering system even work? And when the orders come in online do you receive them in a way that works and makes sense? Can you process them in a timely fashion?

Ask your grandmother to try to order something. Ask your neighbors. Watch them use the site. Listen to their comments and make the appropriate changes.

Register with Search Engines

Unless you're Coca Cola, nobody's going to check your Web site out randomly. Registering with search engines is vital. If somebody's looking for a graphite golf club on AltaVista, you want your site to pop up on the list, preferably near the top. There's an entire subspecialty devoted to the how to of getting your Web listed first on search engines. Some search engines catalog words, some catalog links.

- Use the <TITLE> tag to accurately describe each page.
- Use <META> tags to describe pages, especially pages that are frame based. Avoid duplicating words on the page in the META tags because some search engines penalize you for that.
- Use the ALT attribute to describe images because some search engines will catalog this content.
- Frames will limit cataloging of your site by Web crawlers.

Ten Rules for Web Site Consistency

One of the sure signs of an amateur Web site is its lack of consistency. Big businesses spend months hammering out designs and page layouts, making sure everything looks just so.

You don't have to go quite that far. We've compiled a list of 10 basic rules that will help give your Web site a consistent flavor.

1. Be consistent in your look and feel. In other words, put text and images in the same place on every page.

2. Use the same background image or background color throughout your site.

3. Keep menu bars and buttons in the same place on each page.

4. Use standardized type formatting. Every headline should have the same font, size, and/or header tag.

5. Use subdirectories to organize your site. If you're selling car parts and shampoo, then have a /carparts and a /shampoo subdirectory.

6. Keep all images in a single subdirectory (/image).

7. Keep it simple.

8. Use frames sparingly. Frames seem like an excellent way to maintain a look-and-feel for a Web site. Unfortunately, there are a lot of people who really don't like frames. There are also browsers that aren't frame enabled. That means you have to create the page twice—once for the frame and once for the non-frame.

9. Avoid long pages, the kind that you have to scroll way down. Aside from the stylistic reasons, you're more likely to forget something when you make changes later.

10. Break any and all rules when appropriate.

Using <META> tags

Place the following code in your HTML document:

```
<HEAD>
<META NAME="keywords" CONTENT="insert keywords
about your business here,....">
<META NAME="description" CONTENT="This is the
description that many search engines will dis-
play when they find your site.">
</HEAD>
```

Each page can have different META tags. For example, a golf pro could have a page on putters and another on drivers...

How People Find Information on the Web

If you already know the Internet address of a site, you type it in the Location or Netsite (in Netscape) or Address (in Explorer) box precisely the way it is. This means no misspellings, omitted letters, spaces between letters, or wrong punctuation. If you don't know the Internet address and don't have it on file anywhere, you have to use a search engine.

As a Webmaster, you probably want people to find your Web site, so it's important to understand how people stumble across search engines, and how those engines identify your Web site.

There are several different ways for the ordinary user to find a search engine.

1. They can click the "search" icon near the top of the screen or the "search Internet" command in the "Edit" menu to bring up a handful of popular search engines like Yahoo!, Lycos, or AltaVista.
2. They can type the Internet address of a search engine.
3. They can click on a bookmarked search engine they have visited before.

How search engines are used

To start the engine, click your browser icon to launch your browser and type the Internet address of the search engine you want, or pick one from the list in the "search" icon your browser probably has.

Type the words or phrases that describe what you're looking for in the Search box, then click Search (or hit the Enter key). A page will soon appear, which lists links to the pages that match your words or phrases and short descriptions. If a list of subject areas appears, click on whichever subject seems appropriate and pages that list subcategory areas will appear. Again, click on whichever link seems closest to narrow the search down to what you're looking for. Results the search engine thinks are closest to your request appear first.

Narrow your search by using terms like "AND," "OR," and "NOT" so you won't be swamped by a huge list of results.

- Using "AND" means both words should be included in the search.
- "OR" means either word can be included, so you'll get a bigger list.
- "NOT" before a word means the next word should be excluded from search results.

For example, if you're looking for Granny Goose, you can type in "Granny AND Goose," which means both words are required to appear in the search results. Use "OR"—"Granny OR Goose"—only if you want a massive list of all the Web pages that include either the word "Granny" plus the word "Goose." If you want a list of Grannies on the Web, just type "Venice."

Putting phrases—words which must go together in order—in quotes also works. For example, "Granny Goose's photos" should turn up only pages listing this phrase; the phrase without quotes will turn up many more pages with the words Granny, Goose, or photos. If you want to avoid all the pages about Mother Goose, add the words "NOT Mother Goose"

Plus and minus signs before words—no space in between—also work the way "AND" and "NOT" do in some search engines. For example, "Venice+California" or "Venice–Italy" will both turn up the California town.

Type your words or phrases in lowercase, unless they are proper names starting with capital letters. A search for Rock Hudson should serve up dish on the actor; lowercase, it will turn up results on the Hudson River, rock music, and rock climbing.

Put Your URL on Your Letterhead

It seems obvious, but don't forget to start using your new Web address everywhere. Put it in your ads. Put it on your sales materials. Put it on your shopping bags. Put it on your answering machine. Your online store is open 24 hours a day; you never know when somebody might call the store just to find the Web address.

Using a wildcard—placing an asterisk or another symbol after a word—means you welcome results with different word endings. Typing "gold+" means golden, goldfinger, and goldfinch are all acceptable. You'll get everything from James Bond movies, birds, the precious metal, and companies and people whose names begin with "gold" or "golden."

Comparing Different Search Engines

There are many different search engines—Yahoo!, AltaVista, Web Crawler, Infoseek, Excite, Lycos, HotBot, Google, and Northern Light. Each has its fans. Each has its own distinctive features, and some are better for certain searches than others.

There are two main types of search engines. The first, called the index type, scours the Internet for the same words or phrases you're seeking by using an automated computer program. These tend to return an enormous list of matches. The second, the directory type (such as Yahoo!), consists of broad subject areas where employees have organized the contents into smaller categories.

Search engines vary in terms of how they display results, how many pages they cover, how they index, and extra features they offer, such as searching newsgroups as well. Each offers detailed advice on how to best use its specific service.

An excellent site that compares search engines and offers reviews and news of updates is Search Engine Watch (www.searchengine.watch) from Mecklermedia, the Internet trade magazine publisher.

Many Web sites—companies, news, community to personal home pages—have their own internal search functions so you can easily look through the databases on their sites. Their rules and tips are often posted as well.

How Do I Register with a Search Engine?

Nearly every search engine has an "Add URL," "Add Page," or "Register Site" link. We recommend the following strategy to prepare for registration, and to use whenever you visit a search engine.

Preparation
- Know your Web site.
- Devise a standard 25-word summary for your Web site.

- Make a list of the 25 key words that will help people find your Web site.
- Consider what categories the site falls under. Get very specific.
- Be sure to <TITLE> your pages.
- Put <META> terms in your page headers.
- Be sure to put <META> and <TITLE> tags before any JavaScript. Some search engines will stop cataloging when they reach a JavaScript.

Search engine registration

- Every time you visit a new search engine, learn how to register. Ask your browser to find the words "Add," "URL," or "Register."
- Click on that link.
- Follow the registration instructions. Paste in your already prepared information.

Paying to register

Naturally, there are services on the Web that will, for a fee, register your Web site with search engines. These services typically cost less than $100 and will register your site with hundreds, if not thousands, of search engines. Never mind the fact that there are that many search engines out there, the question you need to ask yourself is "How much time do I want to spend doing this boring work, or should I spend some money and have a computer do it for me?"

Some pay-to-register sites:

World Submit (www.worldsubmit.com/)
Submit-it (www.submitit.com/)

Time is money, and if you have it, consider spending it.

Some Popular Search Engines

Search engines are crucial to your work on the Web. Some people will come to your Web site as a result of your business cards or e-mails, but most of your visitors will arrive from a search engine.

As you read this section, and as you browse search engines, ask yourself, "Who is looking on this page? What type of information are they trying to find?" We've also given you some Webmaster tips to help you improve your standing in the search engine's registry.

> **Tip**
>
> The most important tip on getting good results from search engines: Read the search engine's own help and tips sections for clear advice on how it works. Because search engines are owned by different companies, they don't work exactly the same way.

Yahoo! (www.yahoo.com)

In 1994, Yahoo! began humbly enough as Jerry and David's Guide to the World Wide Web, a directory of favorite Web sites compiled by two Stanford University graduate students in computer science and engineering with time on their hands.

Fast forward to today. Yahoo! Inc. went public in 1996 (it's listed on NASDAQ), was getting over 50 million page views per day (that's one billion per month) in 1997, and has over 25 million users per month in the United States according to Mediamark Research. It's a partner in a popular magazine, *Yahoo! Internet Life*, with the magazine publisher Ziff-Davis. Its Web site has become a hot spot for advertisers, from computer makers to booksellers. The first guide to navigate the Web, Yahoo! also became the first search engine to broaden its services well beyond searching. Other search engines have followed in its path in efforts to convince users to stay a while on their sites, which makes it better to win advertisers. Yahoo! now offers a spate of services, from free e-mail for anyone, chats, Internet guides for other countries such as Scandinavia, Japan, Korea, Italy, the United Kingdom/Ireland, a Chinese-language guide, an instant messaging paging system to reach other Internet users without using e-mail, and My Yahoo!, a customized home page of news and sports scores based on users' interests.

In 1998 it even launched its own commercial online service, powered by MCI Internet, offering lower rates than other commercial online services and ISPs.

AltaVista (www.altavista.com)

AltaVista began as a research project of the Digital Equipment Corporation, a major computer maker, and performed so well the company spun it off as a separate product. The biggest search engine in terms of the number of pages it indexes, over 100 million in early 1998, AltaVista can search newsgroups as well as the Web and searches in 20 different languages. Without the variety of categories and extra features on Yahoo!, AltaVista's home page is rather naked and unadorned. AltaVista is a tool for the serious searcher and is famous for scaring off novices by turning up millions of results for keywords or phrases.

AltaVista is known for its "refine" feature. This presents results arranged in different categories; you choose which to require or exclude to get a closer match. If you're ready to see more results, click "search"; if not, keep refining to narrow your search further. Plus and minus signs, "AND," and "NOT" are important in your original request since AltaVista is so literal minded.

Results—which appear with name, Internet address, and description—can also be limited by date or in the form of a question in its Advanced Search section.

Excite (www.excite.com)

Much like Yahoo!, Excite allows you to search by typing keywords or phrases or choosing a topic category. Excite also offers another helpful feature. Click "Search for more documents like this one" after a match you particularly like after a keyword search and similar results will obligingly appear, with name, Internet address, and description. Excite claims its search system understands synonyms and related concepts thanks to intelligent concept extraction technology. For instance, it knows pet grooming sites should be included in a search for dog care without your typing those exact words.

Categories of topics, or channels, include links to newsgroups and articles as well as Web sites. Channels range from autos, home/real estate, money/investing, relationships to travel. Today's news headlines, a people finder, a product finder (prices and reviews for products from computer equipment, games and toys, home and garden supplies), chats, and an instant messaging paging system are also found on its home page. In addition, Excite also offers free Web-based e-mail accounts to anyone, plus its own commercial online service for Internet access with special content, powered by MCI Internet. But Excite boasts a really nifty feature, NewsTracker, which acts as a free automatic clipping service. Pick a topic and NewsTracker will scan hundreds of top newspapers and magazines on the Web, fetching articles for you like a digital dog. But like any dog, it requires training. Click the "learn what I like" button after clicking several "liked it" buttons when it has behaved well, and it will retrieve more on-target articles for you. Look for it under "my NewsTracker topics."

Webmaster Notes

Yahoo allows you to register your Web site and have a measure of control over the content it displays. You will, however, have to spend a good deal of time figuring out the form and which category your site falls under.

Excite does not recognize <META> tags. Instead, it looks for common words and themes on the page and generates its own description. Be concise.

Webmaster Notes

Since Google prioritizes by links, the best way to improve your listing is to generate many links to your page. Ask a lot of people to link to you.

<META> tag usage is limited to a 200 character description and 1,000 characters. InfoSeek penalizes you for excessive duplicate word usage in your <META> tag.

HotBot supports <META> tags. You can send them e-mail if you don't think you're ranked as highly as you'd like.

Google (www.google.com)

Google is a relative newcomer to Web search engines. It claims to "delivers the most relevant search results—first and fast!"

It is speedy. Google's front page has no garbage sales pitches, ads, or extraneous links on it, so the page loads quickly. The first 10 hits are returned almost instantly. Google also claims to cache many of the pages that it visits. It's possible that a page that was deleted from its home server may still exist on Google.

A Web crawler search engine, Google ranks its links "based on the link structure of the Internet itself." In other words, it uses a complicated algorithm. You can't buy positioning on Google, and META tags are almost useless. More bad news for Webmasters: Google doesn't crawl the Web quickly, so it may take months for a site to register.

InfoSeek (www.infoseek.com)

Accompanying its categories—from Good Life (food and drink, home and garden, classical music, theater) to Kids & Family—InfoSeek features a healthy selection of recommended sites for each, like Zagat Survey and Epicurious for Good Life, and Parent Soup for family advice, plus appropriate tips and chats.

Besides searching newsgroups, newswires, and the Web, InfoSeek also uses intelligent agents, which it claims understand phrases and full questions in plain English. Plus and minus signs can also be used here. A helpful reference section includes a dictionary, thesaurus, and stock ticker symbols.

HotBot (www.hotbot.com)

Indexing over 80 million pages in early 1998, HotBot, owned by the company that owns *Wired* magazine, is the second biggest search engine in terms of number of pages covered. Nifty features allow you to specify a search on front pages of Web sites, or front and index pages of directories on sites, to limit the results. Or you can specify page title, time frame, which words may or must appear in the results, country, and even type of media (image, sound, or video files).

Besides these vast choices, you may opt to use the category directory. Top news sites, newsgroups, people finders, and classified ads are also available.

Lycos (www.lycos.com)

The only search engine that can look for sound and image files, Lycos also offers handy Web guide categories, its list of the top 5 percent quality Web sites, and free personal Web pages as well. (Lycos bought Tripod, a community site with free home page building tools, in 1998.) You can also choose if all your keywords must appear in the search results, if the exact phrase must appear, or if a close match is desired.

A helpful City Guide lists local events, restaurants, news, people finders, and company finders in your area.

WebCrawler (www.webcrawler.com)

Owned by America Online, this search engine is also organized into categories such as Arts & Books, Business & Investing, Careers & Education. WebCrawler rates the relevancy of its results on a scale from zero to 100. Another nice touch is its list of recommended sites, as well as chats and message boards, for each category. For example, the Louvre, Pulitzer Prize, and Dance Online sites appear on the Arts & Books page. The Entertainment page recommends National Enquirer Online, The Official X-Files Site, and The Smoking Gun (a site which exposes confidential documents from court and public records).

A small search engine compared to the big guns, WebCrawler is easy to use and searches newsgroups as well as the Web. It lets you choose if you want an exact match, partial match, or a match to any word or phrase in your search request, and claims its search system is based on natural language searching—ordinary English. The awkward search syntax of using "AND," "NOT," etc., is not needed. But if you miss using these terms, just click Advanced Search and they're yours, since WebCrawler seems to be in a let's-keep-everybody-happy frame of mind.

A people finder search, today's news headlines, and stock quotes are also offered.

Northern Light (www.northernlight.com)

A newer search engine, Northern Light searches the Web plus a special collection of over 3,400 magazines, journals, books, and reviews not covered by other search engines. Summaries of results found in its special collection are free, but reading each document requires a small fee. A low-cost monthly subscription is also available.

Northern Light automatically organizes its results into folders for easy reference by subject, type (such as product reviews or press releases), source (such as magazine, commercial, or personal Web page) and language, besides listing the results themselves. Click on the folder to read the documents listed by title, type, and Internet address.

Keyword searches can use "or," "not," plus and minus symbols, and quotes for phrases.

Deja News, Reference.com, Cyber Fiber, Liszt (www.dejanews.com, www.reference.com, www.cyberfiber.com, www.liszt.com/news)

Newsgroups are searched by these search engines. So if you want to monitor what's being said about your favorite hot topic in the thousands of discussion groups on the Internet, you can easily search by subject, newsgroup name, date, or writer of the posted messages.

A word to the wise: any gossip or badmouthing about a person or topic may be read by the person or persons involved. You may want to restrict personal comments to private e-mail messages, not public newsgroups.

Multiple Search Engines

It is possible to search using a bunch of search engines at once. Some of the multiple search engines you can use include the following.

Savvy Search (www.savvysearch.com/)

This uses two dozen search engines (like Yahoo!, Excite, and Infoseek), other giant databases (like the Internet Movie Database), and people finder directories. It works several search engines at a time, with results compiled by search engine, unless you specify otherwise.

MetaCrawler (www.metacrawler.com)

This queries only the major search engines—Yahoo!, Excite, AltaVista, Infoseek, Lycos, and WebCrawler—and combines the results in one list, noting which engine found the result. MetaCrawler can scour newsgroups as well as the Web. Searches can be limited to certain domains, a certain number of results from each search engine, or a certain continent.

Dogpile (www.dogpile.com)

Two dozen search engines are used by Dogpile, three at once. Newsgroups and newswires—news media that supply breaking news throughout the day such as Associated Press (AP) and Reuters—as well as the Web can be searched. If it finds fewer than 10 results, it will keep going until it reaches that number.

Updating and Maintaining Your Site

Make certain you have a plan for updating your Web site regularly. One reason for this is to drive return business. The theory is that if people return to your site and see that nothing has changed, they'll just click through. The real reason for this is to make the changes that people have suggested and to continuously refocus your business plan.

Be certain to incorporate customer and user feedback into the site. Consider offering a prize for the user who doesn't buy and tells you why he or she didn't buy. Absolutely update any pages showing time-sensitive sales, new products, and products that are out of stock.

Half a Dozen Web Site Pieces to Update Regularly

1. Event calendars. If you put an event calendar on your Web site, make certain that it's kept current. Nothing

> **Tip**
>
> Create an update policy. Even if you're working on your own Web site, make a solid commitment to yourself to update the site daily, weekly, or monthly. Consider posting this commitment as a way of publicly declaring yourself. Then you'll have to stay current; otherwise your visitors will know when you've been slacking.

Use Large Type

If you are going to read stuff online, make your life easier by blowing up the text size. Maybe I'm just getting old, but even with a 17-inch monitor, I don't like to squint.

In Internet Explorer, go to the View menu and click on Text Size "Large" or "Largest."

In Netscape, go to the View menu and click on "Increase Font" once or twice. Whenever you open up a new window, the font will default back to your original setting. If you like looking at the text at this size, go into your preferences and change the font size there.

disappoints a visitor more than to read about an interesting class or seminar that was held two years ago. Recommendation: Be certain to check and update any calendars monthly.

2. Addresses and phone numbers. Always always always keep your address and phone number current. Recommendation: As soon as the computer's plugged in at the new location, update the pages.

3. Personnel. If your company changes personnel, remove the names of ex-employees from the site and replace with the newcomers. Recommendation: Update every six months.

4. Links. You'll be amazed how many of your links to other people's Web sites die or are broken on a regular basis. It's disappointing to find out that your favorite site touting the artistic benefits of tofu hot dogs is no more, but that's part of life on the Internet. As a responsible netizen, you don't want to send people to dead links. Recommendation: Check all links and update them every 6 to 12 months.

5. Articles. If your site contains articles, try to add new ones and archive old ones on a regular basis. This is primarily a service to old visitors returning to the site, but new visitors will benefit from the increased depth of the site. Recommendation: Update at least every six months. At the very least, update annually.

6. Photos. People like to see new pictures on the Web. It's one of the things that brings people back. Parents or grandparents who post pictures of their kids should plan on doing this on a regular basis, or else they'll hear it from all the friends and relatives. Business site recommendation: Update photos at least every six months. Family site recommendation: For kids age birth—1 year, update monthly; 1—2 years update every three months, 2—4 years update every six months; 4—7 years, update annually; 7 years and older, let the kids do the updating.

Links and Cross-linking Your Site

Once your site is up and running, you might want to consider adding links to other sites. This seems somewhat counterintuitive. If you've spent so much time creating your Web site, why would you want to send someone to another Web site?

Believe it or not, not everybody wants to see your Web site in all its glory. Most Web users are looking for something specific. They want to get in and out quickly. The theory is that you don't want to waste their time on something that they don't need. In practice, however, the only way you'll get other Web sites to link to your Web site is by linking to their sites. This is called a link exchange.

The idea is that if somebody is searching for a clown to work at a birthday party, he or she might hit Adam Gertsacov's site by accident. If Adam can send this person along to another site that provides what he or she is looking for, he'll gain this user's good will as well as a reference from the birthday party clown's site if somebody is looking for a theater piece about fleas.

Web Rings

Web rings are another way to drive Web site traffic. A Web ring is a collection of Web sites revolving around the same subject—for example, martial arts schools, storytellers, and so on.

If you're running a special interest site, Web rings are a good way to connect to other similar Web sites. Just go to your Web page, click on the ring, and see where it takes you. Web rings are very random and aren't the best way to bring people to your site, but if you're not getting many visitors, it may be worth a shot.

Registering in a Web ring involves:

1. Finding the appropriate Web ring. Try visiting RingWorld (www.webring.com/).
2. Applying to join the Web ring. Most Web rings are filtered by human beings to avoid being used as staging areas for pornography. If your Web site is legit, being accepted into the Web ring shouldn't be a problem.

3. Creating your own if no Web ring is available. Details are available at RingWorld.
4. Copying the appropriate HTML and putting it onto your Web page. Web rings usually consist of a graphic and CGI link to the Web ring server. A click on the graphic takes the user to the next site in the ring. Just copy the HTML (which is detailed in the Web ring's instructions) and paste it into the Web page you want the ring to appear on.

Web Site Overhaul

You've got the best Web site in the world! It's fabulous. You're getting hits, you're getting e-mail. People are buying stuff (if you're selling anything). It's working!

Except it's boring. Something's missing. You get the feeling that if you just put a few more graphics on the page, or changed the font, then the whole thing would look a lot better.

Or maybe nobody's paying attention. You've got a great Web site, but nobody clicks on the links. Your home page lacks a certain pizzazz and you know that you can spice it up, but then all the other pages will look pathetic in comparison.

You need a Web site overhaul. (Or, if you prefer to think in cosmetic terms—a makeover.) The problem is that you've got a hundred or so Web pages within your site. It took you months to get them all to look just so.

If you've created a site template, it's easy. Just change the template, make sure it looks good, and then alter the template HTML in all the Web pages in your site.

For example, let's say you're getting married and every page in your Web site has the title "Welcome to my Web site." To change that to "Welcome to our Web site," all you need to do is perform the following find and replace.

Find: <TITLE>Welcome to my Web site</TITLE>
Replace with: <TITLE>Welcome to OUR Web site</TITLE>

You can do this in any text program, but if you've got a hundred pages in your site, this is where having an HTML generation program like Dreamweaver, Home Page, PageMill, or BBEdit

How Do I Get Someone to Link to My Web Site?

Send them an e-mail that says, "Hi there, I'm running a Web site about XYZ. The URL is www.XYZ.MYSITE.COM. Would you mind putting a link on your site?" Believe it or not, that's usually enough. If you want to be nice, send them the entire HTML the way you'd like it written.

```
<A HREF="http://
www.chelmtales
.com">The Brothers
Schlemiel — an
Excellent
Serialized
Novel</A></P>
```

becomes invaluable. The software will search your HTML across the entire site, find the old code, and replace it with the new code.

Quick Fix: Changing the Background Image for the Whole Site

Let's say you've got a background image called "backgroundimage.jpg" that you use in every file in your Web site, but you've gotten bored with it. So you find a new background image you want. Now what?

Rather than altering the HTML in every file and changing the link name, just rename the new background image file to "backgroundimage.jpg" and put it in the images subdirectory. Of course, this won't work if your new background image is a GIF. In that case, do a global search and replace throughout the site.

Debugging and Troubleshooting

After you've posted your Web site, you need to troubleshoot. It may look perfect on your computer. In fact, chances are that it will look and work great on your computer. After all, you've designed your Web site to look and work perfectly on your computer.

Remember, though, the World Wide Web is designed to work on anybody's computer. You don't know what software or hardware visitors to your site are using. Is their modem fast or slow? Is their processor fast or slow? Do they have a big monitor or a small monitor? Are they running Macintosh, Windows, or UNIX?

You need to debug. This is especially true if you have a program that generates your HTML for you. As frustrating as it seems, those time-saving programs, the ones that allowed you to do so much work without learning HTML, are the very ones that are most likely to mess your work up once it gets off your machine and onto the Net.

Troubleshooting Case Study— The Apeiron Photo Page

Here's an example of how a page layout program, with all the best intentions, can make your pages look worse if you rely on it rather than writing (or at least knowing) HTML. We redesigned the

---

External Links Tip

If you don't want to lose your visitors every time they click on a link outside your site, you can use the TARGET="_blank" to open the link in a new window. If you create an entire page of links to sites outside your site, you can use this code as a shortcut:

```
<HEAD>
<BASE TARGET=
"_blank">
</HEAD>
```

Now every link clicked in your links page will open in a new window.

Apeiron Foundation's Web site in Macromedia Dreamweaver. The templates feature was especially useful in creating an entire site that looked and felt the same. Unfortunately, Dreamweaver had some of its own ideas about what the HTML code should look like.

In the Photo Gallery section, we wanted to have direction arrows at the bottom of the page to take viewers through a tour of the Apeiron Foundation's Sustainable Living Model House. We initially designed the page on a Macintosh, and everything looked fine. When we went to our PC, however, we found that the right arrow was so far to the right that it was off the screen. We couldn't figure out why, so we just changed the arrow's alignment from RIGHT to LEFT. That put the right arrow immediately next to the left arrow, and then the text describing the picture immediately following it.

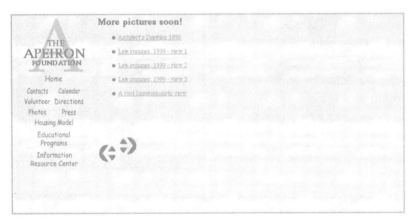

Macintosh Version

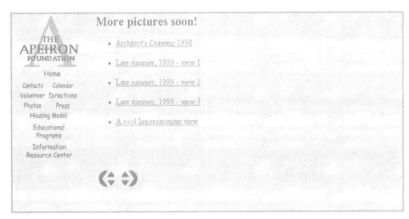

Windows Version

Not the most elegant fix, but a quick one. We adjusted each page and uploaded it to the Web. Then we took another look. This time, however, the page looked fine on our Windows machine, but strange on the Macintosh.

Notice the button bar at the bottom of the page. Rather than spending a half hour trying to troubleshoot this in Dreamweaver—wrestling with the program that writes HTML—we opened the file in SimpleText.

Here's the code we found. The comments we attached (bracketed between the comment tags <!— and ->>) weren't actually in the original Dreamweaver code.

```
<h2> </h2>
<!—the above line is unnecessary—>
<h3 align="center"> <br>
<!—both the h3 and align="center" are unneces-
sary—>
<a href="photo4.htm"><img src="../images/
arrowleft.gif" width="38" height="36"
align="left" alt="Previous Arrow"
border="0"></a><a href="home.htm">
<img src="../images/arrowright.gif" width="38"
height="36" align="left" alt="Next Arrow"
border="0"></a></h3>
<!—Don't forget to remove the close h3 tag —>
</td>
</tr>
</table>
<h2> </h2>
<!—the above line is unnecessary—>
```

So we made some changes directly to the HTML. We deleted the unnecessary lines and tags and adjusted the formatting a little so it would be clearer what the code meant.

```
<a href="photo4.htm">
<img src="../images/arrowleft.gif" width="38"
height="36" align="left" alt="Previous Arrow"
border="0"></a>
<a href="home.htm">
<img src="../images/arrowright.gif" width="38"
height="36" align="left" alt="Next Arrow"
border="0"></a>
</td>
</tr>
</table>
```

Bingo!

(By the way, after that mix-up, we scanned the site on the Mac and PC in both Internet Explorer and Netscape and found that it looked good on them all.)

Macintosh Version Fixed!

How to Update or Fix a Web Page

Updating or fixing a Web page is easy:

1. Open the old page in your favorite editing program.
2. Correct the mistakes.
3. Upload the corrected version.

Test Case: Aikido of Providence— Bad Directions

Directions to your office, business, or event are one of the most useful pieces of information you can post on the Web. When you design your directions, be clear and specific. If you like, use a tool like MapQuest (www.mapquest.com) to create directions to your location from a specific landmark, like another city or a particular highway, and copy them. You can even borrow the maps.

Then check out the directions. Drive them as written and see if you end up where you want to go.

Aikido of Providence spent a lot of time developing the directions to the community center where classes were held. They made sure that you could get to the center from anywhere in the area. Unfortunately, they forgot to include how to get into the building. Again, the fix was simple.

1. Open up the page "directions.htm."
2. Add the piece of information, "How to get into the building."
3. Save the file and upload it to the Web.

The Jewish Community Center of Rhode Island

401 Elmgrove Avenue
Providence, RI 02906
401-861-8800

From I-95

1. Take the Branch Avenue Exit East Towards Providence
2. Cross North Main Street
3. Go up hill onto Cypress Street (Kentucky Fried Chicken on right)
4. Cross Hope Street
5. Left at Morris Avenue
6. Right on Sessions Street
7. JCC is on the corner of Elmgrove and Sessions Street. Parking on street and in the rear.

From I-195

1. Take the Gano Street Exit
2. Head North on Gano Street toward Wayland Square
3. Cross Waterman and Angel Streets
4. Right on Lloyd Avenue
5. Left onto Elmgrove Avenue
6. JCC is on the corner of Elmgrove and Sessions Street. Parking on street and in the rear.

Aikido of Providence
Class Schedule | Class Descriptions | Instructor's Bio
Essays | Humor | Photos | Bookstore | Links
email: info@aikidoprov.com

The Jewish Community Center of Rhode Island

401 Elmgrove Avenue
Providence, RI 02906
401-861-8800

From I-95

1. Take the Branch Avenue Exit East Towards Providence
2. Cross North Main Street
3. Go up hill onto Cypress Street (Kentucky Fried Chicken on right)
4. Cross Hope Street
5. Left at Morris Avenue
6. Right on Sessions Street
7. JCC is on the corner of Elmgrove and Sessions Street. Parking on street and in the rear.

From I-195

1. Take the Gano Street Exit
2. Head North on Gano Street toward Wayland Square
3. Cross Waterman and Angel Streets
4. Right on Lloyd Avenue
5. Left onto Elmgrove Avenue
6. JCC is on the corner of Elmgrove and Sessions Street. Parking on street and in the rear.

Getting into the building

1. Park or walk around to the back of the JCC.
2. Go in the Fitness Center entrance. (This is the Northern-most door. It's not the preschool entrance.)
3. Check in at the Fitness desk.
4. Aikido classes are usually held in the Gymnasium on the third floor, but from time to time may be held in the aerobics room on the first floor. The staff at the Fitness desk will tell you where to go.

Aikido of Providence

Case Study: Aikido of Providence— New Content

In addition to providing lots of information about Aikido and the specific classes offered, Aikido of Providence's Web site includes a number of essays on Aikido and an entire section of Aikido jokes. Developed over a period of several years, these are the kind of in-jokes that only a select group of people (those who study Aikido) are likely to find funny. Nevertheless, the jokes keep coming.

One cold winter morning before class, Mark got the idea for a Letterman-style Top Ten list of the top ten reasons to take an early morning Aikido class. He jotted down the list in FileMaker Home Page and would have posted it directly, but discovered that when he tried to use the VALUE attribute in the numbered list Home Page would alter the tags by adding extra <LI> tags. So he opened it up in a less invasive editor, and marked it up into HTML.

```
<HTML>
<HEAD>
<TITLE>Ten reasons to take an early morning
Aikido class</TITLE>
</HEAD>
<BODY LINK="#660000" VLINK="#FF0000"
BACKGROUND="../images/yellowhaze.jpg">
<H2>Top ten reasons to take an early morning
Aikido class</H2>
<FONT SIZE=+1>
<OL>
<—Use the VALUE= attribute to count down, rather
than count up. —>
<LI VALUE="10">You get to watch the sun
rise.</LI>
<LI VALUE="9">Find out if your newspaper boy
really delivers on time.</LI>
<LI VALUE=8>It's great to get that "exercise
thing" out of the way.</LI>
<LI VALUE=7>Because we don't offer a midnight
class.</LI>
<LI VALUE=6>Be the first on your block to scrape
the ice off your car.</LI>
<LI VALUE=5>Coffee. Lots of coffee.</LI>
```

```
<LI VALUE=4>Gives new meaning to the term "I
just rolled out of bed."</LI>
<LI VALUE=3>You'll only have to shower once
today.</LI>
<LI VALUE=2>"Whuh?" is considered an appropriate
ki-ai.</LI>
<LI VALUE=1>Because you're insane............
(In a good way, of course)</LI>
</OL>
<P><FONT SIZE=-1>
<P> (Note for non-Aikido Students, a "ki-ai" is
that loud shout that they do in samurai movies
before they chop somebody's head off.)</FONT>
<P><A HREF="jokemenu.htm">Return to the Joke
Menu</A>
<BASEFONT>
<CENTER> <FONT COLOR="#660000">
<—Standard Aikido of Providence button bar.—>
<HR>
</FONT><A HREF="../index.htm">Aikido of
Providence</A><BR>
<A HREF="../schedule.htm">Class Schedule
</A> | <A HREF="../class_descriptions.
htm">Class Descriptions</A> | <A HREF=
"../schedule.htm">Instructor's Bio</A><BR>
<A HREF="../aikido_essays.htm">Essays</A> | <A
HREF="jokemenu.htm">Humor</A>
| <A HREF="../photo_album.htm">Photos</A> | <A
HREF="../store.htm">Bookstore</A>
| <A HREF="../links.htm">Links</A><BR>
email: <A HREF="mailto:info@aikidoprov.
com">info@aikidoprov.com</A>
<HR>
</CENTER>
</BODY>
</HTML>
```

Check Your Links!

Before you upload your Web pages, check your links. After you upload your Web pages, check your links. Just click around in your Web site and make sure that you're going to the right page.

After the page was created, he then had to alter the Index Page (to put the joke on the home page) and the joke menu page. Then all three pages were uploaded to the server.

Typical reasons that you're not going to the right page include typos, misspellings, and improper upper and lowercases on UNIX machines. Be sure that you've used the right extension: index.html is a different file than index.htm.

Check external links.

We'll assume that when you post your page all the external links (links to other people's sites) are up and running. Your internal links should never change, but over time other people's Web pages can vanish. You should perform a Web page external link check every six months.

The easiest way is to use an HTML page generation program like GoLive, which will automatically check the validity of any external link. Another method is to visit the web garage (http://websitegarage.netscape.com/), which will check one page for any dead links. Or you can click on all the links on your site. This can take a while.

Correct your mistakes as soon as people notice

When you design your own Web site, you know exactly where everything is. (In fact, one of the problems that corporations without Webmasters have is that nobody knows exactly what's on the site, but that's another story.)

That means that when there's a problem, you're the one who can fix it and fix it quickly. If you can't fix something immediately, then make a list of things to fix and schedule time to do it in the future.

Be aware that the longer this Web site repair list gets and the longer you wait to make the changes, the more likely it is to become a burden. Remember all those little repair jobs you have to do around the house? The lawn and garden chores? Updating, repairing, and fixing your Web site is part of the process of building an excellent Web page. Keep at it.

CHAPTER 13

Business on the Web

The World Wide Web is becoming an integral place to do business. If you're in business and you don't have a Web site, you're missing out on potential customers. Businesses are using the Web as an extension of their sales force—a storefront that's always open.

Creating an Online Presence

Here are the basic steps to creating an online presence for your business:

1. Register a domain name.
2. Begin designing your Web site.
3. Include the following information:
   - The name of your business
   - What you do or sell
   - How people contact you by phone, in person, by snail mail, and by e-mail
   - Events/specials you have planned
   - Questions for Web site content
4. Sign up for an Internet service provider and upload your Web site
5. Register with search engines
6. Improve your Web site on a regular basis; keep things current
7. Go about your business. You probably won't see results from your Web site for 6 to 12 months. If you see results sooner, great!

Before You Open Your Online Store

Is opening an online store easy? Absolutely. Maybe. Sometimes. No.

Well, can you tell me how much it costs? Nope. Not really. There are hundreds, if not thousands of companies out there who will gladly take your money in exchange for setting up an online storefront for your business. Some methods can cost as little as $30 a month. And there are ways of doing everything for free.

Three Quick Questions

1. What's your niche?

    According to Paul Graham at the Yahoo! Store, the size of your product's niche is more important than the types of products you sell. In other words, knowing your target audience and choosing which products to sell to them is vital online. If you already have a branded product, say custom-designed graphite golf clubs, then your target niche is golfers looking for an edge.

2. Who's the competition?

    Who else on the Web is selling what you sell? Don't answer nobody. Assume that somebody else out there has the same exact product and look for them. Look for somebody similar. What are they doing and how can you do it better?

    Perform online searches and find out exactly who your competition is. Examine their Web sites closely. How can you present yourself better or differently from them? How do your products differ from theirs? What do you do better? (If they do something better, steal the idea!)

3. Could you handle the orders?

    What would happen if you were successful beyond your wildest dreams? What if every person in Utah ordered your product for Christmas? Could you deliver within the required 30 days of charging their card? How would you handle returns? Who fills your orders and mails them out? Will you have to hire more help?

    The likelihood of having a massive surge of orders followed by a massive deluge of returns is slim but nevertheless possible. Our experience shows that success can often be as damaging to a business as a lack of sales. When you sell out of your stock, how long does it take to replenish it? If you're a custom-made furniture builder, the answer is a long time. Be aware of these potential problems going in, because you don't want to alienate your current and future customers.

What Is the Downside to Taking Orders on the Web?

In business, the bottom line rules. In other words, whenever you make a decision, you need to decide whether the cost and effort are going to generate a sufficient return within a reasonable period.

We're not talking about whether it's worth it to set up a Web site for your business; we're sure that's worthwhile. We're talking about setting up a Web site on your own server or on an independent Web hosting service. A Web site that's got the capacity to take credit card orders online and promise delivery. Is that worth it, economically? Let's be a little pessimistic as we look at the facts.

1. Establishing a business on the Web is expensive. To establish your own online store correctly, you've got to have your entire catalog online with photos and descriptions. You've got to have up-to-date prices. All sales need to be updated. You need to have a method of handling shipping and returns in-place. If you're going to go all out, expect to pay at least $1,000 to $5,000 on top of all other costs just to sell your stuff online.
2. You'll have to find new customers without cannibalizing your current sales. That means advertising. That means getting mailings out or doing e-mailings. That means generating publicity. How are you going to come up with the $1,000 to $5,000 in new business that the site costs?
3. You'll need to constantly update and maintain your online store. That could mean hiring somebody full time just to handle the online business. Add payroll costs for hiring additional help.

Transaction Net (www.transaction.net/), a Web site dedicated to "Enabling Markets Online," is particularly pessimistic. In their analysis of businesses selling merchandise online, they suggest that profits are "rare."

According to Transaction Net, the businesses that do well are small businesses with a very tightly targeted market, ones that provide excellent value and that specifically cater to Web users (that is, young middle class men).

You Mean I Shouldn't Take Orders Online?

No way! We didn't say that! Your Web site is open 24 hours a day. It has a potential international reach. This is not something you should ignore as a venue for sales. We'd just like you to consider other options before popping for $50 a month in Web hosting plus all the extras.

There are other ways to sell products through your Web site besides taking credit cards online. Most of the information in this chapter will address issues that affect ALL online businesses, not just those who have automated shopping carts.

Creating Your Online Store

What are the minimum requirements for any store?

1. A product
2. A location
3. A customer

What's true in life is also true online.

If you've been in business for any length of time, you've got some sense of your product line. You know what you're selling inside and out. You know what it is, what it looks like, what it's used for, how much it costs to buy, and how much you need to sell it for to earn a decent living.

You're also familiar with your customers. The longer you've been in business, the more aware you will be of who in the world wants to buy your product, and who actually spends the money. Over time you've developed a profile of your customers. You know what their shopping habits are, and you know how to treat them.

Selling online is not very different from selling in your store. It's impersonal, in the sense that you'll never see the face of your

Be Upfront

What do you think when somebody says, "I'm not trying to sell you anything"?

1. It's too good to be true!
2. They're lying.
3. What do they really want?
4. Oh boy, I'm interested; sign me up!

Chances are you didn't pick number four. Remember, online is like the real world. People are suspicious. Don't pretend that you're not in business. The more honest and upfront you are the better.

customer. At the same time, it's very personal. You still want your customers to feel as if they're the most important people in the world to you.

In this section we're going to tell you a number of different ways to sell from your Web site and offer a range of tips, tricks, and advice.

Create a Sales Area

Do you try and close a sale the moment somebody walks into your store? Don't you hate it when you walk into a car dealership and within seconds a vampire sales rep starts hovering by your shoulder?

The same is true of Web sites. People know that all business Web sites want to sell them something. They expect it. They just don't want to be hammered over the head with it.

The Catalog Button

As part of your site's navigation scheme, be sure that there is a link to your online catalog.

You can use catalog buttons, image maps, or just plain text links.

Here are two simple link codes:

```
<a href="catalog.htm"><img src="images/
catalog.gif" border="0"></a>

<a href="catalog.htm">Buy Stuff</a>
```

The first will link to the catalog page from the catalog image. The second will link to the catalog page from the text "Buy Stuff."

The Catalog Pages

These are the last pages visitors will see before they buy. You want to close the deal, right? Make everything simple and crystal clear.

The Keys to Creating an Excellent Business Web Site

1. *Make your site look good.* The more professional looking your Web site is, the more likely someone is going to take a chance and order from you. Don't let an unprofessional site stop you from starting; just continuously improve your Web site.
   - Get a good logo
   - Make page layouts similar
   - Add a search engine to find items within your site
   - Use buttons and fonts

2. *More quick design tips*:
   - Reuse images like buttons on multiple pages. These images will be cached in the viewer's browser's memory and will load quickly.
   - Keep page size small—a maximum page size of 50k including images is a good rule of thumb.
   - Consider a text-only version of the site with no images.

3. *List your prices.* How much does it cost? That's the bottom line, and if you don't list the price for your goods and services online, nobody's going to buy them. They're not going to call you for a price (unless it's a special deal), and they're not going to e-mail you. They're just going to click onto the next site.

   At the same time, be aware that Web buyers are very price conscious. Can you afford to undercut your competition? What happens if your competition reads your price and undercuts you?

4. *Include plenty of pictures in progressive image sizes.* People want to see what they're buying. They're not going to buy a T-shirt without being able to read what's on it. They don't, however, want to wait forever to look at a photo of something they don't want.

   Adopt a strategy of using thumbnails of every single product linked to larger images of products. Depending

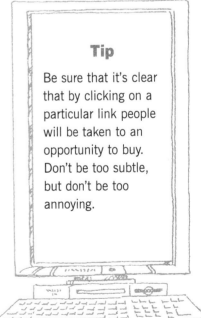

Tip

Be sure that it's clear that by clicking on a particular link people will be taken to an opportunity to buy. Don't be too subtle, but don't be too annoying.

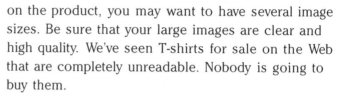

Alternative Ways to Say "We're selling something"

You don't have to call your site an online catalog. Here are just a few of the many alternative names you could give your online sales venue:

Store
Shopping Cart
Shopping Area
Cash Register
Buy Stuff
Checkout Counter
Bob, the Salesman
Sign Up
Order Here
Products
Shameless Commerce
   Division (thanks to
   Click and Clack at
   www.cartalk.com)

on the product, you may want to have several image sizes. Be sure that your large images are clear and high quality. We've seen T-shirts for sale on the Web that are completely unreadable. Nobody is going to buy them.

5. *Don't use frames.* Search engines ignore pages that have frames. That means that if you use frames in your online catalog, your items won't show up on sites like AltaVista.

6. *Go for international sales.* It's just as easy for someone online in Scotland to buy golf clubs from you as it is to buy from somebody in Edinburgh. And if your product is superior and your price (including shipping) is competitive, maybe a whole new sales area will open up for you. Be sure your site looks professional and that it establishes the validity of your service. Before you start selling abroad, get clear about the nitty-gritty details like shipping costs, customs, import and export tariffs, and any trade restrictions. The Yahoo! Store warns about fraud danger from orders placed to the following countries: Indonesia, Belarus, Pakistan, Romania, Macedonia, Lithuania, Russia, Egypt, Nigeria, Colombia, and Malaysia. Given the high risk and low return, they recommend not accepting orders from those countries.

7. *Include a nondisclosure policy.* People online can be weird about their privacy. Create a policy that lets your customers know that you won't be selling their names, addresses, and purchase information.

   If your Web site is at all targeted toward children, you should be aware of the federal law prohibiting the acquiring of information from children without their parents' consent.

8. *Give a physical postal mailing address as well as an e-mail address.* Don't hide out. People are suspicious enough. Let your customers contact you and be vigilant about answering their e-mails. Don't just set up an autoresponder. Customers will tell you what they want. They'll want new products, and they'll want you to improve your Web site. Listen to them.

The Quickest Way to Take Orders from Your Site

If you don't want to take credit cards over the Net, don't want to pay a ton of money for Web hosting, and don't want to spend your time debugging, there's a simple solution: Make an online order form that someone can fax or mail to you.

The simplest method is to just type in the page, have people print it out, and send it to you by fax or snail mail. A slightly more complicated method is to create a form on the page that they can fill out, print, and mail or fax. This method has the disadvantage of being low-tech. It's also the least expensive method we've seen. (*Note:* Don't have people e-mail credit card information to you. There are always rumors of "sniffer" programs that search out credit card sequences and steal them as they pass through the Net.)

This method is best suited for a business with a limited budget and a small product line. The major drawback is that it takes more work than paying by credit card. Don't underestimate this drawback. People are incredibly lazy, and people who are used to pointing and clicking are twice as lazy. (If you are a trusting individual, you could allow your customers to e-mail you this form and then send them a bill or send the merchandise C.O.D.) Still, for 15 minutes' work you could make some money.

1. Make a list of all the products you plan to sell.
2. Research shipping and handling costs.
3. Create an order form page. Feel free to steal and modify ours.
4. Post the page on your Web site and create links to it.

Here is Mark Binder's order form code and how it looks.

The Mark Binder Order Form

Print and fill out this form to purchase copies of our books. Then send it with your payment [personal check or money order only—**no credit cards**] to: Mark Binder, P.O. Box 4062, Providence, RI 02906.

NAME:_____
E-MAIL:_____
STREET:_____
CITY:_____ STATE___ ZIP____

[ ] This is a gift! Send it to:

RECIPIENT'S NAME:_____
E-MAIL:_____
STREET:_____
CITY:_____ STATE___ ZIP____
GIFT MESSAGE(s):_____

I want to order the following books (e-mail us for out-of-USA shipping charges):

[ ] CRUMBS DON'T COUNT (paperback edition) $5.00 (DISCOUNTED!)+$2.50 [book rate] or $3.50 [priority]

[ ] EVERYTHING BEDTIME STORY BOOK (paperback edition) $13.00 + $2.50 [book rate] or $3.50 [priority]

[ ] EVERYTHING BUILD YOUR OWN HOME PAGE BOOK (paperback edition) $13.00 + $2.50 [book rate] or $3.50 [priority]

All books are autographed. If you also wish your copy of any book to be inscribed, PRINT clearly the name of the person to whom the inscription is to be made. **Postage given is for one book only. Add 50 cents (book rate) or $1 (priority) for each additional book (if any) sent to the same address.**

Book Total: $_____

Total Amt Enclosed: $_____ [payment by personal check/money order only]

Mail form & Check to: Mark Binder, P.O. Box 4062, Providence, RI 02906.

This form uses HTML's forms to allow the user to type in information. The form could be printed or faxed. It was easy to make and loads quickly.

On the downside, it doesn't take into account multiple copies of books. And it makes the user fill it out and use a stamp. Results have been limited.

```
<HTML>.
<HEAD>
<TITLE>The Mark Binder Order Form</TITLE>
</HEAD>
<BODY BGCOLOR="#FFFFFF">
<H1><CENTER>
<FONT COLOR="#187534">The Mark Binder Order
Form</FONT></CENTER></H1>
<P><B><FONT COLOR="#AF0000">Print and fill out
this form</FONT> </B>to purchase copies of our
books.<FONT SIZE="-1"> </FONT>Then send it with
your payment [personal check or money order
only—<B>no credit cards</B>] to: <B><FONT
COLOR="#187534">Mark Binder, P.O. Box 4062,
Providence, RI 02906</FONT>.</B>
<HR>
<p>NAME: _____</p>
<p>E-MAIL:
_____ </p>
<P>STREET:_____ </P>
<P>CITY:_____ STATE____ ZIP_____</P>
<P><B><FONT SIZE="+1" COLOR="#AF0000">[ ] This is
a gift! Send it to:</FONT></B></P>
<BLOCKQUOTE>
<P>RECIPIENT'S NAME: _____</P>
<P>E-MAIL: _____</P>
<P>STREET:_____</P>
<P>CITY:_____ STATE____ ZIP_____</P>
<P>GIFT
MESSAGE(s)_____</P>
</BLOCKQUOTE>
<P>
<HR>
<FONT SIZE="+1">I want to order the following
books (e-mail us for out-of-USA shipping
charges):</FONT>
```

```
<P>  [  ] <B>CRUMBS DON'T
COUNT</B> (paperback edition) $5.00
(DISCOUNTED!)+$2.50 [book rate] or $3.50
[priority]</P>
<P>  [  ] <B>EVERYTHING BEDTIME
STORY BOOK </B>(paperback edition) $13.00 +
$2.50 [book rate] or $3.50 [priority]</P>
<P>  [  ] <B>EVERYTHING BUILD YOUR
OWN HOME PAGE BOOK </B>(paperback edition) $13.00
+ $2.50 [book rate] or $3.50 [priority]</P>
<P>All books are autographed. If you also wish
your copy of any book to be inscribed, <B><FONT
COLOR="#AF0000">PRINT CLEARLY</FONT></B> the
name of the person to whom the inscription is to
be made. <B>Postage given is for one book only.
Add 50 cents (book rate) or $1 (priority) for
each additional book (if any) sent to the same
address. <FONT COLOR="#AF0000">Also, please add
7% state sales tax (on price of book only) for
any book sent to Rhode Island.</FONT></B>
<HR>
<FONT SIZE="+1"> Book Total:  $_____</FONT>
<H3>Total Amt Enclosed: $_____ [payment by
personal check/money order only]</H3>
<H3> <b>Mail form &amp; Check to: Mark Binder,
P.O. Box 4062, Providence, RI 02906.</b>
</H3>
</BODY>
</HTML>
```

Auctions—An Alternative Way of Selling Online

Have you ever thought about auctioning off your goods or services? Chances are you haven't. You never even thought about it. It could be outside the traditional sales model for your product or service, but why not?

Online auctions are hot. They offer an inexpensive or free method of connecting buyers and sellers online. Who says that you can't sell your resume writing service in an auction format? Or that your titanium golf clubs wouldn't go for more than what you're

Tip

Give customers an opportunity on every page to go to the store. The Web is a spur-of-the-moment medium. Sales are made or lost in an instant.

currently selling them for? Who knows, maybe you've been under-valuing your goods and services. A free market auction could be the perfect way to find out what you're worth.

1. Choose an auction service. The charges for listing items on eBay, the best known and most popular service currently on the Web, are minimal. With eBay you can pay more to get a better listing. Services like Yahoo! Auctions are free but not as well known.

2. Register yourself.

3. Input your item(s). Your objective here is to list the items as simply and clearly without excessive hype.

   a) Give it a name or title that accurately describes it.

   b) What category does the item or service fall under? Try to be specific and accurate.

   c) Provide a detailed description. Include facts, details, the history of the item, what kind of condition it is in. The more information, the more likely your customer will be happy.

   d) Upload a good clear photo.

4. Choose the shipping method. How are you going to send the item? Do this research in advance.

5. Decide what kind of an auction or sales policy you're going to follow. There are several different methods of selling items in auctions. Pick the one that works best for you. For example, if you're selling multiples of the same item, that's called a Dutch auction.

6. What's the starting price? You want to go low with this to encourage buyers, but not so low that you're going to go broke or undercut your current business.

7. How long is this auction going to go on? How many days will you be selling for?

8. Go over any other options the service offers.

9. Carefully examine the auction page. Make sure that it's got no typos, no broken links, and that the images look good.

10. Submit the page and wait for the bidding to begin.

11. Most importantly, create a link on your home page to your auction! That's what ties your business to the sale.

Taking Credit Cards Online

Unfortunately, taking credit cards online isn't as easy as it ought to be. Or rather, it is easy—if you want to spend a fair amount of money to take orders.

Services are cropping up all over the place. Everyone from Microsoft to IBM wants to get a piece of the pie. In addition to increased domain hosting and service fees, expect to pay between 3 and 5 percent of your sales to the credit card company and Web host. To take credit cards online, you'll need to:

1. Establish yourself as a merchant who takes credit cards. This can be expensive and time consuming.
2. Create a secure storefront. Most Web hosts offer this option, but it will add at least $30 a month to your hosting costs. Web sites that don't require you to establish your merchant status cost at least $50 a month. In other words, you'd better be getting more than $50 a month in new sales from the Web to justify the storefront.
3. Make sure that your online prices are up-to-date.
4. Create a system for getting and filling the orders. You may need to hire someone else.

How Much Will It Cost to Take Credit Cards?

For those of you who have never taken credit cards, you're in for a shock. Here was information we gathered from a few random Web sites and banks:

Site 1

Volume Rate	2.49%
Transaction Fee	$0.30
Statement Fee	$9.95
Monthly Minimum	$25.00
Gateway Fee	$30.00/month
Complete Upfront Cost	$499.00

Site 2

One-time Service Set-up fee	$500 to $1,000
Monthly service access fee	$40 to $80
Transaction fees of	$0.20 to $0.60

Privacy Statements—TRUSTe

In the process of researching this book, we stumbled across TRUSTe, an "independent, non-profit privacy initiative dedicated to building users' trust and confidence on the Internet and accelerating growth of the Internet industry." www.truste.org is a place you can go to build your own privacy statement.

Their online wizard offers a step-by-step method to build a basic privacy/nondisclosure statement based on your Web site's needs and your long-term plans. It even offers guidelines for making sure that children don't accidentally give away information they shouldn't.

Site 3

Minimum—10 products	
Web Hosting (monthly)	$79.95
Transaction Fee	$0.25
Monthly volume charge	2.59%

Kagi.Com

When Mark wanted to sell subscriptions to his serialized novel online, he opted to go with Kagi.com. Established as a shareware clearing house, Kagi has evolved into an inexpensive storefront for everything from non-profits to tiny software developers. In addition to taking credit cards, Kagi also allows for check and fax credit card payment.

The upfront cost is zero, but the transaction cost is steep. Instead of paying $100 a month, you'll pay 15 percent of sales. If your sales are low and slow, this low overhead will be worthwhile, but with sales of more than a few thousand dollars, look into a less expensive per-transaction option.

Also, setting up the site takes a little longer, can be very confusing, and there's no hand-holding. Visit www.kagi.com for details.

Offer Alternative Payment Methods

Some people won't use secure order forms. They don't feel comfortable giving out their credit card numbers online. Don't lose that customer! Give them your phone number. Tell them what days you're open and what time they can call. Give them a fax number to fax their orders to. Never mind the fact that giving a credit card number by fax or phone is just as risky, they'll feel more comfortable and that's what you want.

Here's what one site put on their order form:

To order this product through our secure server, please fill out the form below and click "ORDER NOW." Orders may also be phoned in between noon and 6pm EST daily (555-555-1212) or faxed (555-555-1313).

What about Fraud?

It's a problem. If you're used to running your business face-to-face, then dealing with customers from around the country and around the world will seem very impersonal. How can you tell if someone's a thief? Use your gut instinct, and then check out suspicious orders.

How can I spot a fraudulent order?

It's not easy. If you take credit card orders over the phone or via the mail, you're liable to be defrauded. If you're selling orders online, the chances go up, mostly because it's so easy to submit fraudulent orders online. Here are some danger flags to watch out for:

- Multiple orders of expensive items. (If you're going to steal, why not steal big?)
- Anonymous e-mail addresses. It's very easy to get an almost untraceable e-mail address through sites like Yahoo and Hotmail. Double-check e-mail orders from that type of address.
- Odd or unusual shipping addresses. If you've never received an order from Pakistan, why are you receiving one now? Perhaps it's the global economy, or perhaps it's a stolen credit card number.

How can I avoid fraud?

- Always get authorization codes.
- Double-check strange orders. Try calling or sending an e-mail and see what happens.
- Use the Address Verification System (AVS), to see if the card number matches the billing address. Check an online map system (like MapQuest) to see if the mailing address is a valid one.
- If you think a card has been stolen, contact the person at the billing address.
- Require a signature for all suspect orders. If someone just ordered an entire set of golf clubs to be sent to Indonesia and they say to just leave it at the door, chances are it's a scam.

Getting Sales: Don't Hold Your Breath

If you post your store tonight, you probably won't make a sale tomorrow. It takes time to generate business anywhere. Online is just a bigger version of anywhere. Registering in search engines helps, but even they take time to post their findings.

Instant Stores

For those of you who really do need to sell things on the Web immediately and who have enough volume to justify the cost, here are two ways of managing your storefronts.

The Yahoo! Store

With the Yahoo! Store (http://store.yahoo.com/), you don't even need to build your own Web site. No extra software is necessary. You build the store online on their server using their point-and-click interface. When the site's finished you can choose between using your own address (www.everythingbook.com) or you can use stores.yahoo.com/everythingbook. You can either use their standard interface, which requires **no** HTML knowledge, or modify the site using tags and images.

Customers place secure encrypted orders, and you can receive orders either online from their Web server or they can be forwarded by fax or processed online. If you don't have a credit card merchant account, Yahoo! Store will help you set one up. Users include: NASA, Egghead Software, Vermont Teddy Bear, and Crabtree & Evelyn.

Cost: Stores up to 50 items: $100/month, stores up to 1,000 items: $300/month

Startup fee: None

Cancellation fee: None

Bonus: Store is listed in the Yahoo! Shopping

Note: Store listings must still be submitted to the Yahoo! directory

Amazon.com Auctions and zShop

In September of 1999, Amazon.com made news on the front page of the *New York Times* with their new zShop. zShop was

Case Study: Resumes Online at gresumes.com

The Internet creates demand for new businesses—and different models for old businesses. Kevin Donlin, owner of Guaranteed Resumes, started writing resumes professionally in 1995. His Web site, www.gresumes.com went live in early 1996. Before opening his own business, Donlin wrote marketing materials for FedEx, Pillsbury, and other big-name clients, so he knew how to sell his services. He had also worked in personnel departments, so he decided to combine his skills and experience to help his clients sell themselves in resumes. His motto: "Your Résumé Will Get Results. Or It's FREE."

In the early phases of his Web site, Donlin only took credit card orders via fax. Now, although visitors to his Web site are able to give their credit card information through a secure order form, he still processes the orders by hand. Instead of having an expensive online order processing firm handle the credit card information, the orders are sent to him via a secure order form and via fax from his Internet service provider.

"I don't want to cede control to an online order processing firm just yet," Donlin explained, "My volume doesn't justify it either."

By using this combination of high- and low-tech, Donlin is able to keep his costs way down.

"The secure forms are free from my ISP, www.aitcom.net," he said. "I use a standard swipe terminal and lease it for about $20 per month."

What do you think works best about your Web site?

"The personal touch," Donlin said. "SO many of my competitors say 'we' and 'our' throughout their sites to try to sound like a Fortune 500 company, when in reality it's just a housewife in curlers or a guy in his apartment. I'm one guy giving one-to-one service, and I like to come across like that on the Web. I'm comfortable selling on paper, too, which is an essential skill for creating a Web site that works."

What works worst—but you can't change it because…

"I'd like to ditch my Yellow Pages ad completely, as these are the lowest-paying and highest-maintenance clients I have! Online, I'd like to get a higher alphabetical ranking in Yahoo! to unseat all those clowns with names like "123 Resumes" or "AAA Resumes"—they get loads of hits just because of their name."

designed as an inexpensive way for new businesses to put their wares up on the Web quickly. Basically, Amazon took their auction listing technology and removed the auction element.

They also created the Amazon.com Pro Merchant Subscription, a simple method to bulk upload item listings, and instituted a fixed fee for the service. The theoretical advantage to retailers is that you become a part of the Amazon.com Web. With more than 12 million customers, Amazon is one of the most active sites on the Web.

How much does it cost? As with everything on the Web, the answer is it depends.

- To list individual items in zShop costs 10 cents per 14-day period, or a little over 20 cents a month.
- To list an item in an auction costs an additional 10 cents per 14-day period. Now we're up to 40 cents per month per item.

The introductory Pro Merchant Subscription offer was a steal: $10 setup plus $9.99 a month for a listing of up to 3,000 items! After 12/31/99, Amazon said that the setup fee would be $50 and that listing rates would be as follows:

0—500 items:	$29.99/month
501—1,000 items:	$49.99/month
1,001—2,000 items:	$79.99/month
2,001—3,000 items:	$99.99/month

In other words, as a Pro Merchant, if you listed 100 items, you'd pay 29 cents per month per item. If you listed 200 items, you'd pay 14.5 cents per month per item. If you listed 2,000 items, you'd pay only 5 cents per month per item.

There are extra options you can purchase to improve the chances that somebody will click on your item listing.

Bold listings: $2 per listing. (This puts your item in <B> boldface)
Category features: $14.95 per listing. (With this option, Amazon says, "We'll emphasize your item in a comprehensive Featured List on the pages related to your category.")

Home page featured listings: $99.95 per listing on the Auctions or zShops home page. (This puts your item right on the Auctions or zShops home page, right in the "Featured Today" section.)

Amazon.com will also levee a completion fee. This is essentially the same cost that a credit card company would charge you for their services. For zShops, the fee is based on the sale price. For Auctions, the fee is based on the amount of the winning bid.

Final Price	Closing Fee
$0.00—$25.00	5.00%
$25.01—$1,000.00	$1.25 plus 2.5% of amount over $25.00
$1,000.01 and up	$25.63 plus 1.25% of amount over $1,000.00

Let's say you run a hardware store and have an excess supply of 500 different kinds of high-quality nuts and bolts. Let's say that these babies run an average of $5 retail, but you're willing to sell them for $4.50 plus 50 cents shipping over the Web. (You paid $2.50 per bolt. Never mind the fact that you've got an incredibly overpriced product.)

You don't need a Web site to sell them, just set up a zShop. Assuming that Amazon sticks to its year 2000 price schedule, here's what it will cost you:

$50 setup
$29.99 per month
$0.23 per bolt

To break even, you'd have to sell 22 nuts or bolts to cover the startup costs, plus another 14 per month. After that, you'd make $2.27 profit—not counting the time and effort it takes to set up and upload the system, shipping costs, or the cost of returns.

How do you set up a zShop?

1. Go to www.amazon.com.
2. Click on the zShops tab.
3. Click on "open your own zShop today."
4. Click on "register."

Ignore Get Rich E-mails

Not long ago we got an e-mail like this:

ACCEPT CREDIT CARDS OVER THE INTERNET *** NO SETUP FEES Good Credit / Bad Credit/ No Credit **** NO PROBLEM****!!!

It Just Doesn't Matter— Everyone Gets Approved

No Up front Fees For Application-Processing While Others Charge You From $200 TO $350 To Get Set Up!

WE CHARGE ZERO FOR SETUP FEES!!

We didn't even bother following up. Why? Because they only gave us a toll-free number. No Web site. Any company that will allow you to accept credit cards over the Net has to have a Web site.

5. Enter your name, e-mail address, and a password.

6. Fill out the registration form. *Note:* You'll be asked for a credit card number. According to Amazon, they use this number to "verify your identity." It's their method of tracking you down if you turn out to be a thief or fake. They say that they'll notify you of fees before charging your card. Tip: Use an American Express Card for this.

7. Enter a zShop "nickname." Pick this name carefully, since that's how you'll be listed throughout zShop. Warning: Don't make a mistake here. If you do, you're stuck with it, or have to begin the process again.

8. Read the terms of use carefully. Amazon.com doesn't allow you to sell certain items.

9. Click on "List a zShop listing" or "List an auction."

10. Enter:
    a) zShop title (80 character limit).
    b) Item description (4,000 characters) and you can use HTML.
    c) Add a picture—or rather a pointer—to a URL on your Web site.
    d) Dollar price. How much does it cost?
    e) Quantity—How many are you selling?
    f) Shipping and handling fee.
    g) Select which category the item falls under.
    h) Choose the payment and shipping methods.
    i) Enter your shipping policy.

11. If you have a lot of items to enter, click on "Use Amazon.com's bulk loader."

12. Follow the instructions for:
    a) Building your template.
    b) Reviewing your preferences.
    c) Uploading your file.
    d) Reviewing and submitting items.

Amazon.com's service is new, and during its first few months of operation it was inexpensive enough to warrant a serious look by online sellers. As it moves past the initial offering stage, though, the costs go up, which means your profits go down.

Furthermore, there's a lot of concern that by using Amazon's service you'll be losing valuable marketing information. Amazon keeps all the click-through information secret, so you won't know what other products in your site the buyers looked at and rejected. There was also concern that if Amazon saw a particular product was selling well, they could copy the product and sell their own branded version of it.

Finally, buried in Amazon's Terms of Use was a Velocity Limits clause. Essentially, it says that Amazon sets secret limits on the dollar amount and number of transactions for both buyers and sellers during a set period of time. In other words, if you do too much business, Amazon won't keep processing your stuff. AND they won't tell you until you reach that limit.

Banner Ads

Banner Ads—those annoying, blinking, changing, long-time-to-download advertisements—are a fact of life on the Web today. From a consumer point of view, banner ads are a good thing since they theoretically provide income to Web page designers. That means that somebody is paying America's Finest News Source, The Onion (www.theonion.com) to keep its Web site up and running. From a business point of view, a well-designed banner ad placed on the right Web site or in front of the right person can bring eyeballs to your page, and possibly sales.

Like any form of advertising, banner ads rely on repetition and luck. You have to have the right eyeball at the right time. With banner advertising, however, you might have a little bit of an edge. For example, if somebody does a search on Yahoo! (www.yahoo.com) for pornography, is it any wonder that the banner ads on their search result are for X-rated Web sites? If you search for the palm-top, Palm III, the banner ad is for 3Com, the manufacturer of the Palm. This is direct marketing at its finest and quickest.

Can I Get Banner Ads on My Web Site?

Yes. There are hundreds of firms on the Web that will be happy to clutter up your Web pages with banner ads. Will you get rich this way? Probably not.

One of our biggest problems with banner ads is that they take eyeballs away from your site. Still, if you want to try them, go ahead.

As a Business, How Can I Maximize My Banner Ad Effectiveness and Minimize Cost?

1. Negotiate with your banner service. How are you paying? Are you paying for each time the banner pops up (per impression)? Are you paying each time somebody clicks on the banner (per click-through)? Are you paying per sale (if somebody actually buys something).

2. Design a nice ad. Don't make it too annoying. Give information in the ad. Tell people what you're selling and what the price is. Offer special deals.

3. Make sure you're targeting the right audience. If you're selling power tools, don't get placed on a site for students of Russian literature.

4. Get marketing information back from the service. What demographics are actually clicking through?

5. Re-evaluate the ads frequently. How much money did you make from that ad? Did it work? Is it cost-effective to continue?

For more information on this topic, visit our Web site at businesstown.com

CHAPTER 14

Web Page and Web Site Creation Tools

OPEN

Photo Album

OUR TRIP

RECIPES

BIRTHDAY'S

ANNIVERSARIES

After all those pages on how to write your own HTML code, we're going to give you some good news: **You don't need to learn any HTML.** There are dozens of programs that will generate HTML code based on the text and images you put in.

Then why would you ever want to learn HTML? Because the page generation programs can be quirky. You'll spend hours wondering why you can't do something, or why the application keeps making your pages look strange.

Still, for someone interested in posting a Web site now, without much in the way of study or suffering, a page generator program is the way to go.

This section is going to cover a lot of ground. We're going to look at a bunch of the most common personal and professional home page and site creation tools.

Why? Well, you could learn HTML, or you could just type your pages into one of these tools and mark them up through the software. It's easy, just like using a word processor for the Web.

You can put together entire Web sites without ever learning HTML. We'll say that again. You can write and design entire Web sites without ever learning HTML. We know Web designers who pride themselves on not learning HTML. They'll use any and every tool to put together their sites as long as they don't have to code.

Over time, however, you'll find that every markup and site tool has its own quirks. This one won't display a page correctly. That one will do strange things with images. You may find yourself wrestling with the software, trying to figure out how to get it to do what you want.

Still, we know that most of you don't want to learn HTML. And that's fine with us. We're here to help.

If you're a beginner, we've tried to include reviews and instructions for the software that comes with your computer. We know we won't have touched on every program. By the time we finish writing this book, more, better, and newer programs have already been released. You can go to the Web to find the latest and greatest. Or you can just start with what you've got on your machine. Don't forget to look at your hard drive. You might already have one or more of these applications on your computer for free.

For each tool, we're going to walk you through the creation of a basic home page. We'll also focus on some of that tool's best features. And we'll try to be critical as well.

We'll also take a look at the step-by-step process of how to create a simple HTML code page in a number of editors. We'll scan the features, look at the advantages and liabilities, and take a look at the steps.

Pluses and Minuses of Using HTML Page Generation Programs

PLUS	MINUS
Quick to learn	You may never learn HTML
Web pages in minutes	Software can write bizarre code
You may never need to learn HTML	Takes too long to debug
Link checking—makes sure that all files are there	The more complex the software, the more expensive
Some programs offer external link checking—do the pages you're linking to in other sites still exist?	
Graphics manipulation and control	
Ease of creating image maps	
Site management features	
Many programs contain FTP file upload and download	

How to Use This Chapter

If you already have some of this software, skip to that part of the chapter. If you're shopping for software, skim around and see which program looks best for you. For another look at this subject, see the Web Monkey's article, "The New WYSIWYG Editor Shootout" at http://www.hotwired.com/webmonkey/99/19/index1a.html?tw=eg19991025.

An Expert on Web Site Dreaming and Design

Tiffany Lee Brown (magdalen@well.com) is a writer, editor, and content provider who is obsessed with user experience issues. Here is her advice on creating a Web page.

Really spend some time with the overall architecture (where you'll put what, how it will be navigated) before you do anything else. Let it roll around in your mind; savor it like a fine new idea for a brilliant new book, then:

1. Write down everything you want on your site.
2. Divide it into three categories: things you really need on Phase One of your site, things that are stupid or self-indulgent or unnecessary (trash these), and things you might want to incorporate later on when you have more time/money/whatever.
3. Decide what will go where. Make a sitemap of it. Think about leaving space for those items you might use in Phase Two.
4. Picture yourself clicking through all the stuff you just created. Really follow each path. You'll undoubtedly find trouble spots here.
5. Force someone else to go over it with you, because the outside perspective could be very valuable.
6. Then worry about stuff like Dreamweaver, HTML, and designing of individual pages. The work above can save you tons of time if you do it up front.

Case Study: Uncle Gonzo

Uncle Gonzo is a strange duck. He lives on the fringes of society and enjoys tinkering with many different computer programs. We'll be looking at his work as a method of analyzing a number of different software packages.

Graphics: clip art
Browser: Netscape, Explorer (latest versions)
HTML generators: All of them

Here's the basic page we're going to create. The page title will be Uncle Gonzo's Wacko Home Page. We'll give it a background image. The header will say, "Hi, I'm Uncle Gonzo." The page will have four images: Uncle Gonzo's face, his blender, a picture of the White House, and a pointer.

We're going to put in a table with the box score for the latest Red Sox game. There will also be some text, which we'll change from program to program to keep things interesting.

Before we start, we've already created a directory called "gonzo" with a subdirectory called "images." In the images subdirectory are the following images: gonzoface.gif, blender.gif, whthouse.gif, pointer.gif, and backgroundjpg.

By the way, this isn't the most brilliant page in the world—but it's an easy one to learn with.

Entry-Level HTML Page Editors

Notepad or SimpleText

These two programs are simple text editors. Notepad comes free with Windows, and SimpleText comes free with Macintosh systems. They're nothing more than stripped-down word processors. They are very useful for writing HTML code. But they don't help you at all.

Features
- Small programs that work on any computer; no special memory requirements
- Doesn't add extra or useless code
- Work every time and never crash

Drawbacks
- No WYSIWYG; you have to save and preview
- Minimal text manipulations; limited find/replace
- No spell-check
- No HTML check
- No image adjustment
- No table generation or other cool software features
- Limited file size; you won't be able to open or edit pages with a lot of text

FrontPage Extensions

FrontPage has the capability to create easy CGI-like extensions in Web browsers. If you want to post a spreadsheet on a Web page, simply insert that "component." In order to run FrontPage extensions, the Web host must support FrontPage extensions and the Web browser must be Internet Explorer.

Making the Gonzo page in Notepad or SimpleText—total time: 10 minutes.

1. Type in the HTML basics:

    ```
    <HTML>
    <HEAD>
    </HEAD>
    <BODY>
    </BODY>
    </HTML>
    ```

2. Create the title. Below the <HEAD> tag, add the following (*Note:* you'll need to use the escape sequence &#8217 if you want to use a smart single quote):

    ```
    <TITLE>Uncle Gonzo&#8217;s Wacko Page</TITLE>
    ```

3. After the <BODY> tag, type in the text:

    ```
    Hi, I'm Uncle Gonzo.
    This is my home page.
    I'm a carpenter. I live in a bunker somewhere in the
    United States. I'm very worried about corruption in the
    government. I think they're watching me. Do you floss your
    teeth?
    My Blender.
    This is my blender. I like it.
    Aside from my power tools, this is the one piece of heavy
    equipment I'd take on a desert island. Click on the
    blender for some of my recipes.
    Be Ever Watchful
    Red Sox Yankees
    10 2
    My Next Page.
    ```

4. Now we'll mark it up. Type <H1> tags around the first line. Type <H2> tags around the second line. Type <H3> tags around "My Blender," "Be Ever Watchful," and "My Next Page." Type <P> in front of each paragraph, except "Aside from my power tools..." Type <BR> in front of "Aside from my power tools..."

Making the baseball box score table:

5. In front of the words "Red Sox" type:

    ```
    <TABLE BORDER = 1 WIDTH=T"40%">
    <TR ALIGN = CENTER>
    <TD>
    ```

In front of the word "Yankees" type:

```
</TD><TD>
```

In front of the number 10, type:

```
</TD></TR><TR ALIGN = CENTER><TD>
```

In front of the number 2, type:

```
</TD><TD>
```

After the number 2, type:

```
</TD></TR></TABLE>
```

6. Just for fun, save the file as simplenote_gonzo.htm. Open your favorite browser and open the file. It should look like this.

Adding background, images, and links:

7. Change the <BODY> tag to read:

    ```
    <BODY BGCOLOR="#FFFFFF" BACKGROUND="images/background.jpg">
    ```

8. After the first header, put Uncle Gonzo's face:

    ```
    <CENTER><IMG SRC="images/gonzoface
    .gif" ALT="Me!" ALIGN=bottom></CENTER>
    ```

9. Change the blender header line to:

    ```
    <A HREF="recipes.htm"><IMG SRC=
    "images/blender.gif" ALT="my blender" ALIGN=right BORDER =
    0></A><H3>My Blender.</H3></A>
    ```

10. Change the <P> in front of "This is my blender" to:

    ```
    <P ALIGN = RIGHT>
    ```

11. Change the words, "Be Ever Watchful" to:

```
<A HREF="http://www.whitehouse
.gov"><IMG SRC="images/whthouse.gif" ALT="The Conspiracy?"
WIDTH=135 HEIGHT=123 ALIGN=LEFT></A>Be Ever Watchful<TABLE
BORDER=1 WIDTH="40%" HEIGHT=40>
```

12. Before the words "Next Page" type:

```
<A HREF="nextpage.htm"><IMG SRC="images/pointer.gif"
ALT="Pointing" WIDTH=135 HEIGHT=60 ALIGN=RIGHT></A>
```

13. Change the <H3> tag before "Next Page" to read:

```
<H3 ALIGN = RIGHT>
```

14. Save and take a look!

Your final SimpleText Notepad code should look like this:

```
<HTML>
<HEAD>
<TITLE>Uncle Gonzo&#146;s Wacko Page</TITLE>
</HEAD>
<BODY BGCOLOR="#FFFFFF" BACKGROUND="images/background.jpg">
<H1>Hi, I'm Uncle Gonzo.</H1>
<CENTER><IMG SRC="images/gonzoface.gif" ALT="Me!"
ALIGN=bottom></CENTER>
<H2>This is my home page.</H2>
<P>I'm a carpenter. I live in a bunker somewhere in the United
States. I'm very worried about corruption in the government. I
```

```
think they're watching me. Do you floss your teeth?
<A HREF="recipes.htm"><IMG SRC="images/blender.gif" ALT="my
blender" ALIGN=right BORDER = 0></A><H3>My Blender.</H3>
<P ALIGN = RIGHT>This is my blender. I like it.
<BR>Aside from my power tools, this is the one piece of heavy
equipment I'd take on a desert island. Click on the blender for
some of my recipes.
<H3><A HREF="http://www.whitehouse.gov">
<IMG SRC="images/whthouse.gif" ALT="The Conspiracy?" WIDTH=135
 HEIGHT=123 ALIGN=LEFT></A>Be vigilant<TABLE BORDER=1
WIDTH="40%" HEIGHT=40></H3>
<TABLE BORDER = 1 WIDTH=T"40%">
<TR ALIGN = CENTER>
<TD> Red Sox </TD><TD>Yankees </TD></TR>
<TR ALIGN = CENTER><TD>10 </TD><TD> 2 </TD></TR></TABLE>
<A HREF="nextpage.htm"><IMG SRC="images/pointer.gif"
ALT="Pointing" WIDTH=135 HEIGHT=60 ALIGN=RIGHT></A>
<H3 ALIGN=RIGHT>My Next Page.</H3>
</BODY>
</HTML>
```

FileMaker Home Page

FileMaker Home Page 3.0 (Windows, Macintosh $99, www.filemakerpro.com) used to be one of our favorite home page authoring programs. It hasn't changed much in the past year or so, which is both good and bad.

For basic home page creation, Home Page is excellent. You can have a simple page up with links in a matter of minutes. Its menus are clear, and all the important features are easy to access. With one click you can create a bullet list or insert an image link. It includes a built-in FTP client, so you can upload your site without having to leave the program.

Features
- Easy image adjustment; transparency and interlace tool alters GIFs instantly.
- Import text and images quickly and easily.
- Clip art and template library with more than 2,500 images and 45 ready-to-alter site templates.
- Setup assistants/wizards to help beginners.
- Site management and FTP capabilities.

- Link verification; will check the whole site for broken links and repair them.
- Spell checking.
- Global find and replace throughout single page or the entire site.
- Special Assistant to create forms that connect directly to Web-based FileMaker Pro databases.

Drawbacks
- Although making tables is easy, FileMaker doesn't show tables exactly as they appear in browsers.
- Not recently updated; no support for cascading style sheets.

Making the Gonzo page in FileMaker Home Page—total time: 12 minutes
1. Open FileMaker Home Page
2. Type:

```
Hi, I'm Uncle Gonzo.
This is my home page.
I'm a carpenter. I live in a suburb in the Hinterlands.
I'm very worried about the Internal Revenue. I haven't
paid my taxes since Vietnam.
My Blender.
This is my blender. I use it daily.
I make fruit juice drinks and some soups in it. Click on
the blender for some of my recipes.
Be Vigilant
My Next Page.
```

3. Add a background image and a title by clicking on the Edit menu, "Document Options."

   Click on the "Set" button next to the word "Image" and select background.jpg from the images folder. Click on Parameters tab and type:

```
Uncle Gonzo's Home Page
```

   Click OK. *Note:* If you want to use a smart single quote in Home Page, you'll need to edit the page in HTML and change the dumb quote to the escape sequence ’

Marking it up:
4. Go to the first line and either select Heading 1 from the Format menu or click on the word "Normal" and select Heading 1.
5. Change "This is my home page" to Heading 2 and "My Blender" and "My Next Page" to Heading 3 the same way. *Note:* You can use key commands

1, 2, and 3 to change the headers quickly. (Use the Apple key on a Macintosh and the Control key on a PC.)

6. Select from "My Blender... my recipes" and click the Right Alignment button. Do the same for "My Next Page."

7. Close the space before "I make fruit juice drinks" by clicking before "I make," hitting the backspace key, and then selecting "Line Break" from the Insert menu.

Making the baseball box score table:

8. Click after the word "Be Vigilant," then click on the Table Icon or click "Insert Table."

9. Type "40" into the "Width" box and change "Pixels" to "Percent." Then close the table edit window.

10. Enter the table information:

   Click in the first cell and type "Red Sox." Click the "Center" Icon in the ruler.

   Tab to the second cell and type "Yankees." Click the "Center" Icon in the ruler.

   Tab to the next row, first box and type "4." Click the "Center" Icon in the ruler.

   Tab to the next cell and type "2." Click the "Center" Icon in the ruler.

Adding images:

There are three ways to add images in FileMaker Home Page. You can click on the image button, select "Image" from the "Insert" menu, or you can drag and drop your images onto the page.

11. Open the images folder.

12. Drag gonzoface.gif after the first header. Move the cursor in front of the image and press the return key. Click the Center Icon.

13. Drag blender.gif in front of the words "My Blender." Double-click on the image or select "Show Object Editor" from the Window menu. Type "My blender" in the Alt Label box, in the Border box type a zero ("0"), and select "Right" Alignment. (While we're at it, click on the Uncle Gonzo picture and type "Me" in the Alt Label box.)

14. Drag the files whthouse.gif before "Be Vigilant." Type "The enemy?" in the Alt Label Box, and select "Left" Alignment.

15. Drag the files pointer.gif before "My Next Page." Type "pointer" in the Alt Label Box and select "Right" Alignment.

Adding links:

16. From the Window menu, select "Show Link Editor." Select the blender and in the link editor next to URL, type "recipes.htm."
17. Select the White House and type "http://www.whitehouse.gov."
18. Select the pointer and type "nextpage.htm."

Done! Click the "Preview in Browser" button to see how it looks.

```
<HTML>
<HEAD>
<TITLE>Uncle Gonzo's Home Page
Uncle Gonzo's Home Page
Uncle Gonzo's Home Page</TITLE>
</HEAD>
<BODY BGCOLOR="#FFFFFF"
BACKGROUND="images/background.jpg">
<H1>Hi, I'm Uncle Gonzo.</H1>
<CENTER><IMG SRC="images/gonzoface.gif" WIDTH=80
HEIGHT=135 ALIGN=bottom></CENTER>
<H2>This is my home page.</H2>
<P>I'm a carpenter. I live in a suburb in the
Hinterlands. I'm very worried about the Internal
Revenue. I haven't paid my taxes since Vietnam.</P>
<H3 ALIGN=right><A HREF="recipes.htm">
<IMG SRC="images/blender.gif" ALT="My blender"
WIDTH=92 HEIGHT=135 BORDER=0 ALIGN=right></A>My
Blender.</H3>
<P ALIGN=right>This is my blender. I use it
daily. <BR>I make fruit juice drinks and some
soups in it. Click on the blender
for some of my recipes.</P>
<H3><A HREF="http://www.whitehouse.gov">
<IMG SRC="images/whthouse.gif" WIDTH=135
HEIGHT=123 ALIGN=left></A>Be
Vigilant<TABLE BORDER=1 WIDTH="40%">
<TR>
<TD>
<CENTER>Red Sox</CENTER>
</TD>
<TD>
<CENTER>Yankees</CENTER>
```

```
</TD>
</TR>
<TR>
<TD>
<CENTER>4</CENTER>
</TD>
<TD>
<CENTER>2</CENTER>
</TD>
</TR>
</TABLE>
</H3>
<H3 ALIGN=right><A HREF="nextpage.htm">
<IMG SRC="images/pointer.gif" WIDTH=135 HEIGHT=60
 ALIGN=right></A>My
Next Page</H3>
</BODY>
</HTML>
```

BBEdit

Bare Bones Software (www.bbedit.com), the company that makes BBEdit, has as its motto "Software that doesn't suck." BBEdit is known in Web design circles as the preferred text editor for anyone writing straight HTML code. Marking up is a cinch. It contains an extensive tag list. The table editor in Version 5.1.1 is superb. An excellent text editor with HTML markup and checking capabilities, version 5.0 includes a table generator, FTP support, and more.

Available for Macintosh only.

BBEdit 5.1.1 — $119

BBEdit Lite 4.6 — Free!

Features

- Superb text editor
- Easiest way to mark up text with code
- Table builder
- FTP uploads and downloads
- Superior find and replace
- Choose HTML commands based on HTML version (2, 3, or 4)

Drawbacks
- Doesn't display WYSIWYG
- May be difficult for beginners to understand
- A very confusing menu/tool bar structure until you become accustomed to it, after which it's very useful

Making the Gonzo page in BBEdit—total time: 12 minutes

In BBEdit, you can enter everything just as you would in Notepad or SimpleText, or choose from the menus, tool bars, and buttons.

Enter the basic page:
1. Open BBEdit and click "New HTML Document" from the File menu.
2. Type "Uncle Gonzo's Wacko Home Page" in the Title box. Click OK.
3. After the <BODY> tag, type:

```
Hi, I'm Uncle Gonzo.
This is my home page.
I'm a carpenter. I live in a tree house in the middle of
Arizona. I don't horde food, but I do have 200 jars of
pennies. I live on canned food. Peas and ham are my
favorite vegetable and meat combination.
My Blender.
This is my blender. I use it daily.
I blend my fruit, but not my meat or vegetable (usually).
Click on the blender for some of my recipes.
Be On Guard
My Next Page.
```

Marking it up:
4. Highlight "Hi, I'm Uncle Gonzo" then open the HTML Markup Tool from the Markup menu. Select H1 from the Heading tool button.
5. Select "This is my home page" and click H2. Select "My Blender" and click H3.
6. Select "My Next Page"; click "Heading" from the Heading tool button. Click 3, Align "Right," and OK.
7. Select the line "I'm a carpenter..." and click the Paragraph button then Align "Left."

8. Select from "This is my blender...recipes." Click the Paragraph button then Align "Right."

9. After "This is my blender." click "Break" (or type <BR>)

Making the baseball box score table:

10. Click after "Be on Guard" and click Table Builder.

11. Select "Add Table" from the Table Menu.

12. Type "Yankees" in the first cell.

   Tab to the next and type "Red Sox."

   Tab to the next cell and type "4."

   Tab to the next cell and type "3."

13. From the File Menu select "Send to BBEdit."

Adding images and links:

14. Click after "Hi, I'm Uncle Gonzo.</H1>." From the Markup menu select Block Elements "Center." Click the Image button from the HTML Tool bar. Type "images/gonzoface.gif" in the Src box and "It's me" in the Alt Box. Click apply.

15. Click before the <H3> in front of the word Blender. Click the Anchor button from the HTML Tool bar. Type "recipes.htm" in the Href box.

  Click the Image button. Type "images/blender.gif" in the Src box and "My blender" in the Alt Box.

  Click Border "0" (zero).

  Click Align "Right." Click apply.

16. Before the words "Be On Guard" insert the link to http://www.whitehouse.gov and the image "images/whthouse.gif" with the Alt "Secret Cabal" Align "Left" as in step 15.

17. Insert the link to nextpage.htm with "images/pointer.gif" with the Alt "pointer" Align "Right."

18. Click "Body Properties" from the tool bar and type "images/background.jpg" in the Background box.

Done! Preview your work.

Netscape Composer

This is a surprisingly good page layout program. It does everything you'd want, simply and intuitively. Why is that surprising? Because it's free, bundled with Netscape Communicator (www.netscape.com).

Features
- WYSIWYG Page Composition.
- Clear and logical menus and buttons.
- Table builder.
- FTP uploads through Publish command.
- Very easy to mark up text.
- Nice access to keyword and META tags without coding.
- Spell checker.

Drawbacks
- Inaccurate WYSIWYG—the page in the browser will often look different than it does in Composer, especially around images.
- No drag and drop movement of images.
- Does some strange and unexpected things. Inserts <DIV> tags at its own whim.
- Makes copies of images without asking you.

Making the Gonzo page in Netscape Composer—total time: 14 minutes

Enter the basic page:

1. Open Netscape Composer and select Page Title from the Format menu. Type "Uncle Gonzo's Wacko Home Page" in the Title box.
2. Click on Colors and Background. Click the Image box in the Page Background section. Choose the file /images/background.jpg. Click OK.
3. Type:

```
Hi, I'm Uncle Gonzo!
This is my home page.
I'm a carpenter. I carve bears out of giant
logs with my chainsaw. I live in a log
house in the Pacific Northwest. My own
smoked salmon straight from my wood-smoker
 is the best. Especially on the bagels I
have flown in from New York City.
My Blender
```

```
This is my blender. I call him Gus. We once
tried blending a salmon, like they did on
Saturday Night Live when it was good.
Blended salmon wasn't good. I do have some
excellent blender recipes. Click on the
blender for some of my better recipes.
Be careful
My Next Page
```

Marking it up:

4. Go to the line that says "Hi, I'm Uncle Gonzo." Click the menu box that says "Normal" and select "Heading 1." Find the alignment button on the menu bar and choose Center, or select Align/Center from the Format menu.

5. Go to the line "This is my home page" and select "Heading 2." Go to "My Blender," and "Be Careful" and select Heading 3 for each of them.

6. Go to "My Next Page" and select Heading 3. Click the alignment button on the menu bar and choose Right, or select Align/Right from the Format menu.

7. Select from "This is my blender...recipes." Click the alignment button on the menu bar and choose Right, or select Align/Right from the Format menu.

8. Click after "This is my blender." [QA]Type: <Shift><Enter>

Making the baseball box score table:

9. Click after "Be careful" and click the Table Icon.

10. Set the Number of Rows to 2 and the Number of Columns to 2.

11. Click the Table Width box and type "40" percent of window.

12. Click Insert.

13. Type "Red Sox" in the first cell. Tab to the next and type "Yankees." Tab to the next cell and type "12." Tab to the next cell and type "4."

14. Highlight and select the text from Red Sox through the number 4 and choose Center from the alignment Button.

Adding images and links:

15. Click after "Hi, I'm Uncle Gonzo." Type <Enter> key. Click the image button from the menu bar, or select Image from the Insert Menu. Choose

"images/gonzoface.gif" in the Image File Name or Location box. Type "It's me" in the Text box. Click OK.

16. Click the image button from the menu bar, or select Image from the Insert Menu. Choose "images/blender.gif" in the Image File Name or Location box. Type "Gus the blender" in the Text box. Click the right alignment option in the "To see wrapped text, view page in Navigator Window" box. Click the Link tab and type "recipes.htm" in the URL (Page Location) or File box. Click OK.

17. Before the words "Be careful," insert the link to http://www.whitehouse.gov and the image "images/whthouse.gif" with the text "The Trilateral Commission Headquarters," wrapped text left as in step 16.

18. Insert the image "images/pointer.gif" with the text "pointer," Align "Right," and link to nextpage.htm.

By now, you've noticed some weird stuff happening. Netscape Composer has scrawled some weird text link next to the White House image and created links on the text "My Blender" and "My Next Page."

19. Clean up the page by deleting the weird link line. Select "My Blender." Choose Link Info from the Format menu and delete the text in the URL box. Select "My Next Page." Choose Link Info from the Format menu and delete the text in the URL box.

Done! Preview your work.

Once again, you'll notice a significant difference between the way the page looks in Composer and in the browser. This is one of the primary frustrations users have with most page layout applications—they don't always do what they're supposed to do. What you see on the page isn't what's in the HTML code. And they add strange stuff. Make any adjustments you want directly to the source code, or fiddle around in Composer until you get it the way you want.

AppleWorks

AppleWorks is the latest version of the program suite ClarisWorks. As a one-stop program suite, it is superb, including an excellent word processor, a drawing program, a paint program, a database program, and a spreadsheet program.

Included free with every iMac, the latest version of AppleWorks allows its users to create and maintain Web pages with relative ease. There is also a Windows version of the software, although at this time Apple is no longer actively marketing the product to non-Macintosh owners.

Features
- Ability to design complex pages, including graphics
- Superior word processing
- Spreadsheets in the document can perform calculations
- Ability to create GIFs easily from drawing or painting program
- Easy to create text GIFs (type text, copy it, click the arrow tool, and paste the text image into the document)
- Excellent on-screen help

Drawbacks
- Doesn't display WYSIWYG; the way the page looks in AppleWorks bears only some resemblance to the way it looks in a browser.
- Not a true HTML development package.
- Can't label images, align images, or get rid of borders
- In AppleWorks, images are part of the document and not contained in a separate folder. In other words, it doesn't hold a pointer to an image the way an HTML file would. When generating HTML, these images are converted into GIF format and saved in the root directory.

Making the Gonzo page in AppleWorks—total time: 15 minutes
Enter the basic page:
   1. Open AppleWorks and select Word Processing. Type:
```
Hi, I'm Uncle Gonzo.
This is my home page.
I'm a construction worker. I work long
hours on the tops of skyscrapers, and when
I come home, I like to relax and work on my
web page.
My Blender
This is my blender. I never used to use my
blender, but then my wife left me and took
my false teeth with her. For a long time, I
couldn't eat anything unless it was run
```

```
through the blender. I have new teeth now,
but I've gotten used to the texture.
They're Going To Get Us
My Next Page.
```

2. Select "Show Button Bar" and then choose "Internet" from the button bar options.

3. Set the background image by click on the Configure HTML Button (it looks like a little globe with a few musical notes below it). Click on "Set Background Image" and choose "images/background.jpg."

Marking it up:

AppleWorks is a word processor first and an HTML generator second. It doesn't take advantage of HTML heading tags in its Style menu. Just arrange the page as you would a word processing page.

4. Select "Hi, I'm Uncle Gonzo." Click the center button. Adjust the font size to 18 using the Font menu.

5. Select "This is my home page." Adjust the font size to 16 using the Font menu.

6. Select "My Blender." Adjust the font size to 14 using the Font menu. Do the same with "They're Going To Get Us" and "My Next Page."

7. Select from "My Blender" to "... I've gotten used to the texture." Click the right justify button.

8. Right Justify "My Next Page."

9. Click after "This is my blender." Type <Enter>.

Making the baseball box score table:

10. Click the Spreadsheet button in the Tools Bar. (It looks like a non-religious cross.)

11. Click anywhere on the page and drag until you have a two-by-two grid.

12. Type "Yankees" in the first cell. Tab to the next and type "Red Sox." Click on cell 2A and type "4." Tab to the next cell and type "3."

13. Highlight and select the text from Red Sox through the number 4 and choose Alignment/Center from the Format Menu.

14. Click on the entire spreadsheet, select "Cut" from the Edit menu. Then click the Word Processing icon on the tool bar. (It looks like an uppercase A.) Click after "They're Going To Get Us." Type <Enter> and then paste the spreadsheet into the document.

Adding images and links:

15. Click after "Hi, I'm Uncle Gonzo." Type <Enter> key. Choose Insert/Image from the File Menu. Select gonzoface.gif from the images folder.

16. Click after "My Blender." Choose Insert/Image from the File menu. Select images/blender.gif.

17. Select the blender image. Click the Create URL button from the Internet Toolbar. Type "recipes" in the name box and type "recipes.htm" in the URL box. Click OK.

18. Click before the words "They're going to get us." Follow the instructions in step 15 to insert the image whthouse.gif and a link to http://www.white-house.gov.

19. Click after "My Next Page." Follow the instructions in step 15 to insert the image pointer.gif and a link to nextpage.htm.

20. Click Save As HTML. Call it "Uncle Gonzo's Wacko Page.htm." Select "Overwrite Image Files."

21. Preview the document.

You'll see that the general page layout is close to what we've been working for, but that image features like BORDER=0 and ALIGN=RIGHT aren't working. There are no image names either. Also, AppleWorks has created a slew of images from its own memory rather than references to the images in the images directory.

Adobe PageMill

PageMill (*www.adobe.com*) was one of the first HTML markup applications on the market. Designed to be used by beginners, it tends to be simple and easy to work with. It continues to be updated and improved. Features include building and enhancing Web pages, uploading and managing your site, and simple management of images and sounds. For Windows or Macintosh; Adobe PageMill 3.0—$79

Features
- Excellent WYSIWYG
- Built-in FTP and site management
- Link checking includes verifying the existence of external links
- Useful tool bar; can easily click and modify most text/graphics
- Good documentation/help files

Drawbacks
- Darn few
- Occasional differences between WYSIWYG and browser appearance

Making the Gonzo page in Adobe PageMill—total time: 12 minutes

Enter the basic page:

1. Open Adobe PageMill. Type:

```
Hi, I'm Uncle Gonzo.
This is my home page.
Some of my best friends think I'm crazy as
a loon. They don't know that I won the
Michigan lottery in 1987. That's why I have
my old car up on blocks. Nobody comes
looking for you that way.
My Blender
This is my blender. It doesn't work any
more. I've been thinking about going down
to the hardware store to buy a new one, but
I'm not sure that's where they sell
blenders. Someone told me I could buy one
online. That might be smarter. Then, only
the UPS guy would know that I was receiving
packages. Click on the blender for some of
my recipes.
The IRS is Our Enemy
My Next Page.
```

2. Click the Title box and type "Uncle Gonzo's Wacko Page."
3. If the Inspector isn't open, click "Show Inspector" from the View menu. Click the page tab. Click the "File" button and select "background.jpg."

Marking it up:

4. Click on "Hi, I'm Uncle Gonzo." Click on the Paragraph tool option and select "Heading/Largest" (or select it from the Format menu). Click the center button.
5. Select "This is my home page." Click on the Paragraph tool option and select "Heading/Large." Repeat for "The IRS is Our Enemy."
6. Select "My Blender." Click on the Paragraph tool option and select "Heading/Large." Click the right alignment button.
7. Select from "My Blender" to "... some of my recipes." Click the right alignment button.

8. Click after "This is my blender." Type <Enter>.

9. Right Justify "My Next Page." Click on the Paragraph tool option and select "Heading/Large."

Making the baseball box score table:

10. Click in front of "The IRS is Our Enemy." Click the table button.

11. Set Rows to 2, Columns to 2, and Table Width to 40 Percent. Click OK.

12. Type "Red Sox" in the first cell. Click the center button. Tab to the next and type "Yankees." Click the center button. Tab to the next cell and type "3." Click the center button. Tab to the next cell and type "1." Click the center button.

Adding images and links:

13. Click after "Hi, I'm Uncle Gonzo." Type <Enter> key. Click the Insert Object button or select "Object/Image" from the Insert menu. Select images/gonzo-face.htm. Click on the image and type "It's me" in the Alternate Label box.

14. Click after "My Blender." Click the Insert Object button or select "Object/Image" from the Insert menu. Select images/blender.htm. Click on the image and type "It's a broken blender" in the Alternate Label box.

15. Select the blender image. Click the Right Align button or choose Align Object/Right from the Format menu. Click in the Link To box, or select "Make Link" from the Edit Menu. Type "recipes.htm."

16. Click before the words "The IRS is Our Enemy." Follow the instructions in step 14 to insert the image whthouse.gif with the alternate label, "Where's the party?" and a link to www.whitehouse.gov.

17. Click after "My Next Page." Follow the instructions in step 14 to insert the image pointer.gif with the alternate label "pointer" and a link to nextpage.htm.

Done! Save and preview in the browser.

Microsoft FrontPage 2000

Microsoft FrontPage (www.microsoft.com) is a top-notch HTML generation program. Entering and editing the page is quick and simple. Markup is easy. It includes new HTML features like dynamic HTML and cascading style sheets, an automatic spell-checker, and site management. One of Microsoft's selling points is its interactivity with other Microsoft application components, such as Word, Excel, and

PowerPoint. It's possible to create a report in PowerPoint and manage it on the Web in FrontPage. For work groups, FrontPage can allow multiple users to work on the same "Web." Also, FrontPage has seamless integration with ActiveX components and with Microsoft Access databases stored on your Web site.

Microsoft FrontPage 2000—$149

Windows 98, Windows NT

Features

- Quick access to Microsoft ActiveX components
- Easy interactivity with other Microsoft applications such as Word, Excel, and PowerPoint
- Quick database connectivity
- Nice link checking, site view

Drawbacks

- Many features require hosting on a Windows NT server
- Requires a lot of clicks to make changes; element modification windows don't stay open

Making the Gonzo page in Microsoft FrontPage—total time: 11 minutes

Enter the basic page:

1. Open Microsoft FrontPage. Type:

```
Hi, I'm Uncle Gonzo.
This is my home page.
I'm an unemployed spy for the former Soviet
Union. Ever since the fall of the Berlin
Wall, I've had a hard time. Nobody believes
me when I tell them, because nobody could
imagine what a Soviet spy would be doing in
Kansas. Well, I can't tell you.
My Blender
This is my blender.
I use my blender primarily as a method of
foiling the listening devices various
intelligence agencies have planted
throughout my home. It's also great for rum
drinks. Click on the blender for some of my
recipes.
The Conspiracy Lives
My Next Page
```

2. Right click anywhere on the page. Click "Page Properties." Click in the Title box and type "Uncle Gonzo's Wacko Page."

3. Click the Background tab. Click the Background Picture checkbox. Browse for or type "images/background.jpg." Click OK.

Marking it up:

4. Click on "Hi, I'm Uncle Gonzo." Click on the paragraph formatting section of the ruler (it's the leftmost box with the word "Normal" in it) and select Heading 1.

5. Click to "This is my home page." Select Heading 2 from the same box. Click to "The Conspiracy Lives" and select Heading 3 from the paragraph formatting box.

6. Select "My Blender." Select Heading 3 from the paragraph formatting box.

7. Select from "My Blender" to "... some of my recipes." Click the right alignment button.

8. Click to "My Next Page" and select Heading 3 from the paragraph formatting box. Click the right alignment button.

Making the baseball box score table:

9. Click after "The Conspiracy Lives." Click the table button and select a 2 x 2 table.

10. Right click on the table and select "Table Properties." Change Specify Width to 40 percent.

11. Type "Red Sox" in the first cell. Click the Center button. Tab to the next and type "Yankees." Click the Center button. Tab to the next cell and type "5." Click the Center button. Tab to the next cell and type "4." Click the Center button.

Adding images and links:

12. Click after "Hi, I'm Uncle Gonzo." Type <Enter> key. Click the Insert Picture From A File Button or select "Picture/From A File" from the Insert menu. Select images/gonzoface.htm. Right click on the image and select Picture Properties. Type "It's me" in the Alternative Representations Text Box.

13. Click after "My Blender." Click the Insert Picture From A File Button or select "Picture/From A File" from the Insert menu. Select images/blender.htm. Right click on the image and select Picture Properties. Type "My blender eats bugs" in the Alternate Label Box.

14. Type "recipes.htm" in the Default Hyperlink Location box. Click the Appearance tab. Select "Right" from the Layout/Alignment box. Click OK.

15. Click before the words "The Conspiracy Lives." Follow the instructions in steps 13 and 14 to insert the image whthouse.gif with the alternate label "Capitalistic Cabal" and a link to http://www.whitehouse.gov. Select "Left" from the Layout/Alignment box. Click OK.

16. Click after "My Next Page." Follow the instructions in steps 13 and 14 to insert the image pointer.gif with the alternate label "pointer" and a link to nextpage.htm.

Done! Save and preview in the browser.

America Online

America Online offers two methods of creating a home page: the incredibly simple but limited and the more complex. Type in Keyword: Publishing Tools. AOL has an assortment of Web publishing tools available.

1-2-3 Publish is a Web-based method of setting up very simple home pages using only your AOL browser. Hotdog Express is a more advanced page development tool that is available for free for 32-bit Windows 95 and Windows 98 users.

Making the Gonzo page in 1-2-3 Publish—total time: 5 minutes

1-2-3 Publish is very limited but also fairly quick (if you don't count the time you spend waiting for AOL).

1. Type in Keyword: Publishing Tools and click on 1-2-3 Publish, or go to http://hometown.aol.com/hmtwn123/ index.htm.

2. Choose a background color for the page.

3. Choose the top picture. (Select "No Image.")

4. Type "Uncle Gonzo's Wacko Page" in the Web Profile.

5. Choose a divider style (pick one).

6. In the basic facts sections type:

```
Title: Hi, I'm Uncle Gonzo
Text: This is my home page.
I've been living in a root cellar for
fifteen years. Now I've got access to their
personal computer and I'm messing with
their finances. If you find this page,
```

```
don't tell anyone.
Title: My Blender
Text: Sam is my blender. It's amazing what
you can do with a blender in a root cellar.
Dirt makes a great binding.
Title: Bar the Doors
Text: Yankees 5, Red Sox 0
```

Under "Online Links" type the following:
```
Title:           My links
Link Name:       My Recipes
Link Address:    recipes.htm
Link Name:       The Enemy's Home
Link Address:    http://www.whitehouse.gov
Link Name        My Next page
Link Address:    nextpage.htm
```
7. Click "Preview My Page."
8. Click "Save."

Done! As you can see 1-2-3 Publish is pure AOL, that is to say it works but severely limits your options.

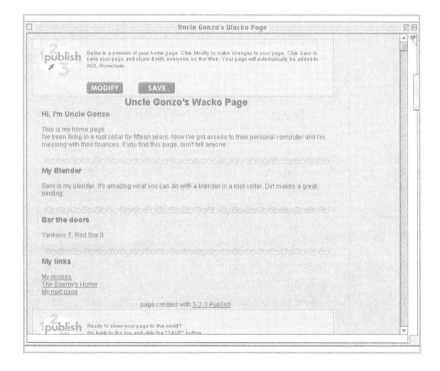

Professional-Level HTML Page Editors

These next two page editors can more than handle Uncle Gonzo's requirements. In fact, for beginners, they're probably overkill. If you're just maintaining a simple site, you don't need to spend the $299 on Macromedia's Dreamweaver or Adobe's GoLive. On the other hand, if you're maintaining a number of sites, interested in creating complex page layouts, or making site-wide changes, these tools might be just the trick.

To decide which tool you want, read our blurbs, read some reviews, and download the demos from the Web sites. Be aware that once you get one of these professional-level HTML page editors, it may be hard to go back to simpler times.

Macromedia Dreamweaver

www.macromedia.com
$299—Mac and PC
Bundled with BBEdit for the Mac and HomeSite for PC.

Dreamweaver has long been considered one of the premier page development tools. Its main selling point to HTML coders is the fact that it won't mess with your code—unless you tell it to. That means it won't go around adding and deleting tags just because its internal logic tells it to. After you've played around with some of the entry-level page editors, you'll understand the reason that this is important.

Some of Dreamweaver's strongest features are its Template and Library tools.

We have already discussed the benefit of creating a basic template for your site with basic background images and links already set up. Instead of rewriting the same code every time you create a new Web page, you open your template file and modify that.

Dreamweaver's Template tool allows you to easily create templates and apply them to new pages. Even better, though, when you modify the template, you are given the option of modifying every page in the site that uses that template. In a matter of minutes your entire Web site can have a completely different look and feel.

The Library tool is very similar to the Template tool. You create a set of content elements, say a tool bar, and save them in the library. This tool bar can be dragged and dropped into any page. When you change the library version of the tool bar, that tool bar changes on every page.

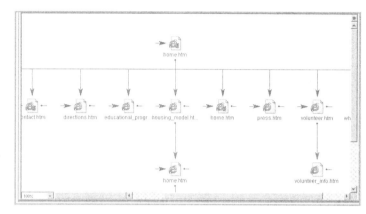

Dreamweaver also allows easy management of multiple sites. It has extensive cascading style sheet support. For graphic designers, you can create pages with pixel precision and then adapt them for any browser you like. Programmers can modify Dreamweaver's default coding to change the way it handles tags. And even though you can get at the background HTML directly in Dreamweaver, it still comes bundled with BBEdit and HomeSite, two premier non-WYSIWYG HTML coders. Dreamweaver also has excellent link checking, including a fine external link checker to be sure that all your links are live.

Adobe GoLive

www.adobe.com

$299—Mac and PC

GoLive lets you take two different approaches to designing Web pages. You can lay them out the traditional way, from the top down, inserting elements as you go. Or you can use the Layout Grid to place images, text, and other elements directly where you want them on the page.

This Layout Grid is GoLive's coolest feature. You drag a grid onto a page, and then drag and drop your elements. When you preview your page, it should look exactly as it does in GoLive. The Layout Grid works by creating some very complex tables within tables. It can make your HTML very, very long, but it looks great in a browser.

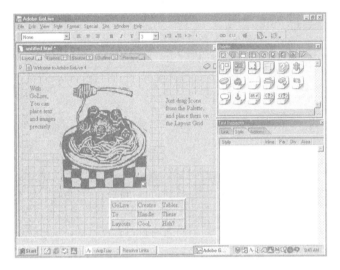

GoLive has excellent bug checking, with a cute little green bug that gives you a quick visual read on which pages have links that are dead. Click the green bug in any page and GoLive immediately takes you to the unruly link for quick repair.

One of the problems with GoLive, though, is click overkill. Sometimes it seems to take much longer to make changes in elements than it might to just rewrite the HTML code in the first place. Once again, though, site-wide changes are easy to make. GoLive works well with other Adobe products.

Other Professional HTML Page and Web Site Editors

As with anything on the Internet, new tools appear almost daily. Here are some of the other HTML editors and site management tools currently available.

HoTMEtaL Pro
SoftQuad (www.SoftQuad.com)
$129—PC Only

Fusion
NetObjects (www.netobjects.com)
$299—PC Only
Bundled with HomeSite

Drumbeat
Macromedia (www.macromedia.com)
$499—PC Only
Designed to assist with e-commerce

CHAPTER 15

Special Features

Calendars, E-Mail Lists, and a Few Cool Tricks

In this chapter we'll tell you how to set up online calendars and e-mail lists, and give you a few extra cool Web site tricks that are mostly just for fun.

Web-based Calendars

In the Internet world, where everyone and every business is online, the first place to check for the date of an event is the World Wide Web. What time was that seminar in New York? Check the Web site. When do they offer aerobics classes at the local gym? Go online.

Here are some uses for online calendars:

- Post regular events, like class schedules, sales, or meetings
- Announce special events. When is that money management seminar? When is your band going on tour, and where?
- Notify your family about your barbecue.
- Keep track of anniversaries.
- Coordinate your schedule with others, like your boss, coworkers, or family.
- Check your own calendar from anywhere in the world.

Important Note about Web Calendars

No matter where you put your Web calendar, whether it's on your site or with a commercial or free service, be certain to keep it current and up-to-date. There's nothing worse than going to a Web site and finding out all the wonderful events you missed from last year.

- Plan on updating calendars monthly. Pull off events that have passed; add new events.
- If your calendar changes frequently, consider using a "new" graphic to point to the changed items.
- And if nothing's happening, be sure to say so on your calendar. "Nothing happening this month. Check back later." People appreciate honesty.

A Do-It-Yourself Calendar

There's no reason to pay someone else to post your business or personal events calendar online. The main advantage to using a service like eGroups (see below) is the ability to modify calendar events online and link them with automated e-mails. But a simple Web-based calendar is easy enough to create.

Would you like a list view calendar, which is the easiest to create, but tends to blur long lists of events? Would you like a monthly calendar, which gives a clear visual picture of a given month, but takes a bit more time to set up?

List view calendar

This is one of the simplest pages to set up: Just type in your list of events and then turn it into a bullet list using the <UL> tags.

```
<UL>
<LI>October 31, Halloween Party</LI>
<LI>December 25, Christmas Party<LI>
<LI>December 31, New Year's Eve Party</LI>
<LI>January 1-31, Recovery month</LI>
</UL>
```

These lists have the advantage of being easy to create and maintain. Whenever you want to make a change, either add or delete the item.

List view example

The Apeiron Foundation e-mailed us a list of their events and we put together this calendar.

In the HTML code below, we've stripped out the standard components of the Apeiron Foundation's site—the images and cross-links.

As you'll see from the screen shot, the list is extensive, complete, easily printable, and somewhat mind numbing. The repetition of the word

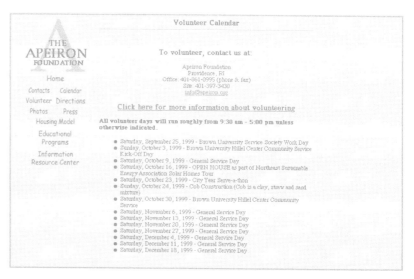

"Saturday" blurs and becomes almost invisible. However, since time was at a premium when this page was put together, and since the maintenance is likely to be by unskilled Web administrators, trying to make the page more interesting looking didn't make much sense.

```
<HTML>
<HEAD>
<TITLE>Apeiron Foundation Volunteer
Calendar</TITLE>
</HEAD>
<BODY BGCOLOR="#FFFFFF">
<H2>Apeiron Foundation Fall 1999 Volunteer
Calendar</H2>
<H4>All volunteer days will run roughly from
9:30 am—5:00 pm unless otherwise indicated.</H4>
<UL>
<LI>Saturday, September 25, 1999—Brown
University Service Society Work Day</LI>
<LI>Sunday, October 3, 1999—Brown University
Hillel Center Community Service Kick-Off
Day</LI>
<LI>Saturday, October 9, 1999—General Service
Day</LI>
<LI>Saturday, October 16, 1999—OPEN HOUSE as
part of Northeast Sustainable Energy Association
Solar Homes Tour</LI>
<LI>Saturday, October 23, 1999—City Year Serve-
a-thon</LI>
<LI>Sunday, October 24, 1999—Cob Construction
(Cob is a clay, straw and sand mixture)</LI>
<LI>Saturday, October 30, 1999—Brown University
Hillel Center Community Service</LI>
<LI>Saturday, November 6, 1999—General Service
Day</LI>
<LI>Saturday, November 13, 1999—General Service
Day</LI>
<LI>Saturday, November 20, 1999—General Service
Day</LI>
<LI>Saturday, November 27, 1999—General Service
Day</LI>
<LI>Saturday, December 4, 1999—General Service
Day</LI>
```

```
<LI>Saturday, December 11, 1999—General Service
Day</LI>
<LI>Saturday, December 18, 1999—General Service
Day</LI>
</UL>
</BODY>
</HTML>
```

Monthly calendar

A monthly calendar uses Table tags to create the month's grid on the page. While visually more useful, the monthly calendar is more difficult to maintain.

Here are the steps to follow:

1. First create a blank template calendar using a page generation program.
2. Set the columns Vertical Alignment to the top. VALIGN=Top
3. Set Widths for each column to 14 percent. WIDTH="14%."
4. Add day numbers from 1 to 31.

Apeiron Foundation Fall 1999 Volunteer Calendar

October 1999

Sunday	Monday	Tuesday	Wednesday	Thursday	Friday	Saturday
					1	2
3 Brown University Hillel Center Community Service Kick-Off Day	4	5	6	7	8	9 General Service Day
10	11	12	13	14	15	16 OPEN HOUSE as part of Northeast Sustainable Energy Association Solar Homes Tour
17	18	19	20	21	22	23

5. Save this file and use it as a template. (month_template.htm)
6. Create each month by opening a copy of month_template.htm and then saving it as the individual month (calendar_00_10.htm). The advantage of using a YY_MM system is that the calendars will appear in order in a subdirectory/index view.
7. Change the date numbers and calendar events.
8. Save your changes.
9. Repeat steps 6 through 8 until all the information is entered. *Note:* To prevent null/blank grid spaces in Netscape, use   in frame cells that would be otherwise empty.

```
<HTML>
<HEAD>
<TITLE>Apeiron Foundation Volunteer
Monthly Calendar</TITLE>
</HEAD>
<BODY BGCOLOR="#FFFFFF">
<H2>Apeiron Foundation Fall 1999
Volunteer Calendar</H2>
<H3><CENTER>October
1999</CENTER></H3>
<H3><TABLE BORDER=1 HEIGHT="100%">
<TR>
<TD VALIGN=top WIDTH="17%">
<CENTER><FONT
COLOR="#CC0000">Sunday
</FONT></CENTER>
</TD>
<TD VALIGN=top WIDTH="13%">
<CENTER><FONT
COLOR="#CC0000">Monday
</FONT></CENTER>
</TD>
<TD VALIGN=top WIDTH="13%">
<CENTER><FONT
COLOR="#CC0000">Tuesday
</FONT></CENTER>
</TD>
<TD VALIGN=top WIDTH="14%">
<CENTER><FONT
COLOR="#CC0000">Wednesday
</FONT></CENTER>
</TD>
<TD VALIGN=top WIDTH="14%">
<CENTER><FONT
COLOR="#CC0000">Thursday
</FONT></CENTER>
</TD>
<TD VALIGN=top WIDTH="14%">
<CENTER><FONT
COLOR="#CC0000">Friday
</FONT></CENTER>
</TD>
<TD VALIGN=top WIDTH="17%">
<CENTER><FONT
COLOR="#CC0000">Saturday
</FONT></CENTER>
</TD>
</TR>
<TR>
<TD VALIGN=top WIDTH="17%">
<P> </P>
</TD>
```

```
<TD VALIGN=top WIDTH="13%">
<P> </P>
</TD>
<TD VALIGN=top WIDTH="13%">
<P> </P>
</TD>
<TD VALIGN=top WIDTH="14%">
<P> </P>
</TD>
<TD VALIGN=top WIDTH="14%">
<P> </P>
</TD>
<TD VALIGN=top WIDTH="14%">
<P>1</P>
<P></P>
</TD>
<TD VALIGN=top WIDTH="17%">
<P>2</P>
</TD>
</TR>
<TR>
<TD VALIGN=top WIDTH="17%">
<P>3</P>
<P>Brown University Hillel Center
Community Service Kick-Off Day</P>
</TD>
<TD VALIGN=top WIDTH="13%">
<P>4</P>
</TD>
<TD VALIGN=top WIDTH="13%">
<P>5</P>
</TD>
<TD VALIGN=top WIDTH="14%">
<P>6</P>
</TD>
<TD VALIGN=top WIDTH="14%">
<P>7</P>
</TD>
<TD VALIGN=top WIDTH="14%">
<P>8</P>
</TD>
<TD VALIGN=top WIDTH="17%">
<P>9</P>
<P>General Service Day</P>
</TD>
</TR>
<TR>
<TD VALIGN=top WIDTH="17%">
<P>10</P>
</TD>
<TD VALIGN=top WIDTH="13%">
<P>11</P>
```

```
</TD>
<TD VALIGN=top WIDTH="13%">
<P>12</P>
</TD>
<TD VALIGN=top WIDTH="14%">
<P>13</P>
</TD>
<TD VALIGN=top WIDTH="14%">
<P>14</P>
</TD>
<TD VALIGN=top WIDTH="14%">
<P>15</P>
</TD>
<TD VALIGN=top WIDTH="17%">
<P>16</P>
<P>OPEN HOUSE as part of Northeast
Sustainable Energy Association
Solar Homes Tour</P>
</TD>
</TR>
<TR>
<TD VALIGN=top WIDTH="17%">
<P>17</P>
</TD>
<TD VALIGN=top WIDTH="13%">
<P>18</P>
</TD>
<TD VALIGN=top WIDTH="13%">
<P>19</P>
</TD>
<TD VALIGN=top WIDTH="14%">
<P>20</P>
</TD>
<TD VALIGN=top WIDTH="14%">
<P>21</P>
</TD>
<TD VALIGN=top WIDTH="14%">
<P>22</P>
</TD>
<TD VALIGN=top WIDTH="17%">
<P>23</P>
<P>City Year Serve-a-thon</P>
</TD>
</TR>
<TR>
<TD VALIGN=top WIDTH="17%">
<P>24</P>
<P>Cob Construction (Cob is a clay,
straw and sand mixture)</P>
</TD>
<TD VALIGN=top WIDTH="13%">
```

```
<P>25</P>
</TD>
<TD VALIGN=top WIDTH="13%">
<P>26</P>
</TD>
<TD VALIGN=top WIDTH="14%">
<P>27</P>
</TD>
<TD VALIGN=top WIDTH="14%">
<P>28</P>
</TD>
<TD VALIGN=top WIDTH="14%">
<P>29</P>
</TD>
<TD VALIGN=top WIDTH="17%">
<P>30</P>
<P>Brown University Hillel Center
Community Service</P>
</TD>
</TR>
<TR>
<TD VALIGN=top WIDTH="17%">
<P>31</P>
</TD>
<TD VALIGN=top WIDTH="13%">
<P>1</P>
</TD>
<TD VALIGN=top WIDTH="13%">
<P>2</P>
</TD>
<TD VALIGN=top WIDTH="14%">
<P>3</P>
</TD>
<TD VALIGN=top WIDTH="14%">
<P>4</P>
</TD>
<TD VALIGN=top WIDTH="14%">
<P>5</P>
</TD>
<TD VALIGN=top WIDTH="17%">
<P>6</P>
<P>General Service Day</P>
</TD>
</TR>
</TABLE>
</H3>
<H3><CENTER><A HREF="vol_
november.htm">Click here for Next
Month's Calendar</A></CENTER></H3>
</BODY>
</HTML>
```

E-mail Lists

E-mail is the least expensive way to communicate with your customers. It's also the least expensive way to keep in touch with friends, family, and neighbors.

An e-mail list is just like a snail mail mailing list. It's a list of e-mail addresses for a group of people related in some way.

There are two kinds of e-mail lists on the Web: one-way and user-participatory. One-way e-mail lists are exactly that, lists that issue from one source to a number of other people. User-participatory lists are more like free-form discussion groups that occur via e-mail. In both types, a message goes to all the people who subscribe to the mail, which may be hundreds or thousands worldwide.

User-participatory list subscribers are usually passionate about the interest or hobby that is the subject under discussion. If you crave a full mailbox, you may want to join a mailing list or two. But be aware, many are not totally open to the public and may be local, regional, or screened by a moderator who may want to know more about you before you join. Some mailing lists from organizations also include events, jobs listings, and positions wanted.

The chief difference between a one-way and a user-participatory e-mail list is that if you reply to a one-way e-mail list, that message isn't repeated to everyone else on the list. Examples of one-way e-mail lists include:

- Immediate family
- Extended family
- Christmas/holiday greetings list
- Neighborhood action committee
- Shameless self-promotion
- Polka band touring list

Many special interest groups also maintain their own e-mail lists. Professional and topic-related mailing lists are discussions on certain topics conducted entirely by e-mail. Examples of user-participatory e-mail lists include lists on:

- Internet and the Web
- Art

- Television
- Movies
- Books
- Jobs
- Marketing
- Computers (all aspects of)
- Education
- Philosophy
- History
- Bands (fan lists)
- Politics
- Environmental Activism
- Human Rights
- Games
- Sports
- Religion
- Biology
- Kids

Using Existing User-Participatory Mailing Lists

The biggest list of mailing lists on the Internet is Liszt (named after the Romantic composer and pianist), which features more than 90,000 lists. At the wonderfully organized Liszt (www.liszt.com), you can search for a mailing list by name or by category. Categories include arts—with subcategories like literature, movies, comics, and theater—business, politics, computers, culture, and more. Liszt shows short descriptions and how to obtain more information about the list.

For example, look up "Internet" and find dozens of mailing lists, many of which are willing to e-mail you information about everything from Web design, managing graphics, the latest info about Flash vector cartoons, Webzines, and even how to manage an adult Web site. Notice that Liszt thoughtfully includes links to related newsgroups, books, Web pages, and hardware or software at the top of the page. Click one to see the listings. (There may not be listings in every category for every topic you pick.)

If you look up the Web designers mailing list "designers," you'll see the following:

Listname:	designers
Hosted at:	designers
Contact person:	owner-aris-humor@mylist.net
Description:	Fully moderated, free list, providing about one joke a day to its subscribers.

You now know whom to e-mail to join this mailing list. When you join a list, carefully follow the instructions you are given. Usually, you send an e-mail to the list manager with "subscribe" or something similar (sometimes, "subscribe" plus the name of the list) in the message body. If you later wish to be deleted, you send an "unsubscribe" message.

Setting Up Your Own E-mail List

First you need to decide what kind of a list you're setting up. Are you planning a one-way or a user-participatory list? Do you want to do it yourself, or use a commercial or free e-mail service?

The advantages to doing it yourself are the level of complete control you'll have over your e-mail addresses. From time to time we've heard stories about hackers breaking into e-mail address databases and sending spam to everybody. If you do it yourself, keeping addresses on your computer, you won't be trusting somebody else with that potentially valuable information. Finally, if you maintain your own e-mail list, you won't be vulnerable to commercial service power outages.

The problem with doing it yourself is that it takes more work. You'll have to check and make sure everything works properly. If your computer crashes, you can't use your e-mail list. If you have way too many e-mail addresses, you may have problems with your Internet service provider, or your e-mail software

Do-it-yourself user-participatory e-mail list

You'll need to buy e-mail listserve software like Lsoft's LISTSERV software for Windows or LetterRip Pro from Fog City Software for the Macintosh. You also need to run this software constantly, either in the background or consistently on a daily basis. User-participatory e-mail lists thrive on consistency and instant responses. Somebody says something boneheaded in an e-mail and somebody else immediately fires back a reply. In a matter of minutes, a flame war develops and hundreds of e-mails beam back and forth around the world. We recommend that you use a commercial or free service for running a user-participatory e-mail list. (See below.)

Do-it-yourself one-way e-mail list

One-way e-mail lists are easy to create and relatively easy to maintain.

1. You'll need to set up at least one, if not several, new e-mail accounts to manage the list. Check with your Internet service provider about how to do this. If possible, set up three e-mail accounts:
    *   mylist@everythingwebsite.com—this will be the e-mail address you use to send the e-mails from. If you can only set up one e-mail address, then use this one.
    *   subscribe_mylist@everythingwebsite.com—this will be the e-mail address people use to automatically be added to your e-mail list.
    *   unsubscribe_mylist@everythingwebsite.com—this will be the e-mail address subscribers use to automatically be removed from your e-mail list.

Naturally, you can name these e-mail addresses any way you want. The advantage to using the words "subscribe" and "unsubscribe" is that they are clear.

Users with only one e-mail address can still start e-mail lists. You will use the subject line of e-mail to manage the list.

2. You will also need a robust e-mail program to manage the list, such as Microsoft's Outlook, CE Software's QuickMail, Bare Bones Software's Mailsmith, or Qualcomm's Eudora Pro. The features to look for in a program to manage your e-mail are:
    *   The ability to handle multiple accounts

America Online Users

Setting up a new e-mail address on America Online is easy. Use keyword "Screen Names" and create a new screen name called something like "MyElist." The difficulty, however, will be managing the e-mail. AOL's e-mail program is sufficient for ordinary use but doesn't have the robust qualities of commercial e-mail programs.

- The ability to filter, manage, and file e-mail addresses
- The ability to automatically respond to e-mail messages
- The ability to quickly enter, import, export, or delete e-mail messages
- The ability to create groups of addresses

3. Set up a Web page in your site that gives detailed information about your e-mail list and explains how to subscribe, unsubscribe, and get more information.

My email list

Welcome to my email list.

This email list goes to more than 1,000 people in 15 countries on 3 different continents!

About this list

If you subscribe to this email list, you'll:

- Learn all about my pets
- Get cool recipes
- Find out what the weather is like in my home town
- Hear about the movies I've seen lately
- Listen to me complain about my lumbago
- Learn all about my business selling used hubcaps
- Whatever else I feel like sending

For more info

Send an email to mailto:mylist@everythingwebsite.com

To Subscribe

1. To subscribe, send an email to subscribe_mylist@everythingwebsite.com
2. or send an email to mailto:mylist@everythingwebsite.com with the word "SUBSCRIBE" in the subject

To Unsubscribe

1. To usubscribe, send an email to unsubscribe_mylist@everythingwebsite.com
2. or send an email to mailto:mylist@everythingwebsite.com with the word "UNSUBSCRIBE" in the subject.

Thanks for joining!

```
<HTML>
<HEAD>
<TITLE>My email list</TITLE>
</HEAD>
<BODY BGCOLOR="#FFFFFF">
<H1>My email list</H1>
<P>Welcome to my email list.</P>
```

```
<P>This email list goes to more than 1,000 people
in 15 countries on 3 different continents!</P>
<H3>About this list</H3>
<P>If you subscribe to this email list, you'll:</P>
<UL>
<LI>Learn all about my pets</LI>
<LI>Get cool recipes</LI>
<LI>Find out what the weather is like in my home
town</LI>
<LI>Hear about the movies I've seen lately</LI>
<LI>Listen to me complain about my lumbago</LI>
<LI>Learn all about my business selling used
hubcaps</LI>
<LI>Whatever else I feel like sending</LI>
</UL>
<H3>For more info</H3>
<P>Send an email to <A HREF="mailto:
mylist@everythingwebsite.com">mailto:
mylist@everythingwebsite.com</A></P>
<H3>To Subscribe</H3>
<OL>
<LI>To subscribe, send an email to <A HREF=
"mailto:subscribe_mylist@everythingwebsite.com">
subscribe_mylist@everythingwebsite.com</A>
</LI>
<LI>or send an email to <A HREF="mailto:
mylist@everythingwebsite.com">mailto:
mylist@everythingwebsite.com</A>
with the word "SUBSCRIBE" in the subject</LI>
</OL>
<H3>To Unsubscribe</H3>
<OL>
<LI>To unsubscribe, send an email to <A HREF=
"mailto:mylist@everythingwebsite.com?subject=
SUBSCRIBE">mailto:mylist@everythingwebsite.com</A>
</LI>
<LI>or send an email to <A HREF="mailto:
mylist@everythingwebsite.com?subject=UNSUBSCRIBE">
mailto:mylist@everythingwebsite.com</A>with the
word "UNSUBSCRIBE" in the subject.</LI>
</OL>
<P>Thanks for joining!</P>
</BODY>
</HTML>
```

The Web page we just created assumes that you've got three e-mail accounts associated with your e-mail list. If you only have one e-mail address, then you will be using the subject line controls.

While we included the ?subject="SUBSCRIBE" attribute in the html code, you should know that this code doesn't work in every e-mail program. So be sure to give the specific instructions also.

Managing Your Own E-mail List

Every e-mail program handles this differently, so we're going to help you understand what's necessary. First of all, set up an e-mail address group called "Subscribers." Then create mail actions that do the following:

- If the subject of an e-mail says "SUBSCRIBE" or if the address the e-mail is sent to is subscribe_mylist, then add the sender's e-mail address to "Subscribers" and send a welcome message.
- If the subject of an e-mail says "UNSUBSCRIBE" or if the address the email is sent to is unsubscribe_mylist, then remove the sender's e-mail address from "Subscribers" and send a good-bye message.

Add people you know would like to receive this e-mail to the "Subscribers" group. Send them a welcome message that includes information about unsubscribing.

Invite people you think might like to be on your e-mail list by sending them an information note about how to subscribe.

Start sending out your email list notices! Compose and send your e-mail list to your subscribers. (Be sure to proofread.)

Adding Your E-mail List to Liszt

If you're not interested in having perfect strangers subscribe to your e-mail list, don't do this. If you're interested in building world-wide interest in your list, then go ahead. Suggestion: Before you register your list, see if there's already one in existence that covers the same topic.

1. Go to www.liszt.com/submit.html.
2. Enter your e-mail list's address.
3. Enter a one-line description of the group with a maximum of 100 characters.
4. Enter an e-mail address for problems with the list.
5. Enter an address where someone can send an e-mail to get more information.
6. Enter a subscribe command/address. What is the e-mail address that someone can send e-mail to to begin getting e-mails?
7. Enter an unsubscribe command/address. What is the e-mail address that someone can send e-mail to to be removed from the e-mail list?
8. What is the e-mail list's home page?
9. Are there any other home pages about the list?

Liszt-specific questions:

1. Would you like to add your list to Liszt Select, a browseable directory of public mailing lists?
2. Would you like free Web archiving of your list?
3. Would you like Liszt to help you find paying sponsors for your list?
4. Would you like to be added to Liszt's extremely low-traffic owners-announce mailing list?
5. Would you like to receive the Liszt newsletter with mailing list tips?
6. Would you like to receive occasional paid ads and announcements specific to the mailing list industry (e.g., ads for mailing list software)?

A Free Calendar and E-mail Service— eGroups

eGroups (www.egroups.com) is one of our favorite Web-based services. Unlike Yahoo!, it doesn't try to be everything to everyone.

Spamming

Spam is the junk mail of the e-mail world. It's all those unsolicited e-mails you receive from companies promising credit cards, weight loss, and lurid photos.

You don't want your friends and customers to think of you as a spammer. Here are some simple tips to avoid being lumped into this category.

1. Invite people to subscribe to your e-mail list rather than automatically subscribing them. (The only exception might be close friends and family.)
2. Be clear that you'll remove people at their request.
3. Don't send out too many messages. Listen to your list and find out whether they're getting overwhelmed.

eGroups offers both e-mail lists (known as eGroups) and online calendars in a number of different flavors and configurations. Once you've joined, you can search for already existing eGroups or start your own.

When you start your own eGroup email list, eGroups keeps track of your subscribers and handles all the maintenance and bookkeeping. Even better, they keep all the e-mails online, so it's easy to go back and search for a message.

Combine that with the only calendars feature that allows you to schedule events and send e-mails out to everyone on your eGroup list and it's very easy to see why this service has become so popular. Best of all, eGroups are free. Well, mostly free.

eGroups makes its money in one of two ways. If you set up a free eGroup, you may find an advertisement attached at the bottom of the e-mails sent through the group. Or you can pay a small fee of $4.95 a month for the no-ads option.

And, if your eGroup gets huge, they've got a service called eGroups Power List, which can help you mange email lists with more than 1,000 subscribers.

Disadvantages to eGroups

There aren't many disadvantages to using eGroups.

- You'll get ads with your emails, but you can ignore them.
- There is a security risk if you keep your personal calendar on the Web, but no more so than with any other information you keep online.
- One Monday morning we were unable to access our eGroups calendar for several hours. This could be a huge problem and ought to be considered before putting time-sensitive information with the service.

Joining eGroups

There are two ways to join eGroups—either through their Web site or by signing onto an eGroups e-mail list. To sign up on their Web site, go to www.eGroups.com.

1. Click on the New User? Sign up—it's free button.
2. Enter your e-mail address.
3. Check your e-mail for the validation number they just e-mailed you.
4. Fill out the rest of the form, including a password.
5. When you return to egroups.com, use your e-mail address and password to log in.

Creating an eGroup

1. Click on "Start an eGroup."
2. Enter the group address. eGroups will automatically add @egroups.com to the e-mail group address. (Example: everything-book@egroups.com.)
3. Select an egroup name.
4. Give it a description.
5. Tell them you were referred by us.
6. Select the subscription type (anyone may join the group or approval is required to join the group).
7. Select the posting rule (only members may post to the group, only the group moderator [you] may post to the group, or anyone can post to the group).
8. Choose the moderation option. (When somebody sends an e-mail message to the group, that message is either immediately distributed to the group or sent first to the moderator for approval.)
9. Choose who can read the messages on the Web (anyone or group members only).
10. Decide whether you want the group to be listed in the eGroups directory.
11. Choose whether the members will be able to see who else is on the e-mail list.
12. Decide whether you're interested in the $4.95 a month no-ads option.
13. Click "Create it."

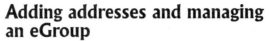

Adding addresses and managing an eGroup

As soon as you create your eGroup you'll be able to add e-mail addresses to the list.

You then choose whether to invite new members to join or simply join them without asking first.

If you invite someone to join, he or she will receive an e-mail with a description of the e-list. This person will then have to reply to the e-mail before joining the list and receiving any more messages. If you simply sign someone on, he or she will also receive an e-mail with a description of the e-list and details on how to stop receiving messages.

Then send out emails, and wait for the replies.

Using eGroups Calendar

You can set up both personal and eGroup-related dates on your eGroups calendar. If you have multiple eGroups, you can set your calendars to overlap so that you can see all the events at the same time.

1. Log onto eGroups.
2. Click on Calendar.
3. Click on "New Event."
4. Enter the Event Name, date, time, duration, and description.
5. Choose between one-time event and repeating event.
6. Choose whether and when you'd like to receive an e-mail reminder of the event.
7. Select the users you'd like to notify about the event. They will receive an e-mail message about your event. (Hint: This is an excellent way to remind a spouse about an upcoming anniversary!)

8. If you want, you can enter all your event information into egroups, save the page as HTML, strip out the eGroups elements, and upload the page into your Web site.

Other eGroups Features

In addition to free e-mail lists and a calendar, eGroups offers chat, Internet talk, a database system, and 20 megabytes of upload space. You can spend a lot of time with this service.

Cool Web Site Tricks

Here are a bunch of cool tricks that you can do on your Web site.

Instant Weather

Do you want the people who visit your Web site to know what the weather's like?

The Weather Channel's Web site offers a "Weather Magnet" image that shows the current weather conditions for the city of your choice. It'll also link you directly to the Weather Channel's detailed information about your local weather. Handy!

If you go to their Web site, they'll give you a whole "Sign up now" rigamarole, but if you live in the United States you don't have to do that. Just add and modify the HTML code below and try it out.

Here's the code for Holbrook, Massachusetts, the home of Adams Media Corporation, publisher of the Everything Book series. Just change "ma_holbrook" and "MA_Holbrook" to your state's initials and city name. If you live in a really small town, pick a nearby population center.

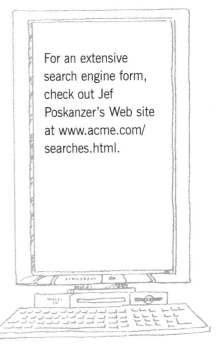

For an extensive search engine form, check out Jef Poskanzer's Web site at www.acme.com/ searches.html.

```
<A href="http://www.weather.com/weather/cities/us_ma_
holbrook.html"><Img border=2 SRC="http://autocobrand.
weather.com/autocobrand/weather_magnet/MA_Holbrook.gif">
</a>
```

Instant Search

Don't you hate having to go to your search engine's site every time you want to perform a search? Wouldn't it be swell to have access to their huge database from your own Web site?

It's easy. Here's the code to set up a simple search window into AltaVista, one of the most comprehensive search engines on the Web. Just put this into your Web site. If you want to place it in a specific spot on the page, put it into a cell in a table.

```
<!Alta Vista Search Engine Form>
<FORM ACTION="http://www.altavista.digital.com/
cgi-bin/query" METHOD=GET>
<P><INPUT TYPE=hidden NAME=pg VALUE=aq>
<INPUT TYPE=hidden NAME=what VALUE=web>
<INPUT TYPE=hidden NAME=kl VALUE=XX>
<INPUT TYPE=text NAME=q VALUE="" SIZE=25>
<INPUT TYPE=hidden NAME=r VALUE="">
<INPUT TYPE=hidden NAME=d0 VALUE="21/Mar/86">
<INPUT TYPE=hidden NAME=d1 VALUE="">
<A HREF="http://www.altavista.digital.com/
cgi-bin/query?pg=aq">Alta Vista</A>
</FORM>
```

CHAPTER 16

Sight, Sound, Pages, and Java

OPEN

Photo Album

OUR TRIP

RECIPES

BIRTHDAY'S

ANNIVERSARIES

In this chapter we're going to briefly touch on a lot of material. We'll take a look at how you can get multimedia like movies and sound files onto the Web, how to create PDF documents that will display and print just the way you want them to, and a little bit about Java.

Videos Online

If you want to put movies on the Web you'll need three things:

1. The hardware to get the movie onto your PC. The latest method for doing this is called FireWire, and it lets you dump directly from a digital video camera directly into your computer. For older model computers, you'll need a video input card.

2. Software to manage the video. Chances are that if you have the FireWire connection, your computer comes with video editing software. Sony's Vaio line, for instance, comes bundled with Adobe Premier 5.1 LE and Sony's own DVgate Motion, a digital video editing application. The latest iMacs include a program called iMovie that allows you to perform amazing video editing that until recently could only be done in a multimillion-dollar studio.

    If you have an older computer and have installed a video input card, see if that card comes with software or check with the manufacturer about compatible software options.

    If you still need to buy video editing software, we recommend looking at QuickTime (see below).

3. You'll need plenty of hard disk space. Putting 30 seconds of a full-motion movie onto a hard drive takes about 10 megabytes. If you're going to become the next Spike Lee, editing your movie and putting it on the Web, you'd better have a lot of hard drive space. A two-hour movie would take up 2.400 gigabytes!

QuickTime 4

Apple (www.apple.com/quicktime)
QuickTime 4: Free, Mac and PC
QuickTime 4 Pro: $29.99, Mac and PC

If you see a video clip on the Web, chances are you're watching a QuickTime movie. QuickTime is Apple's cross-platform browser and video presentation software. With QuickTime 4 Pro, anyone has an inexpensive method of creating movies for online viewing. QuickTime 4 Pro allows you to perform Copy and Paste editing and to save your movies in a variety of compressions and formats that can be played by any Web browser with the Free QuickTime 4 plug-in.

Sounds

Until recently, the most common sound files are Audio Player (which end in ".au"), wave (".wav"), MIDI (".mid" or ".midi"), and AIFF (".aif" or ".aiff"). For a while, it seemed as if RealAudio (www.realaudio.com) was going to be the top dog in Internet sound. And, as of the turn of the millennium, the hot sound format on the Web is MP3. (Who knows what'll be hot by the time you read this!)

Generally, a sound file will not play until the whole file is transferred to your computer. But in some cases, such as RealAudio—which plays high-quality sound and whose files end in ".ra"—the sound starts to play when the download starts, thanks to streaming audio technology.

How Does Sound Work on Web Pages?

Sounds can be handled in a number of different ways.

1.   They can be set up as links—the user clicks onto the sound link and the file downloads and then plays. The

Web page will note a link is for a sound and often describe the sound type and file size so you can decide to hear it or not. Your browser will often play a sound if you click on the link without your needing to do anything else. In some cases your browser will show a message noting it cannot play the file because you need a plug-in and will note the name of the plug-in. Many Web sites allow users to download a sound file on the spot.

Here's how you'd create a link to a song Mark wrote to promote a book of his:

```
<P>Click here to hear the author sing <A
HREF="http://www.markbinder.com/
sounds/rational2.wav"> "The Rationalization
Blues (888K)"</A>
```

On the page, that looks like this:

Click here to hear the author sing The Rationalization Blues (888K)

The user clicks on the link and viola! The sound downloads and a new window opens to allow the user to play the song.

2. If you want to embed the sound into the page so that it automatically begins downloading as soon as the page is opened, use the <EMBED> tag.

```
<P> Click the Arrow to Play "The
Rationalization Blues"
<EMBED SRC="http://www.markbinder.com/
sounds/rational2.wav" WIDTH="100"
HEIGHT="100" ALIGN="MIDDLE"></EMBED>
```

←—The WIDTH, HEIGHT and ALIGN elements describe the maximum size of the window the sound will open into. Since this window is smaller than the described height, it doesn't take up that much room.—→

How to Create Sound Files

As with all multimedia, there are a variety of ways to create a sound file on your computer. The simplest and crudest way to record short sounds is to plug a microphone into your computer and use the software that's probably already built in. *Note:* Windows users may need a sound card to get this stuff to work. Check your hardware. Macintosh users have everything they need already.

For longer sounds and songs, you'll probably have to buy a commercial or shareware program. Before you do, be sure to check your hard drive. You never know what came bundled with your computer.

To record sounds of up to 60 seconds in Windows 98

1. Open the "Sound Recorder." (It may be buried in your Start Menu under Accessories/Entertainment. If you can't find it there, do a file search.)
2. Click the "Record" button and make noise or sing your little heart out.
3. Click the "Stop" button.
4. Save the file.

HTML Sound Notes

It's good to let your users know how big a sound file is so they can have a sense of how long it will take to download.

If you use the <EMBED> tag, your user must already have the plug-in loaded into their browser for it to work.

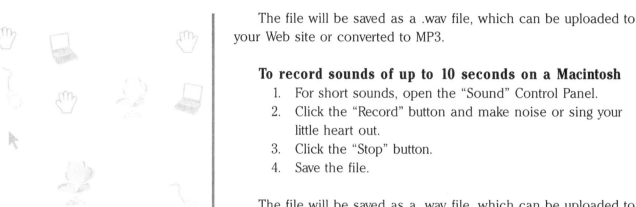

The file will be saved as a .wav file, which can be uploaded to your Web site or converted to MP3.

To record sounds of up to 10 seconds on a Macintosh
1. For short sounds, open the "Sound" Control Panel.
2. Click the "Record" button and make noise or sing your little heart out.
3. Click the "Stop" button.
4. Save the file.

The file will be saved as a .wav file, which can be uploaded to your Web site or converted to MP3.

MP3

MP3 stands for MPEG layer 3. It's a type of audio encoding that allows music to be significantly compressed in digital form with a minimal loss of sound quality. Near CD-quality MP3 is recorded at 128 or 112 kbits per second. MP3 files can be broken into pieces to create digital samples (if you want to sell a compact disc, for instance). They can also be streamed if you have a fast enough Internet connection. On the downside, the people visiting your Web site will need an MP3 player and a 16-bit sound card in order to listen to your MP3s.

To convert a .wav file to MP3:

1. You need an MP3 converter. Windows users can find a free Ripper called MusicMatch at mp3.com. (www.mp3.com). *Note:* The free version of MusicMatch doesn't produce CD quality. You can buy the CD-quality version for $29.99. Macintosh users can use SoundJam MP (www.soundjam.com/) for around $50, which is a combination MP3 player and a robust sound converter. You can also try a $29.95 program called Audiocatalyst from Xing (www.xingtech.com/mp3/audiocatalyst/).
2. Open the .wav file and follow the converter's instructions.
3. Upload the file to your Web site.

Multimedia

"ARRGH! It was working last week!" Beth Hellman looked over her shoulder and shook her head sadly. Her partner, Mark Binder, was testing out his online cyber-novella, *Destroy The World*, and learning a hard fact of multimedia on the Internet—it always takes three times longer to create than you expect.

And, it's expensive. You'll find yourself spending several hundred dollars on software. Plus it helps to have the latest and fastest computers (otherwise you'll be spending more time waiting for your computer). Plus, you might need to get more software (graphics design, sound editing) and more hardware (CD-ROM burners, high-quality digital cameras).

Multimedia tends to require huge amounts of disk space and special players, which means that it can take forever to download and play. People are impatient on the Web. One solution to this is streaming media—the art of playing some of a multimedia piece while the rest of the piece downloads in the background. Even using streaming media takes practice, and isn't guaranteed to work on slow machines with slow connections. So, before you go into multimedia development, think twice then leap.

Macromedia Director/Shockwave Internet Studio

Macromedia (www.macromedia.com)
$999—Mac and PC

Macromedia Director is the premier multimedia development tool today. It allows users to create just about any multimedia presentation or game they can imagine. It allows for animations, buttons, user interaction, and more. With Director, users can create stand-alone applications or Shockwave files that will play on any Web browser equipped with the free Shockwave Player. Nearly every ultra-cool site on the Web has Shockwave. Almost every Web-based game is created in Shockwave.

This level of cool comes at a price. Director 7 Shockwave Internet Studio is expensive. It does come with a complete suite of sound and image management tools. Using Macromedia Director to

---

Making the Leap off the Web

MP3 is one of the first technologies to make the leap from the Internet away from the PC. You can purchase a portable MP3 player at any high-quality electronics store. These Walkman-like devices have no moving parts and can store about an hour's worth of music.

create Shockwaved files is great because it creates high-quality multi-media online.

Drawbacks

There are three main drawbacks to Shockwave:

1. Your users must have the Shockwave Player plug-in installed in their browser **before** they can run your Shockwaved files. While the plug-in is included with most browsers, users may not have the latest and greatest update. To install the player, they'll have to download it (which can take a while), quit out of their browser, install it, and then go back to your Web site. What do you think the chances of that are?

2. Shockwaved files themselves can be very, very big and slow to download. Expect to see minimum downloads of 500K. Bigger files are common. Mark, for instance, wrote a very simple multimedia program called "Destroy The World" (www.markbinder.com/destroy) that sneaked under the wire at just 443K. That still takes a long time to download on even a 56K modem.

3. Macromedia seems to be edging toward selling its Shockwave player. You can already buy an enhanced version of it. Since the Web is currently based on the "give it to me for free" model, putting this barrier up may slow future Shockwave development.

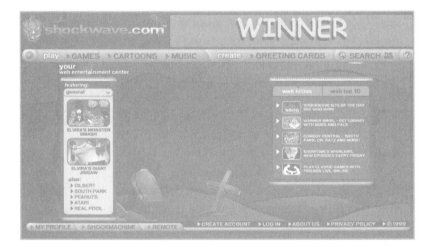

Macromedia Flash

Macromedia (www.macromedia.com)
$299—Mac and PC

Flash 4 is a completely different concept in animation. Flash uses vector graphics to save valuable time and disk space. Instead of taking ordinary drawings and moving them around piece by piece, Flash animations are based on simple shapes that can be drawn and redrawn quickly. As a result, Flash files can be quite compact, less than 50k, and still perform some pretty, well, flashy animations.

Flash does, however, require a player to function (see Shockwave's drawbacks above). If player isn't already built into a user's Web browser, then there's a period of download and registration time that can quickly lose visitors to your site.

Best of all, Flash is fast. Not only do vector graphics load faster than GIFs and JPEGs but you can set up the files to load in a particular order so that the beginning of the animation is running while the rest of it is loading.

Unfortunately, Flash isn't accessible to search engines. In other words, your Web site won't be properly cataloged, and you may lose links. On the other hand, it's cool!

PDF

Adobe Acrobat, Adobe Acrobat Reader
www.adobe.com
Adobe Acrobat Reader: Free PDF enhancement/plug-in for Web
    Access
Adobe Acrobat: Software to generate and modify PDF files. $249,
    $99 upgrade for previously registered owners.

If you really need your audience to see the document exactly the way that you formatted it, then PDF is for you. PDF stands for Portable Document Format. It is an accepted industry standard for transmitting documents across platforms. With Adobe Acrobat, any document you create on your computer is saved into a PDF document. That document may be read by anyone who has either Acrobat or Acrobat Reader.

Flash Instead of HTML

Flash is cool! You can design entire Web sites in Flash without any HTML coding at all. You can place graphics wherever you want them to appear on the page and they show up in browsers at exactly that place. You can create cool buttons that pulse and animations that move around.

To see the best in Shockwave and Flash, go to Shockwave.Com (www.shockwave.com).

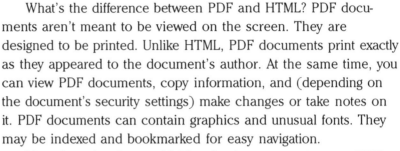

What's the difference between PDF and HTML? PDF documents aren't meant to be viewed on the screen. They are designed to be printed. Unlike HTML, PDF documents print exactly as they appeared to the document's author. At the same time, you can view PDF documents, copy information, and (depending on the document's security settings) make changes or take notes on it. PDF documents can contain graphics and unusual fonts. They may be indexed and bookmarked for easy navigation.

How does Acrobat work? The simplest way to create a PDF document is to drag-and-drop it on the Acrobat desktop icon. Acrobat is designed to automatically create PDF files. Afterward, you can open the PDF file in Acrobat, edit it, annotate it, and create bookmarks.

New features of Acrobat 4 include direct Web-to-PDF creation called "Web Capture" and page-at-a-time downloading, which allows users to download compact PDFs that are smaller than the original source files.

What would I use PDF files for? As you've seen from your work on the Web, HTML and Web browsers frequently mangle the best page layouts you create. Using a PDF file will allow you to create any number of documents and have complete control over the downloader's viewing and printing experience.

You can create catalogs, manuscripts, brochures, sales forms, charts, corporate reports, and anything else. What makes using Acrobat truly easy is that you can create straight from your word processor, spreadsheet, or database and be 100 percent certain that your viewers will see exactly what you're seeing.

For example, if you have to create an annual report for your organization and you want to make that information public, rather than spending an extra week trying to make the HTML formatting work, you can simply drag and drop the report onto Acrobat and call it "annual.pdf."

Now anyone interested in your company can have a clean and printable version of your report.

How Do I Deal with a PDF?

If you want to view and print PDF files, you need to download Adobe Acrobat Reader.

Visit Adobe's Web site or get Acrobat Reader directly at www.adobe.com/products/acrobat/readstep.html.

PDF Case Study—Mark's Brochure

Not long ago, Mark went to the New England Bookseller's Association trade show to sign copies of *The Everything Bedtime Story Book*. While there, he realized that he had the chance to contact dozens of publishers about other projects he was working on.

Rather than babbling incoherently, he took a lesson from the publishers' own marketing departments and created a brochure. After the convention was over, the brochure languished until he realized that posting the brochure in PDF form would make that work immediately available to any potential publishers.

Here's what he did.

1. Since he was working on a Macintosh, he opened the Chooser and clicked on Acrobat PDFWriter. (He could have dragged and dropped.)
2. He printed the file.
3. He opened it to check the document. Something had happened in the translation. Parts of his document had been cut off, and the entire page was over-sized. Also, since the brochure was designed to be printed and then folded in half, like a booklet, viewers immediately saw the back cover and the front cover at the same time.
4. He opened up the Page Setup and discovered that the document scale had been accidentally set to 130 percent. He changed the scale to 100 percent.
5. He changed the page size from a standard landscape size of 11 x 8.5 to 5.5 x 8.5. Instead of showing two pages simultaneously, viewers would now see only one page at a time.
6. He moved the back cover to the end of the document and adjusted the pages until they looked good on the screen.
7. He "printed" it to PDF as brochure_99.pdf.
8. Once the PDF is ready, you need to call attention to it on the Web site. Mark created a subdirectory called "brochure."

9. He uploaded the file into the new subdirectory.
10. Then he put links to the brochure on a subdirectory index page and on several other pages throughout the Web site.
11. He tested the download and was done.

JavaScript

JavaScript is a programming language designed by Sun Microsystems (www.sun.com) and Netscape (www.netscape.com) to extend HTML. Billed as a method of creating platform-independent software (i.e. it doesn't matter what operating system you're running, this will work), JavaScript is mostly used to do cool things on Web sites.

Some of the cool things JavaScript can do:

- Check an online form before it's submitted
- Create a mini-application (like a drawing or painting program)
- Swap images in the browser
- Play a sound or multimedia file
- Run a scrolling banner
- Set and delete a cookie

If you plan on using JavaScript, spend the time to figure it out. If you're not a programmer, the best way to use JavaScript is to steal it. Go to somebody's Web site, look at their source code, copy it, and change it. If it works the first time, you're probably ready to learn PERL.

JavaScript Note

Like everything on the Web, not every browser can run JavaScript. Keep in mind that when you use JavaScript you may be losing users. There are even JavaScripts that let you find out what browser someone is using. (Although this is mostly a process of elimination, since the JavaScript won't be able to tell if you're running a browser that doesn't run JavaScript. Got it?)

```
<script>
function WriteCookie (cookieName, cookieValue,
expiry)
{
var expDate = new Date();
if(expiry)
{
expDate.setTime (expDate.getTime() + expiry);
document.cookie = cookieName + "=" + escape
(cookieValue) + "; expires=" +
expDate.toGMTString();
}
else
{
document.cookie = cookieName + "=" + escape
(cookieValue);
}
}
function setCookie ()
{
var name = document.forms[0].elements[0].value;
var value = document.forms[0].elements[1].value;
var num = document.forms[0].elements[2].value;
var select =
document.forms[0].elements[3].selectedIndex;
if(num == 0)
{
WriteCookie(name, value, 0);
}
else if(select == 0)
{
WriteCookie(name, value, 1000 * 60 * 60 * 24 * num);
}
else if(select == 1)
{
WriteCookie(name, value, 1000 * 60 * 60 * 24 *
num * 31);
}
else if(select == 2)
{
WriteCookie(name, value, 1000 * 60 * 60 * 24 *
num * 365);
}
}
</script>
```

Complex Java Stuff

There are whole books written on JavaScript. It's a miniature programming language based on JAVA, which is based on C++. It can be learned, but be prepared to spend some time at it.

Here's what a chunk of JavaScript looks like. This was taken from a Netscape page explaining how to set or delete a JavaScript cookie (http://developer.netscape.com/docs/examples/javascript/cookies writecookie.html) Don't worry if you don't understand it. We're not even going to try and explain it.

A few JavaScript Rules

Like all HTML tags, scripts begin with a <SCRIPT> tag and end with a </SCRIPT> tag. Everything in between is the script. To specify which script language, use the LANGUAGE="JAVASCRIPT" attribute.

JavaScript command lines end with a semicolon. This enables you to write a very long command line with multiple carriage returns before finishing with the semicolon.

JavaScripts are loaded according to where they are placed in the HTML file. If they are placed in the <HEAD>, they are loaded before any page elements appear. If they are placed before a block of text, they will load before that block. If they are placed after a block of text (or images), they'll load after those images appear.

Here's a simple HTML page with JavaScript to try out. Move it around to see how it loads slightly differently.

JavaScript Alert

This is about the simplest JavaScript we could find. The JavaScript alert command creates a little box that displays whatever text is enclosed between the quotes. Other JavaScript commands that perform similar functions are confirm() and prompt(). These return information to the JavaScript, while the alert() command simply displays the text.

```
<HTML>
<HEAD>
<TITLE>Java Alert</TITLE>
</HEAD>
<BODY>
<H1>All this page does is display a Java
Alert.</H1>
<SCRIPT LANGUAGE="JAVASCRIPT">
alert("Here's an alert. You can modify the
JavaScript and put whatever you want in this
box.");
</SCRIPT>
</BODY>
</HTML>
```

Keep in mind that this alert will play every time somebody reloads the page, so it could get quite annoying.

CHAPTER 17

Legal Issues

Copyright, Trademarks, and More

Throughout this book we've advised you to "borrow" from other Web sites. Now we're going to temper that advice.

Stealing code, that is the software that makes up an HTML page, is not considered theft these days—mostly because there are only so many ways you can lay out a Web page. When somebody invents a new trick, everyone is soon to adopt it. Stealing code from a JavaScript is a bit more sticky. Again, JavaScript is a programming language, and the options in that language are limited and used for the same purposes by just about anybody.

Stealing a photograph or a sound file is something completely different. These involve creative and property rights. Rather than trust the books or Web sites on the legal issues, we decided to interview a professional. Kevin McNeely is an associate with the law firm of Partridge, Snow and Hahn. McNeely specializes in the swiftly changing world of Internet Law and is the author of the privately circulated paper "Internet Law."

What are the primary issues today on the Internet?

McNeely: If you're involved in some kind of commercial venture and you want to run a business, intellectual property is a key issue—trademark and copyright, infringing on other people's intellectual property, and other people taking your creative works and using them for some type of gain.

Intellectual Property

Can you talk a bit about the legal concerns that an ordinary person might have when building a Web site?

McNeely: The issues, which affect both commercial sites and individuals, are the intellectual property issues. The primary areas you need to be concerned with are trademark and copyright.

Copyright protects the author or creator of an original work of art. Typically the period of the copyright runs for 50 years beyond the life of the author. The copyright vests upon creating the original work. In other words, you don't have to make any type of legal filing to create your copyright. The fact that you've created it in a tangible medium makes it your property. That's different from trademark.

In order to receive a federal trademark, you have to register it with the patent and trademark office. A trademark protects the identity of a business owner so that consumers can recognize the source of products or services. It's essential for brand identity. If you're really inventive and you come up with a new e-commerce business model, or a new type of programming method, you can patent that.

A patent gives you the strongest set of legal rights, because it allows you to monopolize an invention for a period of 20 years from the date of the filing. Patent rights are important, but they're also much more difficult to get. It requires very able patent council and a lot more money. There is an extensive review of the invention. The tests for patentability are that first, it must be new—it must have novelty. Secondly, it must be in a patentable category of inventiveness. Finally, it must be non-obvious. In order to be non-obvious, the test that's used is whether or not an inventor skilled in the ordinary category of practice of that invention would have considered it obvious. That's a fairly high threshold to meet.

If you steal something that's copyrighted, what happens?

McNeely: Intellectual property lawsuits are enforced through the federal courts. Typically if you're violating somebody's intellectual property rights, you can receive an injunction. The court will prohibit you from using that intellectual property. You can imagine the dilemma that can put you if you've pirated someone else's invention or intellectual property and you've incorporated that device into your product—you may be required to pull a product off the market. You may also be liable for damages.

Should we worry about clip art and the like? What shouldn't we steal?

McNeely: First you should look for the copyright symbol. Then, you should determine whether or not clip art has a license and what the terms are. Finally, you have to consider what you are using this copyrighted work for. Are you trying to make money or are you merely expressing an idea or a concept? If you're putting it to commercial use and you're making a profit, it's more likely that the company or person owning the work will come after you. And it's more likely that a court will find damages and infringement.

Domain Names

McNeely: One interesting area involves disputes around domain names. When they think about a domain name, they want a snappy name. It could have a prior federal trademark registration. If it does, that trademark holder may want to prohibit you from using that domain name. One way to prevent this from occurring is to do a quick online check. You can do that by getting on the U.S. Patent and Trademark office's Web site (www.uspto.gov) Click over to their trademark section, and you can actually do a search for trademarks.

When we post stuff on the Web, it's there for anyone to see and to take. What can be done if somebody else steals my work?

McNeely: The problem you have if you put a creative work online—say a book—is that it's very difficult to track who actually took the copyrighted work. It's also very difficult to bring a lawsuit and get a judgment. Typically, in terms of logistics, the first hurdle you face is the time and expense of bringing a lawsuit. The second hurdle you face is the fact that you're not just dealing with U.S. law anymore. If someone lives and maintains a Web site in another country, then you've got to deal with a whole other system of laws. It may not be feasible to try to press for some type of legal action.

Business Concerns

According to a recent study, lawsuits for Internet fraud are on the rise. In a storefront business, people exchange money for goods and services, or they sign a credit card slip. Everything is done face to face. What do you see are the problems for businesses online?

McNeely: One of the key hurdles for using a Web site commercially is authenticating who you're dealing with and creating a valid and binding contract. If you engage in commerce, if you run a business on the Web, in order to have a deal with someone you need a binding and lawful agreement.

The law has to change in order to encompass making a binding agreement on line and being able to enforce that agreement.

The keys to that are first of all the contract itself. On the Web, you click on something to bind yourself to an agreement.

In a traditional contract, you sign a piece of paper. It has signatures and other indicia of authenticity. You don't necessarily have those when you're dealing with online contracts. You're dealing with clicks. You're dealing with an electronic record, not a piece of paper. It's something that the courts are wrestling with and the laws need to be change in order to validate online contracts.

A second issue, that's equally important, is who are you dealing with? Can you confirm their identity? Can you ensure that the message is authentic and it hasn't been altered in its transfer? Can you ensure that the person can't deny that they sent it—either it wasn't them or that they didn't send that content.

You're saying that not only are people making binding contracts that are difficult to enforce, but you may not be able to know who you're dealing with? You're talking a bit about hijacking and a bit about fraud—using somebody else's identity or a false identity. Is there any way to be certain that the person you're dealing with is who they say they are?

McNeely: In order to accomplish this, you need a form of digital signature. A digital signature essentially deals with all these issues by using public key encryption. You maintain your public key with a certifying authority. You keep your private key secretly. Other people can use your public key to decrypt a message and send a message back to you. Because there's an independent certifying authority, they can confirm through the certification authority that in fact it was you who sent the message. Because you're using keys of a matched pair, you can ensure the integrity of the message itself.

It's like the three legs of a stool. You need a commercial binding contract. You need to insure the authenticity of a person. And finally, you need to create some kind of digital cash. That's another area in development—creating currencies online that are going to help commerce flow on the Web. Those are the primary issues of conducting a transaction online.

If I've opened a store online, should I worry, or should I let the credit card company worry?

McNeely: Treat it the way you'd accept a credit card over the phone. The problem really is that there's a perception that it's unsafe to give your credit card out over the Internet, that people can eavesdrop and get your numbers and you won't be reimbursed. As a consumer, as long as you follow whatever guidelines are in place—typically you have to report a loss or cancel a transaction within 2 billing cycles—you're covered up to $50 as a consumer. Consumers don't have a lot of confidence in that, even though it's the law. So most people don't buy very expensive items online—for a variety of probably very good reasons.

In this situation, you're dealing more with a consumer confidence issue than a legal issue.

Privacy Issues

What are the legal privacy issues on the Web?

McNeely: When you're building a Web site, one of the key things you want are eyeballs. You want marketing data so that you can attract advertisers and sell that marketing data to others. Or you want to use that marketing data yourself to market your services more effectively.

You have to be careful when you're dealing with children. It's against federal law to knowingly collect personal information from children. Or to have a Web site targeted at children without having a privacy policy that gets parental consent for their children providing personal information. There are a lot of interesting cases and issues on privacy available online at www.ftc.gov. To follow the latest and greatest on what America is doing about privacy policy, cruise their Web site.

Legal Links

Go to the Federal Trade Commission for information about privacy and trade online: www.ftc.gov

U.S. Patent and Trademark Office: www.uspto.gov

See TRUSTe for a nondisclosure policy: www.truste.org

Appendix A: Links

Browsers

- Netscape: www.netscape.com/computing/download/
- Microsoft Internet Explorer: www.microsoft.com/downloads/
- Web Workshop Cross-Browser Cheat Sheet: msdn.microsoft.com/workshop/essentials/versions/cheatsheet.asp
- Opera: www.opera.com/
- Lynx—a text-only browser

    - Lynx for Windows 95/98/NT: lynx.browser.org/ or www.slcc.edu/lynx/current/
    - Lynx Users Guide Version 2.3: www.cc.ukans.edu/lynx_help/Lynx_users_guide.html
    - Macintosh MacLynx (postcardware): www.lirmm.fr/~gutkneco/maclynx/

Business and Online Sales

- The Electronic Commerce Guide—an online magazine about electronic commerce: ecommerce.internet.com/
- Always Open for Business: L A Merchant's Guide to Opening a Store on the Web. This site includes an excellent questionnaire : www.mercantec.com/merchants/AOBweb.html
- eVisa—Visa card's electronic services division: www.visa.com/eVisa
- The Internet Sales Discussion List—an e-mail list discussing Internet sales strategies: www.mmgco.com/isales/
- Transaction Net: www.transaction.net/
- CyberCash: www.cybercash.com/
- How to Sell on the Web: store.yahoo.com/secrets.html
- Internet.com (www.internet.com)

    Excellent features on this site from Mecklermedia, a publisher of Internet magazines, including The List, a directory of over 3,000 Internet service providers, Search Engine Watch, Browser Watch, Product Watch, and an electronic commerce guide with hundreds of links.

- TechWeb (www.techweb.com)

    This site includes daily technology news, product reviews, software downloads, an online store, plus The Net Insider—people profiles and articles on the Internet, with sound clips—and a Net guide from CMP Media, a publisher of a dozen computer magazines.

- ZDNet (www.zdnet.com)

    This site features daily technology news from Ziff-Davis, links to its computer magazines (*Yahoo! Internet Life*, *PC Magazine*, and *PC Computing*), an Internet section, product reviews, software downloads, and an online store.

Clip Art

- Barry's Clipart Server: www.barrysclipart.com
- The Clip Art Connection: www.clipartconnection.com
- The Clip Art Universe: www.nzwwa.com/mirror/clipart
- Photodisc: www.photodisc.com
- Pixelsight: www.www.pixelsight.com
- University of Miami, Richter Library Web Development Resource: www.library.miami.edu/GRAPHICS/browser.html
- Nova Development—Web Explosion: www.novadevelopment.com

Copyright Links

- GNU General Public License: www.fsf.org/copyleft/gpl.html

E-mail List Information

- Liszt.com—huge e-mail list directory: www.liszt.com
- Liszt.com—submit your e-mail list: www.liszt.com/submit.html
- INTERNET & NETWORKING: Internet Mailing Lists Guides and Resources: www.ifla.org/I/training/listserv/lists.htm
- Lsoft—the makers of LISTSERV software (Windows): www.lsoft.com/
- Fog City Software's LetterRip Pro (Macintosh): www.fogcity.com/letterrip.html

Educational and Programming Sites
- CGI Programming Open FAQ: www.boutell.com/ openfaq/cgi/36.html
- The CGI Resource Index: www.cgi-resources.com/ cgi-lib.pl: cgi-lib.stanford.edu/cgi-lib/
- CGI.pm: www-genome.wi.mit.edu/ftp/pub/software/ WWW/cgi_docs.html
- PERL: www.perl.com/
- HTML Tag List: utopia.knoware.nl/users/schluter/doc/ tags/index.html

Free Web Hosting Information and Services
Free Web hosting site lists:
- www.TotallyFreeStuff.com/pages/
- dir.yahoo.com/Business_and_Economy/ Companies/Internet_Services/Web_Services/ Web site_Hosting/Free_Web_Pages/

FTP Software
- Fetch for Macintosh: www.dartmouth.edu/pages/ softdev/fetch.html
- FTP Voyager for Windows: www.ftpvoyager.com/
- WS_FTP for Windows: www.ipswitch.com/Products/ WS_FTP/index.html
- CuteFTP for Windows: www.cuteftp.com

HTML News and Information
- W3C World Wide Web Consortium (the folks who are trying to standardize the Web): www.w3.org/
- W3C's information about cascading style sheets: www.w3.org/Style/css/
- PDF file of HTML 4 recommendations: www.w3.org/TR/REC-html40/html40.pdf

Internet Service Provider and Web Hosting Links
- A list of Web Hosting search engines: dir.yahoo.com/Business_and_Economy/Companies/ Internet_Services/Web_Services/Web site_Hosting/ Directories/
- The Internet List: www.InternetList.com

- Lists of free Web hosting options: www.TotallyFreeStuff.com/pages/*dir.yahoo.com/ Business_and_Economy/Companies/Internet_Services/ Web_Services/Web site_Hosting/Free_Web_Pages/
- Web Host Guild: www.whg.org

Quick Online Web Lessons
- Raggett's 10 Minute Guide to HTML: www.w3.org/ MarkUp/Guide/
- NCSA (at UIUC) Beginner's Guide to HTML: www.ncsa.uiuc.edu/General/Internet/WWW/ HTMLPrimer.html
- Ten Quck Tips for Site Design by Tom Karlo (an excellent resource): www.pixelfoundry.com/Toms/QuickTen/index.html
- Webopedia—an up-to-the-minute encyclopedia of Internet definitions: webopedia.internet.com/
- Web Design Group's Guide to Cascading Style Sheets: www.htmlhelp.com/reference/css/
- Web66 Online Cookbook: web66.coled.umn.edu/ cookbook/

Resources
- Internet Cafes: dir.yahoo.com/Business_and_ Economy/Companies/Internet_Services/Internet_Cafes/ Complete_Listing/)
- TRUSTe Privacy Statement Wizard: www.truste.org/wizard/
- Web Rant—why the web sucks, II: surfin.spies.com/ ~ceej/Words/rant.web.html
- David Strom's Web Informant—A free weekly e-mail newsletter discussing issues around the World Wide Web. To subscribe, send a blank e-mail to: webinfor-mant-subscribe@egroups.com
- The Web Monkey—The Web Developer's Resource: www.hotwired.com/webmonkey/
- W3C HTML Validation Service: validator.w3.org/

Scripts, Scripting, and Perl
- Script Search.Com—A huge script library that includes CGIs and JavaScripts: www.scriptsearch.com/
- Matt's Script Archive: www.worldwidemart.com/scripts/
- CGI Authoring Newsgroup: comp.www.authoring.cgi
- Perl Mongers: www.pm.org

Search Engines, Search Registration, etc.

- Search Engine Watch—Everything you want to know about search engines, including strategies, places to register, and even conventions about search engines: www.searchenginewatch.com/
- Jef Poskanzer's ACME Labs Search Forms. Lots of code that you can steal and use for yourself: www.acme.com/searches.html
- Savvy Search—Site searches multiple search engines: www.savvysearch.com/
- World Submit—A fee-based search engine registration service. Registers with more than 1,000 search engines for less than $100: www.worldsubmit.com/
- SubmitIt: www.submitit.com
- Yahoo!: www.yahoo.com
- AltaVista: www.altavista.com
- Excite: www.excite.com
- Google: www.google.com/ or to add a URL: www.google.com/addurl.html
- Infoseek: www.infoseek.com
- HotBot: www.hotbot.com
- Lycos: www.lycos.com
- WebCrawler: www.webcrawler.com
- Northern Light: www.northernlight.com

Sounds, Videos, and Multimedia

- MP3 made easy: www.mp3.com/help/
- RealAudio: www.realaudio.com
- QuickTime: www.apple.com/quicktime
- Shockwave and Flash Depository: www.shockwave.com
- Macromedia: www.macromedia.com
- Daily MP3: dailymp3.com/
- SoundJam MP MP3 converter for Macintosh: www.soundjam.com
- Audiocatalyst MP3 converter for Mac and Windows: www.xingtech.com/mp3/audiocatalyst/

Useful Links

- Whois (find out whether your domain name is taken): www.networksolutions.com/cgi-bin/whois/whois

- Web Page Backward Compatibility Viewer: www.delorie.com/web/wpbcv.html
- Cookie Central—The last word on cookies, which allow Web sites to track your habits and preferences on the Web. This site also includes privacy protection tips and pros vs. cons of cookies: www.cookiecentral.com
- All-In-One Search Page—A one-stop shopping for many reference sources, here you will find *Bartlett's Familiar Quotations*, Shakespeare's complete works, current U.S. legislation, people finders, and search engines: www.allonesearch.com/

Useful Software

- HTML Tidy—a free HTML clean-up program: www.w3.org/People/Raggett/tidy/#download
- QuicKeys Home Page—QuicKeys is an excellent tool for creating macros and automating tasks within any application and across applications (Mac and PC): www.quickeys.com/

Web Auctions

- www.ebay.com—Sell or buy anything and everything.
- www.onsale.com—Bid on computers and equipment, sporting goods, and consumer electronics.
- auctions.yahoo.com/—A relative newcomer to auctions; a free service with a lot of clout.
- www.webauction.com—Bid on a variety of products, starting at only $1.

Appendix B: HTML Tag List

As of this writing, HTML 3 is the industry standard, but HTML 4 is the coming standard. These tags should be accurate for HTML 3 and HTML 4, except where otherwise noted. We have omitted a number of tags that work only in Netscape or Internet Explorer. Our objective is to minimize the confusion created by writing browser-specific code.

We've also omitted some of the more complex tags and attributes that have not been dealt with in this book or that are automatically handled by HTML design programs, such as the <IMG ISMAP and USEMAP> attributes.

Formal HTML

Formal HTML requires that all tags be closed with a slash tag. Practical HTML doesn't demand this. To make life easier for you, we've omitted the slash tag from those tags that don't require them.

About Attributes

Attributes are inserted within the open tag, not in the close (slash) tag. For example, the FONT= attribute goes inside the <P> tag, not the </P> tag. *Note:* Attributes can be used in any order within a tag. For example these two tags will look exactly the same:

```
<HR WIDTH="50%" ALIGN="CENTER">
<HR ALIGN="CENTER" WIDTH="50%">
```

`<!- ->`	Comment tag. Comments will not be printed by browsers but can be viewed in source code. The correct format for a comment is:`<!- This is a comment ->` *Note:* Tags that are included within a comment will not be recognized by HTML browsers. For example, <H3>This is a test</H3> will display "This is a test" in a browser. <!- <H3>This is a test</H3> -> will not display the header line.
`<A>`	Anchor.
`HREF=`	"URLlink" Hypertext reference location.
`NAME=`	The name of the anchor in the current document.
`TARGET=`	Sets the target window or frame for a document. All links will open in the target window or frame; useful for frames and for links pages. This default will be overridden by the use of a TARGET attribute in a link. Targets may be defined as "targetname" to refer to a particular window or by one of the following:
`_blank`	Link opens a new blank and unnamed window.
`_parent`	Link loads in the frame parent of the document. If there is no parent, the link opens in the current window.
`_self`	Link loads in the same window as the anchor that was clicked.
`_top`	Link loads in the entire window (eliminating any frames). If the document is already the top, then it defaults to _self.
`<AREA>`	Defines the size and shape of a client-side image map area.
`ALT`	Alternative name.
`SHAPE`	Defines the shape of the image map area. Options are CIRCLE, RECT, and POLY.
`COORDS`	Sets the coordinates of the image map area. If SHAPE=CIRCLE, then the COORDS are X-axis location, Y-axis location, and Radius. CORDS="X,Y,R." If SHAPE=RECT, then the COORDS are

upper left corner location and lower right corner location. RECT="X-top,Y-top,X-bottom,Y-Bottom"
If SHAPE=POLY, then the COORDS are X1,Y1, X2,Y2... Don't worry about closing the polygon, the computer will do it for you.

HREF	The link that the browser will go to.
NOHREF	This area has no link.
TARGET	Sets the target for the link. (See <A> above)
<B> </B>	Bold text. Sets the font between the tags to **boldface**.
<BASE>	Alters the base URL. Must be defined in the <HEAD>.
HREF	Specifies the new root URL. All links to other documents, images, or sound will use this new base location rather than the document's actual URL. For example, if the document's URL is http://www.mydomain.com/index, but you want to use a relative location of http://www.yourdomain.com/index, you would write the code like this: `<BASE HREF="http://www.yourdomain.com/index"` All subsequent local URL references would use the new base as their source. A link to "/images/temp.gif" would look in yourdomain.com rather than mydomain.com. However, a link to http://www.theirdomain.com/images/temp.gif would look in theirdomain.com.
TARGET	Sets the default target window or frame for a document. All links will open in the target window or frame. Useful for frames and for links pages. This default will be overridden by the use of a "targetname." Targets may be defined as "targetname" to refer to a particular frame window.
_blank	Link opens a new blank and unnamed window.
_parent	Link loads in the frame parent of the document. If there is no parent, the link opens in the current window.
_self	Link loads in the same window as the anchor that was clicked.
_top	Link loads in the entire window (eliminating any frames). If the document is already the top, then it defaults to _self.
<BASEFONT>	Sets the base font for a particular section of text. If the <BASEFONT> tag is used in a header, it sets the standard font for the entire document. If it is used within the body, then it sets the basefont for all subsequent text.
SIZE=	Set font size. Can be relative to browser default (i.e. <FONT SIZE="+4"> or defined specifically as <FONT SIZE=?> where ? is a number between 1 and 7. *Note:* FONT SIZE is not supported in all browsers.
FACE=	Changes the font. For example, <FONT FACE="Times, Serif" will display the font in Times, if that font is installed, and in a Serif font if Times is not installed.
COLOR=	Changes the base font color.
<BIG> </BIG>	Increases the current font size by one to a maximum font size of 7. Nesting <BIG> tags will add to the increase in the font size. For example, <BIG><BIG>text</BIG></BIG> will make the text font size +2.

`<BLINK> </BLINK>`	Blinks text. All text enclosed within these tags blinks, but only in Netscape Browsers. <BLINK> is considered one of the most annoying HTML tags. It is supported only by Netscape, and other browsers have not adopted it. We include it here, mostly as a warning. Occasionally you'll stumble across a <BLINK> text or feel inclined to use it. Try it out. Watch the screen for a while; very annoying. Then delete the <BLINK> tags from your HTML page.
`<BLOCKQUOTE>` `</BLOCKQUOTE>`, or `<BQ></BQ>`	Used for distinguishing very long quotes. Sets the enclosed text off from the text before and after. The <BLOCKQUOTE> text is usually indented.
`<BODY> </BODY>`	Defines the beginning and end of the body of the HTML document. The <BODY> tag must be after the <HEAD> tag.
BACKGROUND	Defines the background image to be displayed. Background images may be GIF or JPEGs. Example: BACKGROUND="../images/background.jpg"
BGCOLOR	Defines the background color for the page. Background color is overwritten by a background image.
BGPROPERTIES= "FIXED"	Fixes the background image in place so that if you scroll down, the image does not move.
TEXT	Specifies the color of normal text.
LINK	Specifies the color used to display an unvisited link.
ALINK	Specifies the color of active links (one which the mouse has clicked on but not yet released).
VLINK	Specifies the color of visited links.
ONLOAD	Specifies the JavaScript that will be run after all the elements on the HTML page have been loaded.
ONUNLOAD	Specifies the JavaScript that will be run when the user leaves the current HTML page.
`<CENTER> </CENTER>`	Center text and elements between tags. *Note:* ALIGN attribute overrides center tag, but any new unaligned paragraph or header will be centered.
` `	Break line (forced line break). Continues text on new line with no additional space between lines added.
`<CAPTION> </CAPTION>`	Defines a caption for a table. These tags only work within a TABLE.
ALIGN	Specifies where the caption will be placed: TOP, BOTTOM, LEFT, or RIGHT. (Netscape does not support LEFT and RIGHT.)
`<CITE> </CITE>`	Citation text (such as used for a book title; usually displayed in italics.
`<CODE></CODE>`	Computer code; usually displayed in a monotype font such as Courier.
`<DD>`	Definition description.
`<DFN> </DFN>`	Definition text. A logical font style.
`<DIV>..</DIV>`	Defines a division or subsection in the document.
CLASS=name	The name of the span.
STYLE= "attribute:value"	

`<DL> </DL>`	Definition list. A list composed of terms and definitions.
`<DT>`	Definition term.
`<EM> </EM>`	Emphasize text. Usually displayed in italics.
`<EMBED> </EMBED>`	Allows the Web page to play a sound or output from a plug-in, for example, Shockwave or Flash. In order for the <EMBED> tag to work, the plug-in must already be installed in the browser. The content will play automatically. Macromedia Shockwave example: <EMBED src="multimedia.dcr" </EMBED> The EMBED tag has many attributes, including WIDTH, HEIGHT, which define the window size of the embedded content. Other tags may depend on the type of multimedia being embedded.
`<FONT> </FONT>`	Alter font characteristics.
`SIZE=`	Set font size. Can be relative to browser default (i.e. <FONT SIZE="+4"> or defined specifically as <FONT SIZE=?> where ? is a number between 1 and 7. FONT SIZE is not supported in all browsers.
`FACE=`	Changes the font. For example, <FONT FACE="Times, Serif" will display the font in Times, if that font is installed, and in a serif font if Times is not installed.
`COLOR=`	Changes the font color.
`<FORM> </FORM>`	Designates an area of the page as a form. Forms include at least one user input field.
`ACTION`	This attribute tells the browser where to send the data.
`METHOD`	Tells how the data will be sent to the program. Options include GET or POST. Check with the CGI about which option is appropriate.
`ONRESET`	Designates the JavaScript to run when the user presses a "reset" field.
`ONSUBMIT`	Designates the JavaScript to run when the user presses a "submit" field.
`TARGET`	Designates the window in which the forms are opened.
`<FRAME>`	Determines the look and content of a particular frame, including what initially loads into that frame. The <FRAME> tag may only be used within a <FRAMESET>
`BORDERCOLOR`	Sets the border color of this frame. No color will display if FRAMEBORDER is set to 0.
`FRAMEBORDER`	Determines whether a border is displayed between this frame and other frames. FRAME-BORDER values may be 1 or 0. Setting the FRAMEBORDER=0 hides the border between frames. The default is 1.
`NAME`	Defines the name of the frame. While defining a frame's name is optional, we recommend using this attribute because content is typically targeted into a frame by its name.
`NORESIZE`	Including this attribute prevents a user from resizing the frame. If you don't use the NORESIZE, HTML assumes that frames are resizeable by users.
`SCROLLING`	Including the SCROLLING attribute allows users to scroll around the frame. Values include:
`YES`	Always displays a scroll bar.
`NO`	Never displays a scroll bar.
`AUTO`	Displays a scroll bar only when the frames content is larger than the FRAMESET's window's size. In other words, no scroll bar will appear if the frame's content fits in a window.

SRC	The URL that loads when the frame is initially loaded. If no SRC is defined, then the frame is displayed as blank.
\<FRAMESET\> **\</FRAMESET\>**	Defines an HTML document as a frames page. Frames pages have NO \<BODY\> tags. All content displayed from a frames page are contained within the \<FRAME\> or \<NOFRAME\> tags. \<FRAMESETS\> are defined with either rows or columns but may be nested to create more complex frames.
BORDER	Sets the width of frame borders. Can be set to zero.
BORDERCOLOR	Sets the color of the frame borders.
COLS	Sets the number of columns the \<FRAMESET\> will have. COLS are defined by a number of values separated by commas.
ROWS	Sets the number of rows the \<FRAMESET\> will have. ROWS are defined by a number of values separated by commas. Frames **cannot** have both COLS and ROWS attributes.
ROWS/COLS values	COLS or ROWS may have values set as either pixels, percentages, or stars. Using pixel-sized frames can be tricky, depending on the user's screen size. Example: COLS="138,74%" sets two columns, one with a width of 138 pixels and the remainder set to 74% of the page. Example: COLS="1*,2*" sets two columns. The first row will be one-third the width of the screen. The second will be two-thirds the width of the screen.
FRAMEBORDER	Sets the display of borders for the inside frames. Values are YES or NO.
FRAMESPACING	Sets the padding between frames in pixels.
\<HTML\> \</HTML\>	This tag tells your browser that the file is an HTML file.
\<HEAD\> \</HEAD\>	Identifies the header part of your HTML file. This part usually contains \<TITLE\> tags as well as \<META\> tags.
\<H1\> \</H1\>	Heading level 1; used for the most important heading in a document.
\<H2\> \</H2\>	Heading level 2
\<H3\> \</H3\>	Heading level 3
\<H4\> \</H4\>	Heading Level 4
\<H5\> \</H5\>	Heading level 5
\<H6\> \</H6\>	Heading level 6; used for the least important heading in a document.
ALIGN=	Alignment options: LEFT, CENTER, RIGHT. The default is LEFT.
\<HR\>	Horizontal rule.
ALIGN	Left, Center, or Right. Default is Center.
COLOR	Changes the rule's color. Works in Internet Explorer but not in Netscape.
NOSHADE	Creates a gray rule without a 3D/box effect.
SIZE	How many pixels thick the rule will be. Default is 1 pixel.
WIDTH	How wide the rule will be. Either pixels or as a percentage. Default is 100 percent.
\<I\>\</I\>	Italicize text.

`<IMG>`	This tag tells Web browsers to display an image. Images may be stored in GIF, JPEG, X Bitmp, or PNG format.
ALIGN	Aligns the image relative to the text and page.
ALT	Alternative description.
BORDER	Sets the size of the border surrounding the image. Be sure to set this value to zero (0) if you don't want a border.
HEIGHT	Overrides the image's actual height with this pixel size or percentage.
HSPACE	Specifies the amount of space the browser puts on the left and right sides of the image. (in pixels)
NAME	Gives the image a name. Used in JavaScript mouse rollover effects. Netscape and Explorer 4 and above only.
OPTIONS: TOP, BOTTOM, CENTER, LEFT, RIGHT	
SRC	Image source; typically .jpg or .gif files.
USEMAP	Tells the browser to use a client-side image map. Using the # sign tells the browser that the map is within the current page.
VSPACE	Specifies the amount of space the browser puts on the top and bottom of the image (in pixels).
WIDTH	Overrides the image's actual height with this pixel size or percentage.
INPUT	Creates an input control field for a <FORM>. Must be used within <FORM> tags.
ALIGN	Aligns the INPUT field.
BUTTON	Creates a clickable button.
CHECKBOX	Creates a checkbox.
CHECKED	Automatically puts a check mark in the field when used with TYPE="RADIO" or TYPE="CHECKBOX."
FILE	Allows a user to attach a file to the form.
HIDDEN	Information in this input is hidden from the user and not modifiable. Useful for letting you know what page someone is submitting from.
IMAGE	An image submit button, rather than a text button.
MAXLENGTH	Sets the maximum number of characters of a TEXT or PASSWORD field.
NAME	Sets the name of the control field. This name will be part of the data sent to the server.
PASSWORD	Information typed into this field will not be displayed on the screen.
RADIO	Creates a radio button. Every radio button in a group must have the same name, but they ought to have different values. Only one radio button in a group can be checked.
RESET	Resets the form.
SRC	Sets the URL of the image used when TYPE="IMAGE."
SUBMIT	Submits the form.
TEXT	Creates a one-line text input field.
TYPE	Tells what type of input this will be.
VALUE	Sets the value of the element. The Value has different results, depending on the TYPE of input.
RADIO and CHECKBOX value sets the value that will be sent to the server if that radio or checkbox is checked.	
BUTTON, RESET and SUBMIT value sets the text of that button.	
TEXT, PASSWORD and HIDDEN value sets the default value of that field.	
`<KBD> </KBD>`	Keyboard entry. Usually displayed in a bold monotype font.

`<LI>`	List item. Used to designate the start of a new item in a list. Does not need an `</LI>` tag.
VALUE	Assigns a new starting value for this and subsequent items in a list. Allows ordered lists to have mixed-up order.
TYPE	Changes the kind of numbering in an ordered list, or the type of bullet in an unordered list.
`=A`	uppercase letters
`=a`	lowercase letters
`=I`	uppercase Roman numerals
`=i`	lowercase Roman numerals
`=1`	arabic numbers (default)
`="CIRCLE"`	a circle bullet
`="DISC"`	a filled-in circle bullet
`="SQUARE"`	a square bullet
`<LINK>`	Link tag; used to access an external style sheet.
`HREF="stylesheetname.css"`	
`MEDIA="screen"`	
`REL=StyleSheet (the relationship)`	
`TYPE="text/css"`	
`<MAP> </MAP>`	Defines client-side image maps.
NAME	The name of the map; case sensitive.
`<META>`	Meta tags.
HTTP-EQUIV	Sets information about this page's HTML.
`="CONTENT -TYPE`	allows for style sheets.
`="EXPIRES`	Sets the expiration date. Useful if you don't want search engines to keep this page around.
`="REFRESH`	Refreshes the page after a certain number of seconds.
NAME	Allows search engines (and others) to discover the name of AUTHOR, DESCRIPTION, KEYWORDS, or GENERATOR (the program used to generate this page). Format: <META NAME="AUTHOR" CONTENT="Beth Hellman">
	`<META HTTP-EQUIV="REFRESH" CONTENT="10"; url=nextpage.htm>` Takes you to the next page after 10 seconds.
	`<META HTTP-EQUIV="Content-Style-Type" CONTENT="text/css">` Sets the meta tag for a cascading style sheet.
	`<META NAME="keywords" CONTENT="insert keywords about your business here,...."` >
	`<META NAME="description" CONTENT="` This is the description that many search engines will display when they find your site."
`<NOBR> </NOBR>`	No line break. All the text in between the <NOBR> and </NOBR> tags will display on the same line. This can make for some very long lines.
`<NOFRAME> </NOFRAME>`	Defines the content that will be displayed if the user has a browser that either can't show frames or is set to not display frames. Any browser that can view frames ignores content within the <NOFRAME> tags. <NOFRAME> is only used within a <FRAMESET> page. Treat a

<NOFRAME> as a <BODY> command; all <BODY> elements may be included within a <NOFRAME>...</NOFRAME> tag set.

<OL> </OL>	Ordered list; a numerical list.
START	Starts your list from something other than the default of 1. For example, start your list with 7.
TYPE	What kind of numbering do you want?
=A	uppercase letters
=a	lowercase letters
=I	uppercase Roman numerals
=i	lowercase Roman numerals
=1	arabic numbers (default)
<OPTION> </OPTION>	The Option tag defines the value displayed in a <SELECT> input control list.
SELECTED	Sets this <OPTION> as a default value.

VALUE	Sets the value of the OPTION element. Example:
	`<P>Morning or night? <SELECT NAME="Time">`
	`<option value="AM"selected>AM</option>`
	`<option value="PM">PM</option>`
	`</SELECT></P>`

<P>	Signals the beginning of a new paragraph. Does not require a </P> to conclude.
ALIGN=	Alignment options: LEFT, CENTER, RIGHT
<PRE> </PRE>	Preformatted text. Text between the <PRE> and </PRE> tags is displayed in a monotype font. Text is displayed as is, including carriage returns and extra spaces.
ALIGN=	Alignment options: LEFT, CENTER, RIGHT
<S> </S>	Strikethrough. All text enclosed between these tags will be displayed as strikethrough.
<SELECT> </SELECT>	The <SELECT> tag defines a list of input control data from a list of <OPTION>s that may be selected. It is only valid in the FORM element. One example of a select box would allow the user to select the month from a list of 12 months.
MULTIPLE	Allows multiple items from the list to be selected.
NAME	Gives this input field a name that can be used by scripts.
SIZE	Sets the number of lines that are displayed at one time.
<SMALL> </SMALL>	Makes text smaller. Decreases the current font size by one to a minimum font size of 1. Nesting <SMALL> tags will add to the increase in the font size. For example, <SMALL><SMALL>text</SMALL></SMALL> will make the text font size -2.
<SPAN> </SPAN>	Defines a span of text or images. Note: <SPAN> may be used in the middle of another element, for example within a <P> or an <H3>.
CLASS=name	The name of the span.
STYLE="attribute:value"	
<STRONG> </STRONG>	Strong emphasis; usually displayed in boldface.
<STRIKE> </STRIKE>	Strikethrough text.

`<STYLE> </STYLE>`	Style sheet tag.
ELEMENT	Each element may define any page element, such as H1, P, B, etc. `{attribute:value1; attribute2:value2}.`
TYPE	Sets the type of style sheet: text/css, text/javascript
`<SUB> </SUB>`	Subscript text.
`<SUP> </SUP>`	Superscript text.
`<TABLE> </TABLE>`	Tag defines the table.
ALIGN	Aligns the entire table LEFT, RIGHT, or CENTER (default is LEFT).
BACKGROUND	Defines a background image for the entire table. For example: BACKGROUND="images/background.gif"
BGCOLOR	Defines the background color for the table.
BORDER	Defines the tables's border widths.
BORDERCOLOR	Defines the table's border color. This has no effect if BORDER is set to zero. (Internet Explorer only).
CELLPADDING	Defines the space between the stuff in the cell and the cell's border; either a percentage or pixel value.
FRAME	Sets what part of the table's border will be visible. Options include: ABOVE, BELOW, BORDER, HSIDES (left and right border, VSIDES (top and bottom border), LHS (left hand side), RHS (right hand side), and VOID (no borders around the outside, but borders in between cells to create a tic-tac-toe effect). Not valid in Netscape.
HEIGHT	Sets the table's height.
WIDTH	Sets the table's width either in pixels or as a percentage of the remaining width.
`<TD> </TD>`	Table data. Put the text and/or images for each table cell in between the `<TD>` and `</TD>` tags.
ALIGN	Specifies the cell's alignment.
BACKGROUND	Specifies the cell's background image.
BGCOLOR	Specifies the cell's background color.
COLSPAN	Allows a cell to cross more than one column. The default is 1. A COLSPAN=0 allows a header to continue across all remaining cells to the end of the table.
HEIGHT	Defines the cell's height.
NOWRAP	Turns off automatic wrapping. May make cells very wide.
ROWSPAN	Allows a cell to cross more than one row. The default is 1. A COLSPAN=0 allows a header to continue down all remaining rows to the bottom of the table.
VALIGN	Defines the cell's vertical alignment: TOP, MIDDLE, BOTTOM, or BASELINE.
WIDTH	Sets the cell's width. *Note:* To set a cell's width, you must set the table's width.
`<TEXTAREA> </TEXTAREA>`	Creates a text input field of more than one line.
COLS	Sets how many columns (characters) the text window will be.
NAME	Sets the name of the TEXTAREA field. This information will be submitted with the form.
ROWS	Sets the number of text lines shown on the screen.

`<TH> </TH>`	Table header; defines table heading text.
`ALIGN`	Defines the header's alignment (LEFT, RIGHT, or CENTER plus JUSTIFY or CHAR).
`BACKGROUND`	Defines the header cell's background image.
`BGCOLOR`	Defines the header cell's background color.
`COLSPAN`	Allows a header to span more than one column.
`HEIGHT`	Defines the cell's height.
`NOWRAP`	Turns off the automatic wrapping feature.
`ROWSPAN`	Sets the number of rows the header cell spans.
`VALIGN`	Defines the header's vertical alignment.
`<TITLE>`	The document's title is enclosed between the <TITLE> and </TITLE> tags. This is the information that shows up in search engine displays as well as at the top of browser windows. The <TITLE> must be in the <HEAD>.
`<TR> </TR>`	Table row. Tables must have at least one row. Rows contain table data <TD> and may have a table header <TH>.
`ALIGN`	Defines the alignment of all the cells in this row (LEFT, RIGHT, or CENTER plus JUSTIFY or CHAR). The ALIGN=CHAR will create alignment around the decimal point, allowing lists of numbers to line up. To use an alternative character, use the CHAR= attribute.
`BACKGROUND`	Sets the background image for the entire column.
`BGCOLOR`	Defines the background color for the entire column.
`CHAR`	Defines an alternative alignment character when ALIGN=CHAR.
`VALIGN`	Defines the vertical alignment. Options include: TOP, MIDDLE, BOTTOM, and BASELINE.
`<TT> </TT>`	Typewriter text.
`<U> </U>`	Underscore text
`<UL> </UL>`	Unordered list; a bullet-style list.
`TYPE`	Changes the type of bullet.
`= "CIRCLE"`	a circle bullet
`= "DISC"`	a filled-in circle bullet (default)
`= "SQUARE"`	a square bullet

Appendix C: Web Browser Error Messages

It happens to everyone. You're having a fine time surfing around and enjoying yourself when one of those baffling, infuriating error messages appears on your screen. Your computer is misbehaving, telling you it can't connect to the Web site you want or has never heard of it. What nerve.

The most common reason for an error message is simply that you typed in the wrong Internet address—misspelling it, leaving out a punctuation mark, using a back slash instead of a front slash (/), or omitting a capital letter. The exact address is needed without a slip-up, or else your browser can't find the site—one excellent reason to use bookmarks so you just click an often-used Web site with no typing. Checking the Internet address carefully is the first thing to do when an error message appears.

Here are the most common errors, plus tips on what to do next.

401 Access Denied or Authorization Required

This means the person in charge of the site is limiting access to certain people, possibly through passwords. If you feel you should have access to the site—because you've used the password, for example—e-mail the person in charge to ask why you are being shut out. If you don't have the e-mail address, try "webmaster@" followed by the site's domain name.

403 Forbidden

This means the file was set up wrong by the person in charge. Nobody will be able to reach this site. Try later; maybe it will be fixed.

404 Not Found

This means there is no Web page with the name you typed, but a Web site exists at this address. The page may have been deleted or moved around by the person in charge. Type the address of the site's home page, then search through the site to see if the page has been relocated. Another explanation is that the person moved their entire site to a new location.

500 Server Error

This means the server has mechanical problems or something was set up wrong. Try later; maybe it will be fixed.

The Requested URL Was Not Found (or Cannot Open)

This means the Web site cannot be located. Click "reload" to try again. Another explanation is that your cache of already viewed Web sites may be too full. Clean it. In "options" or "preferences," click "advanced" or "browser," then click "empty cache" or something similar. See if you can reach other Web sites. If you can, there is a problem with this site; if not, the problem is with your computer or Internet connection.

Unable To Connect To

This means the site can't be reached. Perhaps the site was taken down or moved to another location and the person in charge didn't include a link to the new address. It may also be the server's fault—it's down or busy. Click "reload" to try again. Try to reach other sites; if you can, the problem is with this site.

Appendix D: Character Entity List

Some characters are not automatically recreated in HTML. In other words, if you want the browser to display a pretend swear word like "%$@!" you can't just type it between a pair of paragraph tags.

Character entities may be reproduced either by using the entity name or the entity number preceded by the ampersand (&) and followed by a semi-colon (;). For example, to have the ampersand appear in an HTML page, you'd need to type either "&" or "&"

This list is an abbreviated version of the complete Character Entities List.

ENTITY NAME	ENTITY NUMBER	RESULT
		non-breaking space
&quot;	&#34;	quotation mark
&ndash;	&#150;	en dash
&mdash;	&#151;	em dash
&tilde;	&#152;	small tilde
&amp;	&#38;	ampersand
&lt;	&#60;	less-than sign
&gt;	&#62;	greater-than sign
&euro;		euro sign
&iexcl;	&#161;	inverted exclamation mark
&cent;	&#162;	cent sign
&pound;	&#163;	pound sign
&curren;	&#164;	currency sign
&yen;	&#165;	yen sign
&brvbar;	&#166;	broken vertical bar
&sect;	&#167;	section sign
&uml;	&#168;	umlaut
&copy;	&#169;	copyright sign
&reg;	&#174;	registered trademark sign
&deg;	&#176;	degree sign
&plusmn;	&#177;	plus-or-minus sign
&sup2;	&#178;	superscript two (squared)
&sup3;	&#179;	superscript three (cubed)
&para;	&#182;	paragraph sign
&iquest;	&#191;	inverted question mark
&times;	&#215;	multiplication sign

Portions © International Organization for Standardization 1986 Permission to copy in any form is granted for use with conforming SGML systems and applications as defined in ISO 8879, provided this notice is included in all copies.

Glossary

ActiveX control. A small add-on program that enhances the ability of Internet Explorer browsers to do specific tasks; similar to a plug-in.

ADSL (Asymmetric Digital Subscriber Line). A speedy way of using the nonvoice part of regular telephone lines to send data, also known as DSL.

AOL (America Online). The biggest commercial online service, it offers special content for members only, plus Internet access.

ARPANET (Advanced Research Projects Agency Network). The computer network developed by the U.S. Department of Defense to survive a nuclear attack; an ancestor of the Internet.

attached file (or attachment). A file sent with an e-mail message, which may be text, images, sound, or video.

attribute. Attributes are the modifiable parts of HTML tags. For example, in the tag <IMG SRC = "image.jpg"> the tag is "IMG" and the attribute is "SRC" ("image.jpg" is the value that is image source value).

bit. The tiniest amount of computerized data. Bits per second (bps) is a common way to measure the speed at which data is transmitted.

byte. Eight bits of computerized data.

bookmark. A way to save favorite Web pages so you don't have to type in an Internet addresses again.

browser. A software program that locates and displays Web pages and other Internet resources.

cache. A place on your computer's hard drive that stores recently viewed documents so they can be accessed quickly.

chat. Communicate by typing and receiving messages to other people in real time, without the delays of bulletin boards or e-mail.

client. A software program that communicates with another computer, called a server, to use its files or programs.

code. The techie term for a piece of a written software. HTML pages are code. JavaScripts are code.

commercial online service. A company that offers special content, plus Internet access, through its computer network to members.

CompuServe. A commercial online service, now owned by America Online, its former rival.

configure. Adjust settings to tailor a device to work with something else. For example, your TCP/IP software needs to be configured to work properly with your Internet service provider, and your modem needs to be configured to work with your computer.

cookie. Information stored on your computer's hard drive by a Web page after you view it, which helps it "recognize" you on your next visit.

cyberspace. Coined by science fiction writer William Gibson, cyberspace is another word for the digital world that exists only in electronic media. The World Wide Web is cyberspace, but so is the pause you hear while you wait for a telephone to connect.

domain name. The name registered for an Internet site. The end is the top-level domain—.com, .org, .edu—which shows what type of entity is behind the site. The part before that is the second-level domain, which is more specific, and is usually the name or shortened name of the company, organization, or person.

download. Copy a file or program from another computer onto your computer's hard drive.

dpi. Dots per inch. One measurement of image resolution/quality. The more dots per inch, the higher the resolution.

DSL (Digital Subscriber Line). See ADSL.

e-mail. Electronic mail, which you can send or receive over a computer network.

emoticons. Punctuation symbols for emotions, used in e-mail and newsgroup postings.

encryption. Scrambling messages so they cannot be read without a decoding device.

FAQs (Frequently Asked Questions). Questions and answers on a topic, common in newsgroups and on Web sites.

filtering software. Software that blocks objectionable material—such as sexually explicit, violent, or hate-filled content—on the Internet, often used by parents to protect children.

flame. A hostile e-mail message or newsgroup posting.

frame. A separate and independent part of a Web page, which not all browsers can display.

FTP (File Transfer Protocol). A way of obtaining or sending files over the Internet from certain sites, which can be public or private.

geek. In computer terms, a geek is somebody who knows far more about computers than anyone really needs to. In carnival parlance, it refers to the sideshow performer who bites the heads off live chickens. How these two terms became synonymous is anyone's guess.

GIF (Graphics Interchange Format). A common format used to display images on the Web.

gigabyte. A hundred times a megabyte, or 1 million bytes of computer data.

graphical browser. A software program that locates and displays Web pages and other Internet resources by letting users point and click a mouse. Mosaic was the first graphical browser.

home page. The front page of a Web site; often used to designate a whole Web site.

IPO. Initial public offering; the stock offering that most Internet startup companies hope to use to get rich.

hypertext. The system of linked pages of related material, created with HTML, which makes up the World Wide Web.

HTML (Hypertext Markup Language). The programming language used to create Web pages that browsers can read.

HTTP (Hypertext Transfer Protocol). The command that moves hypertext pages over the Internet. It is the first part of an address located on the Web ("http://"), and is followed by the domain name.

icons. Pictures that are symbols for functions. For example, a mailbox, envelope, or paper and pen can stand for mail.

intelligent agent. A software program designed to locate information and understand context.

Internet. A network of computer networks that contains countless computers worldwide, each of which can communicate with any other.

Internet Explorer. A Web browser made by Microsoft.

Internet relay chat (IRC). A system that lets people type and receive messages in real time, without the delays of e-mail or newsgroups.

Internet service provider (ISP). A company that sells dial-up access to the Internet.

InterNIC. Agency responsible for the registry of Internet domain names, operated by Network Solutions, an American company.

ISDN (Integrated Services Digital Network). A speedy way to move data over regular telephone lines that is digital, instead of analog, at both ends.

JPEG (Joint Photographic Experts Group). A common format used to display images on the Web.

kilobytes. A thousand bits of data. Modem speeds are in kilobytes per second; for example, a 28.8 Kbps modem moves 28,800 data bits per second.

link. A word, phrase, or picture you can click on to connect to another Web page instantly.

Lynx. A text-only browser, often used on the UNIX operating system.

MacTCP. A Macintosh computer needs this connection software to be on the Internet (similar to TCP/IP for a IBM-type PC).

mailing list. A system that sends incoming e-mail to a group of subscribers who want mail on a specific topic.

megabyte (MB). A million bytes. For example, a computer's memory may be 32 MB, or 32,000,000 bytes.

modem. An electronic device that connects to your computer and telephone line and lets your computer talk to other computers.

monotype font. A fixed-width font in which every letter is exactly the same width. Example fonts include Monaco and Courier.

Mosaic. The first graphical browser, which lets users point and click a mouse to get around the World Wide Web.

MPEG (Motion Picture Experts Group). A common file format used for short video clips on the Internet.

Netscape Communicator. A software package, which includes the Netscape Navigator browser, an e-mail and newsreader program, home page building tools, and other features, developed by Netscape Communications Corporation.

Netscape Navigator. A browser developed by Netscape Communications Corporation.

newbie. A beginner on the Internet.

newsreader. A software program that lets you read and post messages in newsgroups.

newsgroup. A public discussion group on the Internet where you can read and post messages on a specific topic.

one-way e-mail list. An e-mail list that only sends information from its source to subscribers.

page. A document written in HTML on the World Wide Web, which can include text, picture, sound, or video files.

password. A secret word that allows entry; for example, a commercial online service or a Web page may require a password for access.

PGP (Pretty Good Privacy). A software program that scrambles e-mail to protect the user's privacy.

plug-in. An add-on that enhances the abilities of your browser to play sounds, display images or virtual reality, or take part in chat.

POP (Points of Presence or Post Office Protocol). A city or location where an Internet service provider can offer inexpensive dial-up access, often with a local telephone number. Or, a way in which a mail server on the Internet lets a user pick up mail.

PPP (Point-to-Point Protocol). An account with an Internet service provider, which means your computer is connected to the Internet.

proportional font. A font in which some letters are wider than others. Example fonts include Times, Bookman, Comic San Serif.

push technology. A system that sends customized information directly to a computer without the user's immediate request or search based upon previously submitted preferences.

QuickTime. A common file format for short video clips on the Internet, invented by Apple Computer.

root directory. The directory in which all your other directories are stored. This is the default directory that someone gets when they type in your URL.

search engine. A software program that finds topics, words, or phrases on the Web or in newsgroups and displays them as links.

server. A computer that offers services, ranging from e-mail to Web pages, to other computers, called clients, on a network.

SET (Secure Electronic Transaction). A standard used by some credit card companies to scramble information, such as credit card numbers, so a Web site can offer safe shopping.

shareware. Software that is free for a trial period, then requires a nominal fee paid to its developer.

SLIP (Single Line Internet Protocol). An account with an Internet service provider, which means your computer is connected to the Internet; an older version of PPP.

spam. Unrequested junk e-mail.

SSL (Secure Socket Layer). A system that scrambles information to protect privacy, often used by Web sites to offer safe shopping.

status indicator. The icon on a computer screen that shows a browser is active.

streaming media. A term for multimedia (sound, video, or animation) that begins playing while it is still downloading.

tags. Codes in HTML that are commands for certain functions, such as boldface, italicize, and create links. Sample commands include <HEAD>, <BODY>, and <IMG>.

text. In its pure form, words are text. In HTML terms, the text is the portion of the HTML page that is enclosed and modified by tags. Examples include:
```
<H1>This is a Header</H1>
<P>This is how a paragraph begins.
```
TCP/IP (Transmission Control Protocol/Internet Protocol). The system of rules computers connected on

the Internet follow to communicate. Your computer needs TCP/IP software to be on the Internet.

telephony. Technology that allows voice communication over the Internet, which may involve using microphones and computers, not telephones.

thread. A cluster of messages on the same topic in a newsgroup or on a bulletin board.

toolbar. A horizontal row of icons, which stands for browser commands, such as "back" and "bookmark."

traffic. The amount of data transferred from your Web site to users across the Internet. In other words, every time somebody downloads a picture from your site, that's traffic. Typically measured in MB per month.

UNIX. An operating system for computers before Windows was invented, which can still be used today.

upload. Copy a file or program from your computer's hard drive to another computer.

URL (Uniform Resource Locator). The Internet address of a page that includes the protocol needed. For example, "http://www." for a page on the World Wide Web, followed by the domain name.

Usenet. The thousands of newsgroups on many different topics on the Internet. It is an abbreviation of Users' Network.

user-participatory e-mail list. An e-mail list that automatically sends subscriber's replies to all subscribers on the list.

value. The simplest way to understand what an HTML value is is to explain it. In the tag <FONT COLOR = BLACK>, the value is BLACK.

virtual. "Almost" something. For example, virtual reality is a 3-D environment that offers the feeling of being within a real world.

Webmaster. The person responsible for building a Web site. For the purposes of this book, you are the Webmaster, and you'll be doing just about everything from designing the Web site, writing the HTML, finding images, testing it out, and uploading.

WiT. Webmaster in Training.

World Wide Web. The graphical part of the Internet, rich in images, sound, and video clips.

Web site. A group of pages written in HTML on the World Wide Web belonging to one company, organization, or person.

WYSIWYG (what you see is what you get). A Web authoring tool that shows what the Web page will look like before you are finished creating it (pronounced "wizzy-wig").

Index

We Have EVERYTHING!

Available wherever books are sold!

Everything **After College Book**
$12.95, 1-55850-847-3

Everything **Astrology Book**
$12.95, 1-58062-062-0

Everything **Baby Names Book**
$12.95, 1-55850-655-1

Everything **Baby Shower Book**
$12.95, 1-58062-305-0

Everything **Barbeque Cookbook**
$12.95, 1-58062-316-6

Everything® **Bartender's Book**
$9.95, 1-55850-536-9

Everything **Bedtime Story Book**
$12.95, 1-58062-147-3

Everything **Beer Book**
$12.95, 1-55850-843-0

Everything **Bicycle Book**
$12.95, 1-55850-706-X

Everything **Build Your Own Home Page**
$12.95, 1-58062-339-5

Everything **Casino Gambling Book**
$12.95, 1-55850-762-0

Everything **Cat Book**
$12.95, 1-55850-710-8

Everything® **Christmas Book**
$15.00, 1-55850-697-7

Everything **College Survival Book**
$12.95, 1-55850-720-5

Everything **Cover Letter Book**
$12.95, 1-58062-312-3

Everything **Crossword and Puzzle Book**
$12.95, 1-55850-764-7

Everything **Dating Book**
$12.95, 1-58062-185-6

Everything **Dessert Book**
$12.95, 1-55850-717-5

Everything **Dog Book**
$12.95, 1-58062-144-9

Everything **Dreams Book**
$12.95, 1-55850-806-6

Everything **Etiquette Book**
$12.95, 1-55850-807-4

Everything **Family Tree Book**
$12.95, 1-55850-763-9

Everything **Fly-Fishing Book**
$12.95, 1-58062-148-1

Everything **Games Book**
$12.95, 1-55850-643-8

Everything **Get-a-Job Book**
$12.95, 1-58062-223-2

THE EVERYTHING WEDDING BOOK

The ultimate reference for couples planning their wedding!

- Scheduling, budgeting, etiquette, hiring caterers, florists, and photographers
- Ceremony & reception ideas
- Over 100 forms and checklists
- And much, much more!

Absolutely everything you need to know to survive your wedding and actually even enjoy it!

Janet Anastasio, Michelle Bevilacqua, and Stephanie Peters

$12.95, 384 pages, 8" x 9¼"

THE EVERYTHING MONEY BOOK

Personal finance made easy—and fun!

- Create a budget you can live with
- Manage your credit cards
- Set up investment plans
- Money-saving tax strategies
- And much, much more!

Learn how to manage, budget, save, and invest your money so there's plenty left over

Rich Mintzer with Kathi Mintzer, C.P.A.

$12.95, 288 pages, 8" x 9¼"

For more information, or to order, call 800-872-5627 or visit www.adamsmedia.com/everything

Adams Media Corporation, 260 Center Street, Holbrook, MA 02343

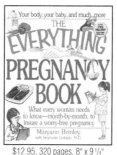

For more information, or to order, call 800-872-5627
or visit www.adamsmedia.com/everything

Adams Media Corporation, 260 Center Street, Holbrook, MA 02343

FIND MORE ON THIS TOPIC BY VISITING

BusinessTown.com

The Web's big site for growing businesses!

- ☑ **Separate channels on all aspects of starting and running a business**
- ☑ **Lots of info on how to do business online**
- ☑ **1,000+ pages of savvy business advice**
- ☑ **Complete web guide to thousands of useful business sites**
- ☑ **Free e-mail newsletter**
- ☑ **Question and answer forums, and more!**

http://www.businesstown.com